PLAN TO STAY™

PEACHTREE CITY LIBRARY
201 Willowbend Road
Peachtree City, GA 30269-1623
Phone: 770-631-2520
Fax: 770-631-2522

THE FALL OF
THE HOUSE
OF FORBES

THE FALL OF
THE HOUSE
OF FORBES

THE INSIDE STORY OF THE
COLLAPSE OF A MEDIA EMPIRE

STEWART PINKERTON

ST. MARTIN'S PRESS
NEW YORK

www.stmartins.com

Library of Congress Cataloging-in-Publication Data

Pinkerton, Stewart.
    The fall of the house of Forbes : the inside story of the collapse of a media empire / Stewart Pinkerton.
        p. cm.
    Includes bibliographical references and index.
    ISBN 978-0-312-65859-5
    1. Forbes, Malcolm S.   2. Businesspeople—United States—Biography.
3. Publishers and publishing—United States—Biography.   4. Capitalists and financiers—United States—Biography.   5. Forbes.   I. Title.
HC102.5.F67P56 2011
338.7'61070572092—dc23
[B]
                                                                            2011024758

First Edition: October 2011

10 9 8 7 6 5 4 3 2 1

For Chloë and Margot

CONTENTS

CONTENTS

A NOTE TO READERS

*F*ORBES WAS MY HOME for nearly twenty years, a privileged tenure working for a remarkable family. It was a great ride. But like so many other jobs in journalism over the past few years, my position became unnecessary, a casualty of the times. Recession and profound Internet-driven change have smashed old media molds and brought uncertainty and fear to those coping with this new environment.

This isn't a "tell-all" book. Or, to quote one of *The Sayings of Chairman Malcolm*, "How can anyone 'tell all' when no one knows all?" Nor is this an act of retribution intended to hurt or embarrass the Forbes family or any of my former colleagues. Quite to the contrary.

It's simply a story, as told by a journalist with nearly a half-century of experience. This is, in effect, a *Forbes* story about *Forbes*. It has a point of view. It's got some attitude. My hope is that it will be seen for what I believe it to be, a tale told fairly, with balance and accuracy—as I experienced events and mapped the journey of a fascinating family, an enterprise full of larger-than-life characters, and a period of fateful change in American journalism.

This book has been in preparation, in one form or another, for the past fifteen years. The inspiration came from my late friend and colleague, Laury Minard, a veteran journalist who once held my title at *Forbes*, managing editor. Coming out of an editorial meeting one day—during which our boss threw pencils in a fit of rage—Minard whispered, "You know, if anyone ever wrote this all down, nobody would ever believe it."

Well, I did, and here it is.

As with any *Forbes* story, there are embedded lessons, including how risk aversion, hubris, and greed can disrupt even the best-intentioned intergenerational transfer of entrepreneurial spirit and corporate mission. As family patriarch B. C. Forbes once wrote, "If you don't drive your business, you will be driven out of business."

To acknowledge all those who have influenced my journalistic career and this book would require many more pages than these. But here are just a few of them, with apologies to those not mentioned.

Professor Hans Aarsleff of the Princeton English Department was in a way probably to blame for all of this, ever since he criticized the tone of a paper I'd written as being "far too journalistic." Though he did not mean it as such, I took it as a compliment. During twenty-four years at *The Wall Street Journal*, I was privileged to learn from some of the most gifted writers and editors in the business: Mike Gartner, Bill Blundell, Steve Lovelady, Bowen Northrup, Jack Cooper, and Jim Stewart, to name just a few. Their work was inspirational for me.

At *Forbes,* the list of people who truly *cared* about their work continued, but only one name really mattered: the brilliant Jim Michaels, who influenced scores of writers and editors over the thirty-seven years he edited the magazine, generating one thousand covers over that span. Fortunate were those who were his students. While incessantly demanding of his staff, he was no less so of himself, setting the highest possible standard of editorial excellence, with a harsh, visceral disdain for excess verbiage and mere assertion.

A legend in the world of literary agents, Al Zuckerman at Writers House patiently walked me through the proposal process and into the doors of St. Martin's Press, where I was delighted to learn my editor would be Phil Revzin, an old colleague from the *Journal,* whose good humor and professionalism made the editing process painless. After departing for *Bloomberg* early in 2011, Phil handed me over to George Witte, St. Martin's editor-in-chief, who ably finished up the job. Laura Chasen and Terra Layton were extremely helpful during the production phase and happily answered my frequent and annoying questions. Former *Forbes* colleague Kristine Smith handled the photo research and matched the images to the words. Tireless work by my devoted researchers, Amanda Schupak and Rosemay Smith, made me look good. Each put up with a demanding barrage of requests, particularly in the final weeks. Heidi Brown did some important Russian translation work and helped fact-check the material on foreign language editions. At critical points, my good friend and coconspirator on many previous *Forbes* efforts, Dirk Smillie, gave valuable suggestions, as did Katherine Tallman, Dr. Heather O'Leary, and Dr. Eric Genden.

I'm particularly indebted to the staff at the Special Collections Library at Syracuse University for their assistance in helping me review the seventeen boxes of letters and papers belonging to B. C. Forbes. I have also relied heavily on the work of a former *Journal* colleague, Christopher Winans, whose book *Malcolm Forbes: The Man Who Had Everything* was invaluable in filling in some gaps in B.C.'s early life. Similarly, Arthur Jones, a former *Forbes* editor and author of *Malcolm Forbes: Peripatetic Millionaire,* was an important source of rich anecdotal material from his own reporting and his extraordinary access to Malcolm, something very few writers had. For the chapter on the purchase of the "Jefferson" wine bottle, I've relied heavily on the reporting of Benjamin Wallace for his wonderful 2009 book, *The Billionaire's Vinegar.*

The brief quotes attributed to Malcolm Forbes that begin several chapters all come from either *The Sayings of Chairman Malcolm* or *The Further Sayings of Chairman Malcolm*, published in 1978 and 1986, respectively, by Harper & Row. Certain puns that may sound vaguely familiar were inspired by and adapted from *David*

Letterman's Book of Top Ten Lists and Zesty Lo-Cal Chicken Recipes, published in 1995 by Bantam Books.

Contemporaneous personal notes taken over the past fifteen years, notations in personal calendars, even scribbles on various scraps of paper, all in the nature of an extended personal diary, helped me reconstruct important conversations, as well as attribute quotes and impart thoughts and emotions to the main characters.

Since leaving Forbes, I have interviewed nearly a hundred people for this book, including many former and current *Forbes* employees, nearly all of whom agreed to speak candidly on the condition that their identities not be revealed. You know who you are. Thank you for your trust and help. For their own reasons, the Forbeses themselves declined to be interviewed or cooperate in any way with fact-checking. As a result, much of the material about the Forbes collections and family historical tidbits comes from the company Web site or various books by Malcolm or others, all cited in the notes section and the bibliography.

Finally, this book could never have been written without the support of my wonderful family. Daughter Chlöe teaches English at a public high school in the Bay Area and therefore knows what it takes to get people's attention. She helped me make the book appeal to the broadest possible audience. Margot, a college undergraduate whose remarkable gifts as a writer far exceed my own, offered her own insights. Being a close student of *Law & Order*, she applauded my decision to begin the story with the discovery of a dead body. And my eternally patient and understanding wife, Meredith Nicholson, who has much more common sense than I do, endured far too many days and nights as a "writer's widow." Without complaint—or having to put Raoul Felder on speed dial—she helped keep me focused on the task at hand. To her go my profound thanks and love, always.

Any sons who inherit a profitable and going business and fail to make a success of it, do not deserve to succeed in making headway in life.

—B. C. Forbes, in a private letter to Bruce, Malcolm, Gordon, and Wallace Forbes, February 8, 1949

INTRODUCTION

BEFORE THEY SOLD THE Fabergé eggs, before they mothballed the yacht, before they drove many loyal subjects from the land, before nobody cared anymore, it was a real kingdom. There was a Moroccan palace, a magical Pacific island, a majestic ranch, a seventeenth-century London town house, a small air force and navy, priceless pieces of art and treasure, plus riches sufficient to fund an extravagant lifestyle that would make any Sultan envious.

There was even a Scottish king who died offstage under tragic circumstances and four princes, one of whom would become regent. On the surface, the royals embodied and personified the rewards of the entrepreneurial capitalism they so vigorously celebrated and preached.

But when great trouble smote the land, panic and greed took hold. The princes were not united in a single voice as to how to proceed. Risk aversion and hesitation took hold. From a foreign land (Silicon Valley) came a charismatic stranger bearing chests of gold for the troubled kingdom. In return for this largesse, however, the stranger demanded conditions. To keep their wealth, the princes had no choice but to accelerate what had already begun during the first signs of trouble—a systematic dismantling of the kingdom, along with increased sibling tension.

This is a business parable with undercurrents of Greek tragedy. It starts in the middle, goes back to the beginning, and hasn't yet ended. It's a story that arcs from Scotland in 1880 to the present, pulling back the velvet curtain on one of America's most iconic publishing families. Recounted here are a family's remarkable achievements as well as the daunting challenges it faces in dealing with the tsunami of change roiling American media today, as publishers cope with the transition to digital from analogue.

This is the story that nobody has dared tell before—and one the family does not want to see published. No doubt because "You shall know the truth, and the truth shall make you mad" (Aldous Huxley). This is a tale of triumph and failure, of brilliance and dysfunction, of honor and hypocrisy, of praise and betrayal, of compassion and cruelty, and of bizarre personal behavior at the highest levels.

This is the story of *Forbes*.

BOOK I

1

DEATH IN THE FAMILY

To ENTER MALCOLM FORBES's second-floor bedroom at *Timberfield*, his forty-acre estate deep in the horse country of New Jersey, was to experience a surprisingly cold, industrial-like space, somewhat jarring and out of place within the traditional Colonial interior of the white-paint-over-brick main house: gray Italian granite interior walls, leather upholstered ceilings, mirrors, and enough chrome, a visitor once noted, "to plate a '57 Caddie."

It was there on Saturday, February 24, 1990, an unusually mild mid-winter day, that Dennis Stewart, the estate's caretaker, found the iconic publishing executive on his bed, unresponsive, "asleep" far longer than he should have been. Stewart must have feared the worst. Was it a heart attack? A stroke? Or something else?

Only hours before, Malcolm's driver, Kurt Shaffer, a former New Jersey state trooper, had dropped him off after picking him up early that morning at Newark airport. Forbes had flown in overnight from London where he'd hosted a bridge tournament at his home near the Thames, *Old Battersea House,* pitting some members of Parliament against a group of celebrity American executives, including Larry Tisch, Milton Petrie, and Alan "Ace" Greenberg. He'd come in on the *Capitalist Tool,* his private Boeing 727—tail No. N60FM—configured to seat only twenty-four instead of the usual 181.

Painted in Forbes's favorite colors—money green and gold—the *Tool*'s lush interior by Jon Bannenberg, the Australian-born yacht designer who did some of the work on the QE2, included plush, cream-colored leather swivel chairs, an L-shaped banquette, a mirrored bathroom with a marble sink, and a stateroom for Malcolm. There was a fully stocked bar and galley, a steward to anticipate and cater to the boss's every need.

Despite the alarming condition in which he found the Forbes editor-in-chief, Stewart did not call 911. That would have dispatched an ambulance from 29 Rescue, the Far Hills-Bernardsville First Aid Squad, located just seven minutes away on Route 202 near Woodland Road. From *Timberfield* it would have been perhaps a ten-to-fifteen-minute sprint to the closest hospital, Somerset Medical Center.

Instead, he dialed the number of Forbes's friend and long-time personal physician, Dr. Oscar Kruesi, an internist whose practice was nearby in Bernardsville. Dr. Kruesi left his office immediately and before long was negotiating the winter ruts in the dirt portion of Old Dutch Road, turning right at number 95, into the familiar driveway. He'd been to *Timberfield* before, of course, and had always enjoyed bantering with his famous patient. But this time, given the urgency in Dennis Stewart's voice, he had a bad feeling. Dr. Kruesi parked his car and hurried to the front door, which he opened without knocking. Stewart was waiting for him. Together they climbed the curved stairway leading up to the second floor and Malcolm's bedroom.

Dr. Kruesi's foreboding proved to be correct. The accepted protocol for pronouncing someone dead is to find cardiac, respiratory, and neurological functions all absent. Dr. Kruesi found no pulse in Malcolm's carotid artery, no heartbeat or breathing from a stethoscope, and presumably, no arousal response to a deep sterna rub. There was nothing for him to do but to pronounce that Malcolm Stevenson Forbes had passed on to his last, most exotic destination. "Mr. Forbes had obviously died in his sleep. He had died very peacefully apparently," Dr. Kruesi told *The New York Times.*

More phone calls. To the family, of course. And to Frank E. Campbell, the iconic Manhattan funeral home that for decades has performed its last rites on the rich and famous, including Rudolph Valentino, Judy Garland, John Lennon, Tennessee Williams, and Jackie Onassis. Stewart then phoned a *Forbes* colleague who was scheduled to visit *Timberfield* later that day. "We have a situation here," he said. "Mr. Forbes has passed away."

Forbes's remains were removed and prepared for cremation at Campbell's facilities. There was no call to the medical examiner, no autopsy. The family held a private service two days later at the Church of St. John on the Mountain, not far from *Timberfield*, followed by a public service of thanksgiving for Malcolm's life on Thursday, March 1, at St. Bartholomew's on Park Avenue. Packing the pews were *Forbes* employees (given priority seating), a contingent of Hell's Angels, and a galaxy of executives, politicians, and celebrities, including, of course, Elizabeth Taylor, Malcolm's frequent companion, Richard Nixon, Barbara Walters, Katherine Graham, David Rockefeller, Rupert Murdoch, and former New York mayor Ed Koch.

The family sought proceeds from Mass Mutual and other insurers on what was later reported to be $100 million in life insurance policies, payouts that were to go toward estate taxes and which a former *Forbes* financial executive confirms were held up, though the executive cannot explain why. Mass Mutual declined all comment, citing confidentiality. But a former *Forbes* senior editor, writing about the matter for another publication six years later, reported that the insurers balked at the payouts because of "curious circumstances" surrounding Malcolm's death. Citing a confidential settlement agreed to by the family after "many months of quiet behind-the-scenes wrangling," this writer said, the payments were finally made, but for far less than what the family sought, about fifty to seventy-five cents on the dollar.

Dr. Kruesi, who died in 2010, personally signed the death certificate. The official cause was heart failure, which the press dutifully reported. Yet, even after all that time, there are questions. For years, there have been whispers and speculation within the corridors of *Forbes* that Malcolm had taken his own life, a tragic scenario two former employees very close to the family now affirm. In his 1990 biography of Forbes, author Christopher Winans noted that after so many brushes with death on his motorcycles and in his balloons, Malcolm's peaceful death in bed defied the odds: "It seemed almost too perfect to be an accident." In retrospect, Malcolm's $2.5 million seventieth birthday bash in Morocco only months before was a fitting, grand good-bye to the world: The standing ovation. The last curtain call. The big finish.

Forbes wanted to be buried in Laucala, a beautiful three-thousand-acre island in the Fiji archipelago reportedly first spotted by Captain Bligh of the *Bounty*. Forbes bought it in 1972 for $1 million and developed it into a small, exclusive resort, complete with a twin engine Piper Chieftain called *Capitalist Tool Too* to ferry guests on and off the island. Forbes marketed Laucala as the "ultimate South Pacific getaway for those into extraordinary deep-sea fishing, scuba diving, or for those who simply want to live the life of Gauguin without the torment."

Forbes hoped that his burial there would prevent his sons from ever selling it. He even hired an architect to design a mausoleum. His ashes did go to Fiji, but that turned out to be just a layover. A few years later, the sons dug him up, reburied him in Scotland next to their grandfather B. C. Forbes, then put the island on the block for $10.5 million. Former Beatle George Harrison was one of those who looked at it.

Laucala eventually sold in 2003 for much less than $10.5 million, to Dietrich Mateschitz, head of the Red Bull energy drink company. But the transaction was delayed by the sound of jungle drums: restless natives, protesting government policies, staged a coup, briefly taking tourists hostage at several Fiji resorts, including Laucala, no doubt conjuring back at the home office *New Yorker* cartoon images of *Forbes* guests simmering in large black pots emblazoned with the company logo.

Though the uprising was directed against the Fiji government, possibly the Laucala hostage-takers were also protesting Forbes's abrupt removal, since he had built for the natives a church and a school—perhaps in compensation for uprooting them from their beachfront homes so he could charge $700 a night for his own guests.

In either case, the uprising was not a good omen. Malcolm's death would touch off a series of cascading changes that would ultimately unseat the family from day-to-day management control and dilute the value of a storied brand—profound events that would have appalled Malcolm's father, Bertie Charles Forbes, the Scottish immigrant who founded the magazine that bore his name in 1917. In a private letter written in 1949 describing how his estate would be split up after *his* death, B.C. wrote, "Any sons who inherit a profitable and going business and fail to make a success of it, do not deserve to succeed in making headway in life."

But to understand the fall, we need to look in some depth at the rise, and especially at the unique life and style, of Malcolm Forbes.

2

"SPARKLING NAUGHTY BOY"

What's unnatural sex? Having none.

—Malcolm Forbes

To those attending Malcolm's standing-room-only service of thanksgiving at St. Bart's, the tribute that seemed to resonate the most came from second-oldest son, Bob, whose longish brown hair caressed the back collars of his striking bespoke pinstripes, always set off by a dashing pocket square.

"He was so many things to so many of us," Bob said, "boss, bon vivant, raconteur, happiest millionaire, leader of the pack, source, mentor, friend, super this, mega that, father, grandfather, father-in-law, uncle, cousin, and sparkling naughty boy."

What exactly did he mean by "sparkling naughty boy"?

Rightly or wrongly, many in the church interpreted the reference as a tacit admission of the side to Malcolm that was widely known but never conceded or discussed by the family. To anyone who knew anything about his private life, it was a given that Malcolm Forbes was conflicted about his sexuality. "I've slept with women, but guys are more fun," he once confided to a friend. As prelude to a kiss, it wasn't unusual to spot Malcolm playing footsie with a handsome young man at a discreet table in one of his favorite downtown eateries. If one is to believe those who were seduced—or at least propositioned—by him, his increasingly indiscreet liaisons were numerous and widespread.

Which of course raised the question—never answered—of whether at his death, Malcolm had AIDS and feared the ghastly and certain death that awaited anyone with the virus in those days before HIV protease inhibitors. Shortly after he died, *Outweek* featured a cover piece entitled "The Secret Gay Life of Malcolm Forbes," and the sensationalist tabloid *Globe* screamed in a classic bait-and-switch headline: "Malcolm Forbes Had AIDS & Killed Himself: His Gay Lover Tells All." The story quoted a twenty-two-year-old body-builder who alleged multiple oral sex and sodomy encounters with Malcolm in the town house at $1,500 per "date." Of course, in the actual story, the bodybuilder said nothing about Malcolm having AIDS or wanting to kill himself, though he did indicate Malcolm thought he might have cancer.

The mainstream press generally steered clear of the whole issue of Malcolm's sexual doings, but in December 1990, Elizabeth Taylor bristled to *People:* "It's nobody's business what Malcolm's sexual preferences were. It's nobody's concern. I respected him, which means I respected his choices, all the way around. We knew each other very well."

For Malcolm's "invitees" to the town house, "drinks" usually consisted of tumblers of vodka and grapefruit juice, followed by a "Would you like to join me?" stroll toward the sauna before dinner, typically passing through what staffers called the "porn room," a space filled with elaborate oil paintings of homoerotica in Old Masters style, depicting naked revelers engaged in various activities. One featured a disturbing "group whipping" of a fellow strapped down on a table. (The whippee did not appear to be enjoying it.)

One evening, after the warm-up vodkas, Malcolm told a handsome young editorial staffer that he was going to "freshen up" before going out to dinner and suggested that the young man use the time to take a sauna, presumably alone. But it wasn't long before Malcolm appeared through the mist, naked and fully aroused. "How about a smooch and a hug?" he asked.

Now what do I do? the young staffer thought in panic. *This is the guy who owns the place, for chrissake.*

When the young man demurred, Malcolm asked if he could "relieve himself." In front of the horrified employee, he then proceeded to masturbate.

Oh my God, it's all over. Now he's going to fire me.

Afterward, the young staffer felt he had no choice but to join Malcolm for what turned out to be a delicious but awkward meal at a fancy uptown restaurant. The next morning, Malcolm was waiting at the security desk when the extremely hungover employee arrived. *Uh-oh. This is it. He's going to can me right here.* But Malcolm was chipper and jaunty, giving a big wave to the staffer, acting as if nothing had happened.

It was a routine Malcolm regularly followed, sometimes handing employees $100 "for cab fare" afterward. One night, Malcolm dropped a staffer off at his apartment via motorcycle and handed him $200 "for being my bodyguard tonight." Was it generosity or simply a bribe to keep things quiet? Occasionally, Malcolm would suggest that a young staffer join the elite "Balloon Ascension Team," which worked Malcolm's big events, went on exotic trips, and, claims one former employee who declined Malcolm's advances, sometimes performed other services for the boss.

Once escorting a group of Japanese businessmen around the edit floor, Malcolm spotted a handsome young man he hadn't seen before. He interrupted his tour and came over. "Excuse me, are you new here?" Malcolm asked. "I always like to take new employees out for a drink." A few days later, in the town house, Malcolm said, "I'm having vodka and grapefruit juice, care to join me?" "Sure." The usual script followed.

Explaining the need for a hot tub soak after a long day's work, Malcolm excused himself, but reappeared shortly wearing only a bathrobe. He called the restaurant to reserve a table for two, using his "cover" name, Stevenson. Then, approaching his guest, he said, "Would you care to join me?" The new hire demurred, but Malcolm persisted, approaching even closer. Grabbing the young man's hand, he turned the prior question into a request: "I'd *really* like you to join me." Again, the answer was no, but Malcolm appeared not to mind. The two had a pleasant dinner, as if nothing had happened.

In those days before workplace sexual harassment and a "hostile work environment" were taken seriously, Malcolm could get away with it. But the behavior was clearly predatory and unnerving to employees—as well as to his oldest son. One evening, a first-time town house "invitee" was washing up in a ground-floor restroom when Steve walked in. "Hey, Steve!" the young man said cheerily. "Guess what? I'm having dinner with your dad tonight!" Forbes's smile turned to a grimace. He went into a stall and slammed the door.

What was that about? the young man thought.

Not again, thought Steve.

3

"THE BARNUM OF BARNUMS"

M ALCOLM'S MISCHIEF AND THE office gossip about it simply
added to his mystique as an intriguing larger-than-life character. *Oh, that's just Malcolm being Malcolm. He's really just a little
kid dressed up in pinstripes having a good time being naughty. He's
just having fun.*

That's the way he came across, and for the most part, Malcolm
was beloved as a boss. Employees felt they were part of a family, and
to a certain extent, they were. Malcolm knew most of them by name,
and called each of them on their birthdays, always making sure that
a corsage or boutonniere was waiting for them at their desks that
day. Malcolm would grant interest-free loans to those in financial
distress and forgave them when he died.

There was free medical coverage. And long before 401(k)s became fashionable, the Forbes Thrift Plan made many employees
very well off. Staffers put up to 10 percent of their salaries into the
plan. For every dollar an employee contributed, Forbes put in $2.50.
It was not unusual for long-time Forbesies to retire as millionaires.

There was a canteen that served hot breakfasts and lunches, but
in a bow to Scottish practicality, there was no place to sit: *Take your*

sandwich back to your desk and get to work. (But perhaps not on those days when a former chef was seen relieving himself in the men's room still wearing his latex prep gloves. "It doesn't get much better than that," says a top executive who now prefers to get his sandwiches elsewhere.) A varsity gymnast at Princeton who knew the value of having healthy, fit employees, Malcolm put in a fully equipped gym on the top floor of 60 Fifth Avenue. There were panoramic city views, televisions, and an in-house trainer to customize workout routines. It was, of course, a free perk, as were *Forbes* "money green and gold" umbrellas from the security desk whenever it rained.

I joined the magazine just months after Malcolm died, so I never worked directly for him. But I'd met him socially on several occasions before and, like most people, was totally charmed. How could you not be? On our second meeting, a party at the Forbes Galleries more than six months after my first being introduced, he came right up and said with a big grin, "We have to stop meeting like this!" My clearest memory of him remains the evening I was a guest on his yacht, *Highlander,* for a dinner cruise around New York harbor. As we were about to shove off, I went up to the bridge and was surprised to find Malcolm sitting by himself on a little bench behind and to the right of the captain's wheel. Swinging his legs back and forth like a twelve-year-old, he made a grand gesture toward the sparkling Manhattan skyline that unrolled as the *Highlander* backed out into the Hudson, tooting its imposing horn. "Isn't this just great," he said, clearly having more fun than I'd ever seen an adult have.

But Malcolm's excessive spending sometimes offended the plantation hands, particularly when they had to endure sitting through his "admire my great wealth" home movies each year at the company annual meeting. The films, which one former senior staffer characterized as flaunting "the most tasteless, grotesque spending imaginable," documented Malcolm's various ballooning and biking trips as well as his extravagant parties. "Here we were," the ex-staffer adds, "not making that much money, and he's rubbing our noses in it, barely giving us a thank-you. It was, 'Have a good year but work harder.' It was disgusting and vile beyond belief."

But Malcolm genuinely wanted to share his fun. It made him happy. And like his good friend Ronald Reagan, Malcolm took his work very seriously, but never himself. Reagan liked to tell the story about walking down Fifth Avenue near St. Patrick's during his Hollywood days when a man coming toward him exclaimed, "I know you . . . you're, you're . . . Ray Milland!" and then asked for an autograph. Reagan smiled, and pulled out his pen, not missing a beat. "And I signed . . . 'Ray Milland!'"

Unlike the "DON'T YOU KNOW WHO I AM?" CEOs who bristle with attitude when the smallest thing goes wrong at a hotel or restaurant, Malcolm always played it cool, and rarely pulled out the ace card. But when he did, it was a thing of beauty.

Late one hot summer night in Tennessee, Malcolm arrived with two dozen bikers at a Marriott, eagerly anticipating drinks in an air-conditioned bar. The group, covered with bugs and sweat, got an icy reception from the bartender, who wasn't amused that they all put their helmets on the bar.

"We'd like a round of daiquiris, please," Forbes said.

"We don't have a blender," the bartender said.

"Oh really? Then what's that?" Malcolm said, pointing to a blender.

"It's broken."

"So how about margaritas, then?"

At this point a man appeared and suggested the group might be "more comfortable" in a nearby conference room, where the staff would bring them "anything they wanted." Malcolm took one look at the setup, which consisted of a big table with folding chairs, and said, "I'd like to speak to the manager, please."

"I *am* the manager."

"Then please call your boss," Malcolm said, still pleasant.

"To say what?"

"Tell him Malcolm Forbes and his friends would like to have a drink at the bar."

"Oh, Mr. Forbes, *I'm so sorry. . . .*"

On the *Tool* one day, Malcolm wanted a white wine spritzer, one of his favorite drinks. When he couldn't find the head steward (who was in the loo) he asked another aide to go find him. The aide returned within moments. "Sir, he said to make it yourself." Malcolm paused, then started laughing. "He didn't say that, *you* did," he said, getting up to make two spritzers, one for himself and one for the aide. "You got me," he added, still chortling.

Forbes didn't like to disappoint people. Billed as a big attraction at a motorcycle event in Pennsylvania one weekend was the appearance by one of Malcolm's favorite hot air balloons—which was shaped like a gigantic Harley. But the winds weren't cooperating. Too dangerous. Malcolm pondered for a bit, then conferred with his helicopter pilot who'd flown him in, a Vietnam flying ace who'd done many precision, low-altitude medivac rescues.

Malcolm grabbed the PA mike. "I know everyone was hoping to see my Harley balloon," he said. "But instead, what I'm going to do is have my helicopter drag race with you!"

Enthusiastic applause.

The Bell Ranger lifted off and aligned itself with the bikers at the start line, its engines revving, tilted at a sharp forward angle to the ground. The pilot waited for the start light. At the signal, he gunned it, quickly reaching two hundred miles an hour—and sending a huge backwash of dust and wind into his competitors, who fell instantly behind. At full speed, the copter skimmed over the crowd in the grand stand, executed a reverse loop, and landed squarely in the middle of the winner's circle. Wild cheers and applause from everyone. Malcolm relished the spontaneity and success of his impromptu show.

Forbes's own well-publicized Harley road trips included Munich to Helsinki via Moscow, France to Norway, Bangkok to Brunei, a romp through Pakistan, Egypt, and going from Xi'an, China, to Beijing. But there were more than a few wipeouts, so many that Steve Forbes, who would get the calls from the hospitals, has forbidden his daughters to take up the sport.

On several of these trips, Malcolm hauled along his balloons, too: a giant sphinx for Egypt; a huge replica of Balleroy for France; a 240-foot likeness of the Minar-e-Pakistan, that country's independence monument, which looks something like the Eiffel Tower; a much-larger-than-life elephant for Malaysia.

Once, attempting a transcontinental balloon trip in North America, Forbes ran into trouble about halfway to the East Coast. He was trying a morning launch in Nebraska, near a line of trees. Balloon physics dictate that when wind rushes over a barrier, it creates a false lift before the balloon is filled with enough hot air to take off by itself.

Malcolm knew that, sort of, but was more focused on just getting a good start, since NBC was covering the trip. "He had the attention span of a butterfly in heat," says former staffer Arthur Jones. Cameras were rolling as Malcolm lifted off slowly, waving happily to the crowd, when suddenly the balloon hit cold air and started down hard. The gondola hit the ground, bounced around, and destroyed five cars.

Malcolm thought it was amusing, though the car owners no doubt failed to see the humor. Said the NBC commentator, "And here are five people who are going to have to tell their insurance companies their cars were smashed by a hit-and-run balloon." There was a tussle with a power line in Virginia, and then a somewhat unceremonious dumping in Chesapeake Bay just short of the Atlantic. As press planes circled like vultures, Tim Forbes filmed away as Malcolm and Bob sloshed in the shoulder-high water. Malcolm cursed, "I don't suppose it's occurred to any of those bastards that it's cold down here."

All this cost Forbes millions. But he knew exactly what he was doing. How can you beat having a big balloon with your name on it splashed all over the evening news, even though the reason was that it wiped out five cars?

"All this sort of stuff brought a lot of publicity to ballooning," he said. And as he might have added, to his magazine. "Malcolm," says Arthur Jones, "was the Barnum of Barnums."

And he liked being naughty. On the motorcycle-balloon trip to China, Malcolm wanted to take one more balloon ride at the end of the day. But Chinese officials didn't want him to. Undaunted, Malcolm climbed back into the gondola and took off, leaving a chagrined Tim having to make amends to the unamused officials. But one of them smiled, and said, "Your father very bad boy!" To break the rule in this case was pure exuberance on Malcolm's part. *I'll follow the rules,* he seemed to be saying, *when they make sense.*

Malcolm was always generous, even when it was clear people were taking advantage of him. On a trip to Moscow, with a planeload of guests, Malcolm apologized for having to make a refueling stop in Reykjavík, this being in pre-*Tool* days. In compensation, he marched the group into the airport's gift shop, plopped down his American Express card, and told the manager to ring up "anything" his guests wanted.

Like those contests where shoppers see how much they can pile into their carts in three minutes, passengers scooped up sweaters with lots of snowflakes and reindeer on them, fur hats, clothing, souvenirs, and luggage to pack all the loot in. It was a feeding frenzy. To one *Forbes* staffer who witnessed the scene, it was all a bit unseemly—like the night on the *Highlander* when some high-powered Wall Streeters feasted on Malcolm's boxes of Cohibas, stuffing fistfuls of the pricey contraband Cuban cigars into the inside jacket pockets of their $4,500 Zegna suits.

The staffer didn't pick out anything himself. Back on the plane, Malcolm asked, "So what'd you get?" When the reply was "nothing," Malcolm feigned irritation. "Are you fucking kidding me? Don't ever disobey a direct order again. I told you to shop!" Malcolm ordered the plane's door reopened so he could escort the chagrined employee back into the shop, where he picked out a snowflake sweater for his mother.

Malcolm was always kind to the families of his staffers. In the early eighties, when he was Washington bureau chief, Jerry Flint brought his son Doug to see the *Highlander,* which happened to be docked on the Potomac that weekend. Flint had a package the New

York office had asked him to deliver to the boat. Malcolm was there, looking fresh and very nautical in white slacks, a knit shirt, and blue blazer. Young Doug, an auto mechanic, showed up in greasy coveralls. "Malcolm treated him as if he were the Prince of Wales," Flint recalled. "I never forgot that."

Sometimes Malcolm's exuberance at spending came at the cost of serious mental anguish for his money handlers. Enjoying Malcolm's sixtieth birthday bash at Timberfield, an event featuring an air traffic controller who had to be brought in to direct all the helicopters, finance man Joel Redler was having a fine time until Malcolm got up on stage and interrupted Elizabeth Taylor, who was talking about her support of AIDS research. "Here's a check for one million to help out," Malcolm proudly announced to clapping and cheers. But Redler wasn't applauding. His stomach had suddenly dropped to his feet: There wasn't enough money in the Forbes Foundation account to cover the check, and Malcolm hadn't said a thing to him beforehand. Since it was a Saturday night before the days of remote electronic transfer, there was nothing Redler could do but head to the bar—and camp out Monday morning in front of Chemical Bank until the doors opened. He never told Malcolm.

Part of Malcolm's sense of humor was publicly messing with those he genuinely liked and admired. After arriving one night by motorcycle to give a speech at the Museum of Natural History, Malcolm spilled soup on his tie during the first course. Not wanting to be seen as "the old guy with soup on his tie," Malcolm asked a staffer who'd come with him if they could sneak out to the men's room and switch ties. Malcolm sported a classic Brooks Brothers rep. The staffer had a flashy Italian silk number. After dinner, a beautiful blond woman walked up to Malcolm and complimented him on his speech. "But I really *love* your tie, Mr. Forbes," she gushed. Malcolm beamed. "Thank you," he said. "I got it in Italy. But look at my friend here. He's got soup on *his* tie! Now if he had one like *mine*, he could get a girl like you."

Each year, Malcolm gave every employee the day off on his birthday, August 19. And he hosted an annual Veteran's Day at Timberfield for all employees who'd worked there for five years or more. It was a tradition begun by his father during the Depression. Held every fall, it was another day off, a much-anticipated big party in the country and a chance to see how the boss lived. There was golf, tennis, swimming, hot-air balloon rides, tours of the motorcycle barn, games, an open bar, and a formidable lunch buffet prepared by the town house chef.

Most important was the handshake from Malcolm—memorialized by the staff photographer—and money, an amount that increased with each year of service. Short of being named a federal judge, working for *Forbes* was considered, for many years, about as close to lifetime employment as one could find.

Employees were fiercely loyal to and protective of the man who was taking such good care of them. If any outsider even hinted at any kind of confrontation with the family, George Tempro, a big bear of a former FBI agent who was Malcolm's long-time head of security, would smile and warn in his quiet gravelly voice, "You have *no idea* what you're up against."

Walking into *Forbes* from any other job in publishing was a little like walking into Oz. Suddenly everything was in glorious color, and the default word was almost always "yes" for practically any request by even the youngest of editorial staffers—money for travel, or for meals with sources. *Fortune* would never have listed *Forbes* in its annual listing of the best places to work, but it would have qualified by any measure.

To be connected to *Forbes* in any way in those days was, in fact, to be a member of a very exclusive club. As a reader, there were valuable insights available nowhere else. As an advertiser, there was access to a vast, unparalleled audience of wealthy entrepreneurs and decision makers at the highest levels of American business. If you were listed on the *Forbes 400*, even if you didn't want to be, it was worthy of country club chatter—and envy.

There was no *Mr. Fortune*, no *Mr. BusinessWeek*. But there definitely was a Mr. Forbes. And if you were a chief executive invited on the *Highlander*, Malcolm's beloved 151-foot yacht, for a Saturday trip up the Hudson for a football game at West Point, or a lucky marketing manager invited to the Colorado ranch for a weekend junket, flown back and forth on the *Tool*, you were assured a splendid experience. Spouses always invited. Small groups. Great food and wine. And very personal service, sometimes from a Forbes. Flying back from a trip, Kip, for example, would often go through the cabin, pen and paper in hand, asking each guest if they needed a car at the airport for the trip home. And, sure enough, there it would be, trunk open for the luggage, waiting at the bottom of the plane's steps. Kip could have easily delegated the task to a steward. *But that's not the way we do things at* Forbes.

For an added touch of fun, Kip would sometimes approach a favored guest and ask, "You want to help land the plane?" The lucky person would then be escorted to the jump seat for a pilot's-eye view of the approach and landing.

"You know why I advertise in *Forbes*?" the marketing head of a big Wall Street investment bank asked a seatmate as the *Tool* began its descent into Newark airport after a pampered three-day trip to the ranch in Colorado. "So I can go on trips like these."

4

HAUNTED HOUSE

NOT FAR FROM WASHINGTON Square in Greenwich Village, near
the very beginning of Fifth Avenue, stands number 60, an elegant nine-story neoclassic building. The Macmillan publishing company built it in 1925, as legend has it, with the profits from H. G.
Wells's *The Outline of History*.

The building's architect, John Russell Pope, had also designed
the Jefferson Memorial and the National Gallery in Washington,
D.C. In its Macmillan days, the likes of Wells, James Michener, and
Sean O'Casey frequently visited "60 Fifth's" oak-paneled offices.
The ghosts of William Butler Yeats and John Masefield are said to
still walk the history-infused halls.

In 1967, the fiftieth anniversary year of the magazine, *Forbes*
moved into the property as its headquarters, along with an attached
town house whose entrance is just around the corner on Twelfth
Street. George Brett, the former president of Macmillan, used to live
there. Then, as now, Forbes used the 1847 town house to entertain
corporate bigwigs, heads of state, U.S. presidents, royalty, and other
notables.

For such guests, the town house liturgy rarely varied from a script that's been followed for years. In the third-floor living room, with windows looking south onto the grounds of the First Presbyterian Church, the guest of honor is invited to sit in a red armchair, positioned in the corner between a fireplace and a yellow-toned three-cushion couch, where the host, almost always a Forbes, sits on the far right, next to the guest. Above the couch is a painting of a young Forbes family at ease at Timberfield.

A white-coated attendant offers cocktails, then passes hors d'oeuvres exactly twice. After an appropriate amount of inconsequential small talk (never rudely short or boringly long), the host waits for a conversation break, and then invitingly says, "Let's see what the chef has cooked up today!"

It's the signal to rise and move to one of two dining rooms, one directly adjacent to the living room or a smaller one on the second floor, each with a round dining table, fine linens, and ceramic centerpieces. To mark the first time a chief executive dined in the town house, Malcolm would present him with a Tiffany silver wine goblet in the shape of an inverted stag's head, with the executive's name engraved on it, to be kept in the Forbes wine cellar for use on future visits—and as a little incentive to buy advertising space in the magazine.

The meals, impeccably prepared and served, often with a nice, crisp Macon-Lugny Les Charmes chardonnay (referred to in-house as "Steve Wine"), rivaled those of any highly rated Manhattan restaurant. For smaller gatherings, there were cocktails in a first-floor library, followed, perhaps, by a meal in the cozy basement wine cellar, lined with row upon row of vintage bottles. They surround a small rectangular dining table, creating the atmosphere of an intimate French *cave*.

The town house, now up for sale for $15.3 million, is also home to the most important office at *Forbes,* that of the editor-in-chief. A dark-paneled room with a fireplace and chintz sofas, its walls are pleasantly cluttered with colorful academic hoods from honorary degrees and the requisite minicollection of fine paintings, including a dramatic Rubens, reportedly done in three days by the master himself as a bribe to the treasurer of the Medicis, who owed the painter money for past work.

The boss's surroundings reflected and celebrated his vast wealth and business success, which Malcolm always explained was attributable "to sheer ability—spelled i-n-h-e-r-i-t-a-n-c-e." If you can pick a parent, he used to say, "who owns a business and be sure he's not mad at you when he checks out, it's a surer way to the top than anything else that comes to mind."

Malcolm's eldest son, Malcolm Stevenson Forbes Jr., known to everyone as Steve, would inherit 51.1 percent of the voting shares. Brothers Tim, Christopher (known always as Kip), and Bob would each get 16.3 percent. Daughter Moira, not involved in running the family business, would get $2 million in cash and 5 percent of the nonvoting shares. (She lives with her husband in Philadelphia, where she's involved in various good works, most notably the Community Coalition.)

It was no surprise the voting stock was distributed the way it was. To prepare for an orderly transition (whenever that would come) Malcolm had made it clear to everyone in the family (and anyone else who asked) that Steve would be taking over.

Tellingly, Malcolm's last will and testament revealed just how he ranked his four sons' abilities, as he perceived them, to be able to run the whole show. If Steve predeceased his father, Tim would have wound up getting the 51.1 percent of the voting shares. Next in the ranking to receive the majority stake if the other brothers had died was Kip, and finally, Bob.

Timberfield went to Kip. Malcolm's ex-wife, Roberta, under terms of their divorce agreement, would get $5 million outright and $4,000 a week as long as she lived (which was until 1992). Among nonfamily beneficiaries, the owners of eight of Malcolm's favorite Manhattan restaurants, received $1,000 each "as a token of gratitude for the joy their skill and genius added to the lives of those who've been lucky and sensible enough" to dine there. The winners included Lutèce, La Grenouille, Chanterelle, The Four Seasons, Le Cirque, Mortimer's, and oddly, Benihana, the original restaurant of what's now a national chain of nearly one hundred Japanese-themed eateries. Who knew Malcolm liked his steaks carved by samurai warrior-waiters?

Twenty-six motorcycle clubs in New York, New Jersey, and Pennsylvania got $1,000 each. The American Motorcyclists Association in Westerville, Ohio, hit the jackpot with $10,000. Five friends who helped Malcolm learn how to play bridge got $1,000 each. And two "treasured friends," Luvie Pearson of Washington, D.C. (the widow of columnist Drew Pearson) and Countess Boul de Breteuil of Morocco, once described by *New York* magazine as the social leader of haute Marrakech, got $10,000 each.

5

THE NEW BOSS

IT WAS AS IF a background music loop by Aerosmith had been suddenly replaced by *Perry Como's Greatest Hits*. No more outrage, no more flamboyance. Just a steady diet of conservative predictability. In February 1990, the editorship passed to Steve, the quiet, unassuming eldest brother, who was a veteran speaker and prognosticator of business trends. Despite two campaigns for president (referred to in-house as the "$75 million sales call"), Steve—unlike his father—could be shy and socially awkward at times, uncomfortable with elevator small talk unless it involved politics or the New York Yankees.

But he inherited his father's self-deprecating humor, and even agreed (during one of his presidential campaigns) to host *Saturday Night Live*, appearing in a skit in which he portrayed a construction worker. Calm, even in crisis, Steve rarely appears to lose his temper. But when he does, it's usually because of a detail out of place or a small glitch in advance work.

As when, in a scene reminiscent of the marching band in *Animal House* that takes a wrong turn and winds up colliding with a brick wall, a small procession led by a bagpiper with Steve and aides in tow marched up the wrong stairway at a *Forbes* CEO conference and ran into a locked door. The procession had to retreat. Red-faced and glowering, the boss was not pleased. His father, on the other hand, probably would have thought it funny.

My first meeting with Steve was right before shaking hands with the editor, Jim Michaels, on a deal to come aboard for what would turn into an assistant managing editor's job. I'd wanted some assurance from Steve that he had no plans to sell out to some big public company. *Forbes* was still small enough in those days that such a meeting, while certainly not routine, was possible, and I was amazed at how quickly Michaels arranged it—he called Steve from his apartment, where we were meeting, and in less than thirty seconds, my meeting was set up. Soon I was sitting down with Steve over Diet Cokes in the imposing second floor director's room, where many years before, Margaret Mitchell held her first meeting with the press about *Gone With the Wind*. Steve, invoking the memory of his father, said the family had "no intention" of selling to an outsider. *Forbes,* he said, would always be family owned.

But that was at the beginning of one of the biggest bull markets in history and well before the disruptive forces of the Internet smashed the old business models. Watching the brothers at work and interacting with them frequently over the years, I had a unique perspective from which to view one of America's iconic publishing companies, and saw firsthand the burdens of running a family-owned enterprise.

Theirs was a formidable challenge, to suppress differences and childhood rivalries and put their own selfish interests behind them. How were they to keep up the momentum their famous father had generated within the highly competitive world of financial journalism? As often happens, hubris, greed, and poor judgment got in the way. "Life is never," Malcolm once said, "as you think it was going to be."

Steve's first instinct was to distance himself, at first discreetly, then more aggressively, from Malcolm. His father's clothes clearly did not fit, so the son undertook a major retailoring. *It's our money now,* Steve thought. *No more nonsense.* Among the first things to go was a project that only a multimillionaire would think of: building a small (one thousand square foot) open-floor-plan house on top of the highest mountain at Trinchera, Malcolm's 256,000-acre Colorado ranch.

With floor-to-ceiling glass, the $1 million Panorama House was to have spectacular views from every vantage point. Malcolm had imagined how fun it would be to be there during thunderstorms or blizzards. And it would be *very* private, the only easy access by helicopter. So complicated was the engineering that Forbes was planning to hire oil rig contractors to do much of the work. As he did with most of his fanciful projects, Malcolm made a practice of running them by his sons, because whatever he did, they'd have to live with it someday. Not that Malcolm took a vote. It was a courtesy, a gesture of familial cooperation.

Because the brothers knew that in the end, their father would probably just do what he wanted to do. Like buy a $250,000 Aston Martin Lagonda (James Bond's getaway car of choice in the eighties), a $145,000 Lamborghini Countach, a Rommel-in-the-desert $120,000 Lamborghini jeep, or a $200,000 vintage 1932 Twin Six Packard touring car. *Just to have them.* Besides, Malcolm said, "I can outvote their . . . votes if it comes to a showdown about slowing down."

"So what do you guys think of this house idea?" Malcolm ventured at one family powwow. Strained silence. The brothers looked at each other. Then one finally piped up, "Uh, how much is this going to cost, Pop?"

Much eye rolling at the "close to a million" answer. But of course, there was no veto. A futile backdoor effort to derail the project soon came from Leonard Yablon, the company's chief finance man, an attack dog known as "The Hammer" when it came to expenses, but often frustrated when trying to restrain Malcolm.

On the sensible theory that Panorama House would be nothing more than a small, well-outfitted "viewing station," Yablon tried out this desperate logic with one of the planners: "Isn't there some kind of prefab shed we can get for around $40,000, and spend another $40,000 to get it up?" *Yeah, that would be great if that's what the boss wanted, but that's not what he wants.* End of argument.

Now that Malcolm was gone, none of the brothers wanted to

proceed with the project. Certainly not Bob, privately referred to by some as "Fredo" for his role as a likeable but unappreciated brother. Bob had few emotional ties to Trinchera and came closer than any of his siblings to living the kind of glamorous life his father did—splitting his time among the high-altitude social worlds of Palm Beach, Manhattan, and London, along with his wife, Lydia, whose son from a previous marriage, the handsome party-loving Miguel Raurell, later Miguel Forbes, Bob adopted and brought into the company.

Tim, a tall, fit former documentary filmmaker who looked uncannily like his father, minus the gray hair, could easily climb through the sagebrush up a Colorado mountain. He often runs into staffers late afternoons as he trudges up and down eight flights wearing a sixty-pound backpack, training for rock-climbing the Shawangunk Mountains in upstate New York, or for skiing in Montana or at Jackson Hole, Wyoming, where the family had a ranch on the Snake River; eighty-five acres of that were put up for sale in the summer of 2010 for $12 million. Like Steve, Tim rarely visited Trinchera.

To the extent any of the brothers would have supported the idea of Panorama House, it would have been Kip, who had his own home at the ranch—Schley House, a large cabin with a dramatic array of elk racks framing the entrance. Kip spent more time at Trinchera than any of his siblings. But he wasn't about to argue for what amounted to a $1 million shack on top of a mountain. So the message to the planners was polite but firm: *None of what you're doing has any bearing on what's happening now. We're not doing that stuff anymore. It's over.*

I got a firsthand taste of the "distancing" when I proposed a marketing gimmick to give some buzz to the magazine's year-end edition that featured an unusually well-managed company on the cover. Why not revive a B. C. Forbes tradition of celebrating top CEOs with a fancy dinner at the Waldorf? The update would be to present the cover "winner" with a "Malcolm Forbes Award." Jim Michaels motioned me to stay after the meeting where I'd pitched the idea. "The family wouldn't like that," he said in a confidential tone. "They're moving away from the past."

6

"WHY IS THAT MAN LAUGHING?"

Paying too much for a bottle of wine spoils the taste.

—Malcolm Forbes

L IKE HIS FATHER, KIP loved spending money, particularly on art. He relished his role as the sort of uber curator of the family's vast collection of paintings, prints, historical documents, ceramics, jewelry, and of course, the famous Fabergé eggs. All of which were worth hundreds of millions of dollars. He was personally responsible for buying most of the four hundred or so paintings that once provided the core of the family's Victorian collection, most of which used to be at Old Battersea House in London.

With dark hair, smartly tailored suits, tab collars, Gucci loafers, and a debonair manner that almost always includes a slight bow when greeting a guest or employee, Kip conveys a totally charming haughtiness that is at once pleasing yet distant, a sense that no one can really ever know the man behind the ready smile, the droll sense of humor, and that perfect bon mot. *I'm a Forbes,* he seems to say, *and you're not.*

His demeanor befits a royal, which he'd certainly like to be. Reflecting his love for things beautiful and lush, Kip's inner sanctum at 60 Fifth is a sensual Victorian retreat, with opulent flowing curtains, lots of dark wood, and a silky feel that echoes his father's old bedroom in the town house, which looked a little like a Moroccan bordello.

After an early marriage right out of college that lasted only a short while, Kip, at twenty-three, married a German baroness fifteen years his senior, Astrid von Heyl zu Herrnsheim, of Bismarck lineage. Like his father, Kip liked to be in the company of handsome young men, some of whom would accompany him on his frequent international trips.

Beyond objets Victoriana, Kip was attracted to the work of William Aiken Walker, a South Carolinian who specialized in genre scenes from the Old South, most of which were done between the 1860s and early 1900s. On the block November 9, 1994, at Doyle & Co., one of New York's premier auction houses, came lot 88, *Levee in New Orleans,* ostensibly by Walker. Kip snagged it for $45,000.

Realizing who'd won the painting, a man in the audience started laughing so hard he had to leave the room. What was that all about? Perhaps a clue something was amiss? Turns out the man was part of a small gang of scamsters who forged paintings on decades-old canvases and then foisted them on unsuspecting auction houses. *Levee* had been one of them. After X-ray analysis proved it was a fake, Doyle gave Kip his money back. "We always do the right thing," a Doyle official later told a reporter.

Levee was a reprise of sorts of Kip's apparent triumph in snagging a bottle of 1787 Château Lafite for his father at a 1985 Christie's auction in London. The bottle had supposedly belonged to Thomas Jefferson, quite the oenophile himself in his day. Malcolm had read about the auction and was determined to get the bottle to include as part of an exhibit of Jefferson memorabilia, including three letters about wine, to launch the opening of the Forbes Galleries.

Kip got into a bidding war with Marvin Shanken, the publisher of *Wine Spectator,* who was dismayed to learn he'd be bidding against the deep-pocketed Forbeses—especially after Len Yablon, the guardian of the purse strings who came along with Kip, told Shanken before the auction they were there to "pick up" the bottle and fly it back to New York that night on the *Tool.* To Shanken, Yablon's presumptive arrogance that they'd prevail and simply whisk away the bottle on a private jet was infuriating. *Hey, I'm the wine guy here!* Shanken was willing to pay up to $30,000, almost as much as the then-record $38,000 paid a year earlier for a jeroboam of 1870 Mouton Rothschild at a Dallas auction.

Kip had his own angst about the auction, since he knew all too well that bidding on his father's behalf was always tricky. Malcolm had once become furious at Steve for paying $396,000 in 1982 for the original survey marking the Mason–Dixon Line.

As recounted in *The New Yorker* and Benjamin Wallace's *The Billionaire's Vinegar,* the auction provided some high drama. Kip and Yablon figured they could get the bottle for around £5,000, or $7,500. But the bidding for lot 337 began at £10,000 and rose quickly to £50,000. From the back of the room, Shanken jumped in at £52,000, and the war was on. Forbes and Shanken ping-ponged back and forth in £2,000 increments until Shanken finally caved after Kip had bid £105,000, an astounding $156,000. The entire process had taken ninety-nine seconds.

Malcolm dropped the phone when Kip called from London to tell him how much it cost. "We did what you told us," Kip began. But Malcolm was enraged: In a hold-the-receiver-away-from-your-ear tirade, he chewed out Kip—then his trusted finance guy who was supposed to take care of his money.

Perhaps propitiously, a father-son confrontation that night back in New York was avoided; the extraordinary sale price meant a departure delay from Heathrow. Why? Forbes now had to obtain an export license as well as a certification from a museum that the bottle wasn't a national treasure. By the time all that paperwork was assembled and the *Tool* lifted off, there was no chance to make the party.

The purchase, excessive even in the "greed is good" eighties, simply wound up creating more buzz for Malcolm. Appearing on a television program later that night, to talk about business and the economy, Malcolm found the wine bottle, news of which had hit the wires, to be the main topic of inquiry. "The Forbes family would have been far better off if Mr. Jefferson had drunk the damn thing," he said.

But by the time Kip and Yablon arrived the next day, Malcolm was basking in the media attention over his latest acquisition. Which to him merely cemented the Forbes name more solidly to wealth. Or as Kip would later say, "It's more fun than the opera glasses Lincoln was holding when he was shot. *And we have those, too!*" So there.

But the $156,000 investment "in a piece of history" proved to be somewhat dubious. Questions almost immediately surfaced as to the bottle's provenance. For one thing, the archivists at Monticello were highly skeptical that the bottle belonged to Jefferson, who kept meticulous daily logs and memos on virtually every purchase or transaction he ever made. But there was no reference to a 1787 Lafite.

The bottle's seller, a German collector named Hardy Rodenstock, became the focus of inquiry after another purchaser of "Jefferson bottles," the famously litigious billionaire William Koch, got suspicious about the four bottles he had. He launched an investigation of his own, with the help of some former FBI agents. They concluded that Jefferson's "Th.J." initials were probably engraved with some kind of modern power tool like a dental drill. Koch wound up suing Rodenstock in U.S. federal district court for fraud, but was unable to convince the Forbes family to join the suit. That wouldn't have been the kind of follow-up publicity they needed. A judge ultimately dismissed the suit on jurisdictional grounds, but by dint of the suit's allegations, Rodenstock was branded a "con artist," as the suit alleged.

Whether the bottle was a fake or not, the Forbes curatorial staff inadvertently made sure nobody would ever sample what was inside. The bottle was inexplicably kept under a bright spotlight in the Galleries, basically cooking the contents into a big jar of salad dressing. Now useless for drinking or resale, the bottle resides in a temperature-controlled curatorial vault at 60 Fifth, along with one of Lincoln's stovepipe hats, presumed authentic.

7

INSIDE THE MONEY PIT

More than enough is too much.

—Malcolm Forbes

F ORBES IS TO ART, bric-a-brac, toys, and anything collectible what a magnet is to iron filings." So Christopher Buckley wrote about Malcolm's once immense collection, one that prompted more than one essayist to speculate on the reason behind his obsessive behavior—was it an extraordinary level of sensation-seeking? Or the strenuous efforts of one man to accumulate a material sense of self-identity—like Citizen Kane?

Malcolm's trove of Fabergé, including at one point eleven Imperial eggs (one more than the Kremlin, he'd boast), began modestly enough, with the early 1960s purchase in London (for less than $1,000) of a small gold cigarette case with the double-eagle Russian Imperial seal on the lower left-hand corner. It was a "presentation piece," the Czarist equivalent of the modern-day goodie bag item. Forbes gave it to his wife for Christmas, followed at Easter by a small white "jelly bean" Fabergé egg from A La Vieille Russie, the Fabergé specialist at the corner of Fifty-ninth and Fifth, just up the street from Tiffany's.

Before long, Malcolm wasn't holding back. At auction, he paid $50,000 for an egg that was originally a gift to the Duchess of

Marlborough. After the bidding was over, the man who lost out came up and introduced himself. It turned out to be the owner of A La Vieille Russie, who showed Malcolm some Imperial egg treasures in his vault. That did it. He was smitten.

Except for Kip's passion for Victorian art, the family really didn't start out wanting to be a collector of anything. As with the eggs, it just sort of happened. Seeing a box of toy soldiers at an auction one day that looked like the ones he used to play with as a kid, Malcolm bought the lot. Other purchases soon followed. Bob Forbes recalls his father saying, "Up went my hand and it has stayed mostly up ever since." "Eventually," Malcolm said, "I ran out of shelf room, and out of excuses that I was buying them for my children."

Sold at auction at Sotheby's in the fall of 2010, the Galleries' soldier collection once numbered ten thousand: British and French troops on parade, marching bands, sailors, Aztec warriors, Trojans battling Greeks, Revolutionary War figures, medieval knights, Kaiser Wilhelm reviewing his troops, George Washington doing the same, William Tell (complete with bow, arrow, and apple), Alexander the Great, Caesar and Cleopatra, Buffalo Bill, countless cowboys and Indians, the U.S. Calvary coming to the rescue, farmers, fox hunters, Bengal lancers, bagpipers, stage coaches, covered wagons, coronation coaches, airplanes, antiaircraft gunners, elephants, camels, and even a village idiot.

They came from makers like George Hyde of Dresden, Heinrichsen of Nuremberg, Mignon of Paris, Harold Pestana of the U.S., and the U.K.'s William Britain, who figured out in 1892 you could make hollow soldiers by shaking the molten lead out of the cast before it totally set.

Malcolm had a particular passion for autographed documents, and at one point the family had over three thousand of them, including the Treaty of Versailles, the Emancipation Proclamation, Truman's famous letter to the music critic who panned his daughter's piano playing, and even Paul Revere's expense account—covering the costs of his 1774 roundtrip between Boston and New York, including "horse hire." (The total expenses of £14.42, equivalent to-day to more than $1,500, were approved.)

Also auctioned off recently were Malcolm's five hundred toy boats, mostly metal and wood (no plastic), dating from the 1870s up to the mid-1950s, representing the most storied of European makers, like Marklin, Bing, Carette, and Fleischmann of Germany, and Ives, Orkin, Brown, and James Fallows & Co. in the U.S. There were sailboats, steamships, and battleships, and the L'Amphibio, a charming 1906 French contraption made of tin and wood, powered by a rubber band. It could run either as a car or float on water.

Writing in his introduction to his 2004 book *Toy Boats,* Bob Forbes, a former "bathtub admiral" himself who helped his father gather the collection, talked about his fascination with toy boats: "I look at them as a reflection of the world they came from, a world still linked by water: Passenger liners carrying immigrants to a new world or the wealthy to visit the old; warships that protected boundaries or helped annex new ones; and pleasure boats that existed for just that, for messing around in boats."

But Malcolm's favorite toy boat couldn't fit in the Galleries.

Built at the De Vries Lynch shipyard in Holland, the 151-foot *Highlander,* the fifth so-named company yacht, went into service in October 1985. It had always been the family's most distinctive signature symbol of wealth and power. With a crew of fourteen, it was able to comfortably entertain up to one hundred passengers. In any one May–November season, the boat would host some eighty events and serve eighteen fourteen-ounce tins of Beluga caviar to guests like Buzz Aldrin, Mick Jagger, Paul McCartney, Margaret Thatcher, Andy Warhol, Elizabeth Taylor, the Reagans, Prince Charles, President and Mrs. George H. W. Bush, plus dozens of chief executives, marketing executives, media planners, and any other people the family wanted to soften up, including key members of the New York City police department.

There are five guest staterooms and six salons, each displaying several appropriate pieces of maritime-themed art, including three *verre églomisé* panels from the main salon of the *Normandie,* a stained-glass door from Queen Victoria's Royal yacht *Osborne,* set in the ceiling in the dining salon, and a painting by Sir Noel Coward entitled *The Lighthouse, Dover.*

A trip on the *Highlander* was an extraordinary experience no competitor could possibly come close to matching. Marketing executives, media planners, and chief executives were excited and honored to be piped aboard—whether it be for an elegant dinner cruise around lower Manhattan, or a trip up the Hudson to West Point on Saturdays for an afternoon of football, food, and booze. For added drama, the *Highlander*'s resident helicopter, a Bell 206 JetRanger named the *Highland Fling,* often delivered or removed Malcolm or Steve while the boat was underway. For ports of call there were two BMW motorcycles, plus a nineteen-foot cigarette boat and a twenty-three-foot Donzi to serve as tenders.

To help fend off possible IRS inquiries as to just how the boat was used, Forbes went to great lengths to always assert that "99 percent of the *Highlander*'s use is for business," mostly arm-twisting for ads. But the other 1 percent, likely much more, certainly made for family fun. Miguel Forbes, Bob's stepson, has used the *Highlander* for trips to St. Barts over Christmas and New Year's. And Steve would routinely use the boat to take his family up to New England in the summers.

On one particularly epic 1987 "I'll see your kings and raise you" voyage up the Amazon, Malcolm brought along the king and queen of Bulgaria. Following along in his own yacht, the *Virginian,* was the late media mogul John Kluge, whose guests included the king and queen of Greece. Malcolm knew Kluge's yacht well, since he used to own it as the *Highlander IV.* The hosts on this particular trip would take turns entertaining each other's passengers. Perhaps with the IRS in mind, there was a meeting with the president of Brazil and a press conference in which Malcolm gave his views on the country's then $100 billion debt ("it needs to be restructured").

But otherwise, the twelve-day adventure, inspired in part, Malcolm said, by Jacques Cousteau's 1983 Amazon trip, consisted of crocodile spotting, fending off mosquitoes and very large bats, a machete-wielding trip or two into the jungle, a little skeet shooting by the royals, lots of good food and wine, Bloody Marys, and air-conditioned comfort.

Just in case, Malcolm brought along a doctor who specialized in tropical diseases. For good company and amusing discussion came Christopher Buckley, who delighted in unsettling his fellow passengers by reading aloud from a book that described, in graphic medical detail, the different ways the Amazon could ruin your entire day: "nose dropping off, blindness from insects crapping in eyeball," and "toothpick-size catfish with fondness for 'mammalian orifices,'" which must be surgically removed." Buckley was about to continue, reading from sections on snakes and furry spiders, but was told to shut up.

If Forbes's guests weren't wined and dined on the boat, at Trinchera, or in the town house, there was always Balleroy, the family château in Normandy, built by François Mansart between 1626 and 1636. The signature event there was Malcolm's annual balloon weekend, an invitation-only event that included an array of the world's best hot-air balloonists and the usual galaxy of bold-faced names: Liz Taylor, Jann Wenner, Dominick Dunne, Abe Rosenthal, the king and queen of Romania, Jay Leno, Walter Cronkite, Rupert Murdoch, and Gianni Agnelli.

In Tangier was Malcolm's Palais Mendoub, a sprawling ten-acre Moroccan gem that once belonged to the governor of Tangier. Not far from the site of the Battle of Trafalgar, the palace has views of the Mediterranean, Gibraltar, and the southernmost tip of the Iberian Peninsula, the port city of Algeciras, Spain. Inside are magnificent rooms, including a stunning space laced with intricate mosaics for receiving important guests. Malcolm used Mendoub for his over-the-top $2.5 million seventieth birthday party in 1989, notable for many excesses, but particularly for the transportation provided: a chartered Concorde (from Los Angeles), two 747s, and the *Tool* to fly in his friends. Wildly extravagant by any measure, the party included eight hundred guests, six hundred drummers and dancers, balloons, bagpipers, and three hundred Berber horsemen, who rode in firing their muskets as a grand finale. Beverly Sills sang happy birthday. There were fireworks by Grucci. Calvin Klein came in all white. Robert Maxwell wore a big turban. Henry Kissinger came dressed like Henry Kissinger.

The party, widely covered in the media, had its behind-the-scenes moments. Morocco in the summer is basically a blast furnace. But the hotel where most of the guests were staying had no central air. Rather than turn their guests into walking shish kebabs, party organizers dispatched a fleet of vans to buy up all available oscillating fans in Tangier. Still, there were complaints from the high-end guests, not only about the accommodations but also about the noise from the tethered hot air balloon in the lobby. Well into the night, it would erupt in an enormous roar every time the giant flame kicked in to keep it aloft.

Confronting a protocol nightmare as to how to seat eight hundred people, Forbes decided to solve the problem by having everyone file past two giant Moroccan urns, reach in, and pick out their table numbers. Sucking it up, kings and queens waited in line patiently with commoners. But when Gianni Agnelli found out how the seating would be handled, he grabbed his wife and walked out.

King Hassan II, knowing that this would be Morocco's big moment, wanted his country to be the model of hospitality and generosity—especially to Malcolm and Elizabeth Taylor. Merchants were instructed to provide them with whatever they wanted. Thus on Liz's various shopping trips for jewelry, clothes, and gifts—during which all roads were closed to allow her three-car armored caravan to pass smoothly without hitting any camels or donkeys—she didn't have to pay for a thing. The standard line was "Please accept this . . ."

But a moment of panic set in at one store when Ms. Taylor asked where the bathroom was. Shuddering at the prospect of Elizabeth Taylor walking down a spiral staircase to a grungy room with a hole in the floor, the security detail's walkie-talkies came instantly alive. Within minutes Taylor was in her car being whisked to a nearby marbled penthouse restroom, fresh flowers and chocolates awaiting her reemergence. Nothing was left to chance. During the visit, Malcolm presented her with a velvet-lined box from Harry Winston. Wearing her best "You spoil me" smile, Taylor opened it to find a pair of paper earrings made of photographs of priceless jewels. "You shit!" she exclaimed, beating Malcolm on the head with the box while he convulsed in laughter.

Old Battersea House, the family's seventeenth-century Georgian home in London, is now on the market for $19.5 million. Of Christopher Wren design, it once contained an elaborate collection of Victorian art, assembled over the years by Kip. There's a display of ceramics by William De Morgan, the English potter whose distinctively complex lusters and underglaze painting techniques made him famous in the late nineteenth century. Befitting any old English abode, there's a resident ghost, once spotted by Steve's daughter Moira, and a very large pair of undergarments that once belonged to Queen Victoria. They reside in a glass frame inside a discreet cupboard above a vintage Thomas Crapper device in a second-floor bathroom, off the state bedroom. The undies are hidden so as not to embarrass the Prince of Wales, a family friend who sometimes visits.

Counting Trinchera, Balleroy, Battersea, Mendoub, and Laucala, what Malcolm once said was undeniably true—that the sun never sets on the houses of Forbes. No more.

8

THE MELTDOWN BEGINS

O N A MILD, LATE October evening in 2002, the family assembled a group of some sixty employees and guests in the Galleries for a rollout of a Forbes Wine Club, a line extension intended to enhance the brand's high-end image. It was a typically splendid Gallery event. As the wine flowed, white-coated servers glided through the crowd, refilling glasses and offering the signature array of hot cheese puffs, broiled chicken on skewers (with Thai dipping sauce), and fresh jumbo Gulf shrimp. Even to cynical journalists who'd seen this movie (and any number of its sequels) before, the evening's elegance was a reminder they were part of a very special organization, one that provided them with a hot meal prepared by the town house staff every other Friday night (when the magazine was in its final production phase) and a ride home afterward in a black town car.

Events like this, choreographed so as to suspend the real world for a couple of hours, made everyone feel as if they were at one of Gatsby's parties or on a small cruise ship bound for some distant, magical port. But looming that evening was an iceberg only a few senior managers at the party knew about. For what was to happen the next morning would make the night before seem eerily like that scene in *Titanic* when the string quartet fiddles away on deck as the ship disintegrates.

Sampling the wines and thoroughly enjoying themselves that night were a handful of the magazine's veteran writers, including Dyan Machan, a tall, drop-dead blonde who specialized in quirky profiles and stories about successful money managers. Her date that night was Donald Kendall, the former chairman of PepsiCo. Brigid McMenamin, an alluringly distant woman with black hair and dark, piercing eyes, had left a Wall Street law firm to become a *Forbes* reporter and fact-checker. Her intensity, skepticism, and formidable attention to detail made even the most accomplished senior writers sweat when she checked their work. Promoted to senior editor, McMenamin made her mark uncovering scamsters and shady offshore tax dodges—complex, hard-to-report stories most *Forbes* writers avoided. Coming down from his third-floor office to join the party was Bill Baldwin, then the magazine's editor, a man with a quick sense of humor, a formidable brain, and a clever wordsmith's touch. Unlike top editors at most magazines, Baldwin literally edited *every* story, whether changing a few words here and there or rewriting pieces from top to bottom, often inserting for the writer challenging questions, the answers to which invariably resulted in the stories being much more numerate and sophisticated.

Baldwin's cerebrum can instantly retrieve obscure parts of the U.S. tax code, fees charged by various mutual funds, anything to do with math or physics, and all things geeky. His recall both scared and amused his staff, some of whom referred to the bearded Harvard graduate as the "Unabomber" for his strange behavior in stressful situations. That's a characterization that resonates with some of Baldwin's high school classmates from New Canaan, Connecticut, who remember Billy as being aloof, obviously too smart to be seriously challenged by any of the work, and sometimes very odd.

Example? Less than an hour after the second plane hit the World Trade Center, incinerating thousands of people only blocks away and sending the entire country into panic, Baldwin refused to postpone the regular 11:00 A.M. editorial meeting. He openly doubted the attack was worth extensive coverage in *Forbes,* later that day refused to believe the Towers had collapsed, and ended the meeting by telling his puzzled editors, "Have fun!" Having a meeting with Baldwin, a former executive says, was "like visiting an uncle in a VA ward. He's sort of there, but not. And there were always miniature Japanese crawling out from under the bed."

Often uncomfortable with social interaction, Baldwin rarely left his office to wander around to talk with staffers, keeping salt-and-pepper shakers on his desk for solitary lunches and dinners. That night he particularly avoided engaging with Machan and McMenamin. Because he knew the next day he'd have to tell them and a dozen other editorial staffers they no longer had jobs.

During the Great Depression, founder B. C. Forbes kept everyone on, using the "Scottish vacation" solution—work four weeks, get paid for three. In 2002, even though there had been a prior round of layoffs the year before, most employees, at least those not privy to the numbers, felt *Forbes* was still at the top of its game, holding on to its number-one position in ad pages against rivals *Fortune* and *BusinessWeek.*

With a global audience of 38 million in Web, video, and print, including fourteen foreign language editions, *Forbes* had long sought to make its readers richer and smarter by delivering unique insights: mapping the smart places to put money; exposing the traps that await the unwary; drawing inspirational portraits of those who find opportunity where others see only adversity; and pointing a powerful searchlight in the faces of any who seek to exploit, mislead, or defraud.

Embedded with evidence and logic, *Forbes*'s edgy stories were always highly numerate, told with clarity and brevity. Like well-crafted jury summations, they proved, never asserted. Typically contrarian to what the rest of the press was reporting, *Forbes* would question where others applauded, find the silver lining when others derided. Surprise was a constant litmus test for whether a writer's story idea would be approved.

The payoff for the reader was always a lesson to learn and/or profit from—an obscure mutual fund that's outperformed the market; a company beating the pants off the competition because it embraces a technology or distribution technique the others dismiss or haven't thought of; a new way of using an old tax code provision to get a bigger refund. The *Forbes 400* list, the "franchise issue" each year, ranks the country's richest people and dissects the reasons behind their successes and failures. It has, Bill Gates once told publisher Rich Karlgaard, "an MBA between its pages."

But unbeknownst to many employees, the company was in a tailspin. In 2000, at the height of the tech frenzy, the magazine was bulging with 6,081 pages of ads, more than any other magazine that year, including the bride books. The problem was that 1,500 of those pages came from companies that didn't exist at the end of 2001. And without the lucky push of the nineties economy, there was no more cover for the owners' management missteps. After the hammer of 9/11, the ad slump turned into a free fall, and for all intents and purposes, the phones on Madison Avenue simply stopped ringing.

9

THE DISMANTLING

ONLY A FEW PEOPLE at 60 Fifth knew just how close *Forbes* was to financial ruin. In addition to the layoffs, *Forbes* stopped matching employee 401(k) contributions and cut senior managers' salaries by 5 percent.

Before long, the family launched what could only be called a systematic yard sale of its most valuable and visible assets: the Fabergé eggs to Russian energy tycoon Viktor Vekselberg for $110 million in 2004. Before they were shipped off to Russia, Forbes arranged for a last private showing of the eggs for the staff at the Sotheby's gallery at Seventy-second and York on the Upper East Side. At the end of the evening, when nearly everyone had left, Steve walked slowly around the exhibit, silently saying good-bye to each of the eggs. He looked crestfallen, on the verge of tears.

A potential lifeboat appeared briefly that same year from Condé Nast, which was looking for ways to expand its appeal to male readers. The Newhouse family thought *Forbes* might be a good fit with its prestigious stable of titles that included *The New Yorker, Vogue, Vanity Fair,* and *Architectural Digest.* The rumored number was $400 million, not enough at the time to satisfy the Forbes family, though in retrospect, it would have been a smart thing for them to do. On the other hand, Condé Nast knew that $400 million would be just the beginning: many more millions would be needed to retool *Forbes* for its own purposes.

Flirtatious but ultimately bowing to celibacy, Condé Nast backed away from *Forbes* and announced it was starting up its own business magazine, to be edited by Joanne Lipman, a high-powered *Journal* talent who'd been in charge of the paper's popular *Weekend* section. Si Newhouse promised patience and what *New York* magazine called "breathtaking resources" (industry gossip was that Newhouse was willing to spend $100 million over five years). The glamorous-looking *Portfolio* fell victim to poor timing. The magazine launched just as the country was plunging into recession. Reliant on luxury advertising, all Condé Nast magazines were slammed, and the company couldn't afford to sustain its investment. With great sadness, Si Newhouse pulled the plug in April 2009.

So the fire sale continued. Trinchera went to New York hedge fund manager Louis Bacon for $175 million in 2007. Sixty Fifth has been sold to Greenwich Village neighbor New York University in a sale/five-year-leaseback deal for $65 million, about half the original asking price.

Under the gavel went a stash of Victorian art: over three hundred pieces in 2003 for $35 million, and another dozen paintings in 2009 for $8 million. The sales included works by Burne-Jones, Holman Hunt, Hughes, Millais, Landseer, Leighton, Rossetti, and a James Abbott McNeill Whistler portrait of the daughter of *Charley's Aunt* playwright Walter Brandon Thomas.

At the time, Kip publicly professed not to be sad about the sale, noting that "for a long time, I was always the brother who spent money, but when my brothers saw what things have sold for they decided I wasn't quite as stupid as they thought." Kip once told his father that he could amass a definitive Victorian collection for about the same price that Malcolm once paid for one of Monet's water lilies.

"We've all been pretty good at spending the money," Kip said, "but now one is having, like everything else, to be constrained."

Privately, however, Kip was miffed, bitter, and unhappy with the dismantling of a collection he'd spent a good part of his life accumulating. He refused to attend the auction. I can only speculate about the shouting matches that divestiture must have triggered, as a major family fault line was opening up: Kip and Bob wanted to maintain their lifestyles and preserve as much of their money as possible; Tim and Steve, neither of whom spent much money on "stuff," were more concerned about the future of the company.

Then came the most wrenching fund-raiser of all: On Monday, August 7, 2006, *Forbes* employees awoke to read a shocker in *The New York Times,* leaked exclusively to that paper over the weekend: Elevation Partners, a Silicon Valley private equity group, had purchased 40 percent of *Forbes.* The price, never announced, was $250 million, which valued the company at about $650 million. Given that only a few years later, both *Newsweek* and *BusinessWeek* would sell for the price of a ham sandwich and some debt, the brothers now look smart. But the sale was and is still seen as the family's first step in its own exit strategy, though they have repeatedly denied that. Whatever the driving force behind it, this much is clear: they badly needed the money.

Given their differences, my sense is that Tim was the one pushing for the Elevation deal, whereas Steve probably initially resisted, finally reluctantly accepting that selling part of the company was a painful but necessary step. It was a stunning move for a company that had long pledged to remain independent and family owned.

The *Highlander* is now in mothballs, its crew laid off. Now that Old Battersea House is moving out of the family's inventory, Balleroy will be the only part of the kingdom left in Europe. Gone are Palais Mendoub, Laucala, *Capitalist Tool, Capitalist Tool Too,* an Augusta 109-A helicopter, and *Highland Fling.* There are no more birthday calls or corsages, no more Friday night dinners for editorial staffers, no more black car rides home, no more free umbrellas on rainy nights. For many *Forbes* employees, the most insulting cut was the elimination, starting in 2009, of Veteran's Day and the Veteran's Day money.

It wasn't so much that Veteran's Day wasn't held. Most people would have understood the cost-cutting move, particularly with an explanation from department heads. But even that wasn't done, for fear it'd immediately leak to Gawker or Mediabistro. And as it did with practically everything, the family approached cost-cutting *incrementally*, one round of layoffs at a time, followed by another, one more, then yet another, leaving those who still remained twisting in apprehension. By contrast, Barney Kilgore, the longtime head of the *Journal*, believed in reducing costs *fast*. "My father used to say it is a mistake to cut off the cat's tail an inch at a time," Kilgore once said. "Doesn't help the cat."

Forbes, which used to burst at the seams with three-hundred-page back-to-back issues, now rarely gets above 120, except for special issues, and is typically now held together by staples rather than being "perfect bound," a process by which separate sections are glued to the spine, like a book. Editorially, the magazine, once characterized as a publication for "the little greedy about the big greedy," has fewer edgy, groundbreaking stories than before, largely because there's now only a handful of writers left who know how to do them. Freelancers are being recruited now to do covers.

Rather than focus on substantive, analytical stories on its Web site, *Forbes* succumbed to the typical Web site addiction of focusing on "hits," how many viewers can be lured to click on a story on any given day, prompting a push to churn out such heavyweight stories like: "Ten Top Topless Beaches"; "Ten Ways to Avoid Gastric Bloat Over the Holidays"; and "Ten Famous Victoria Secret's Models: Where Are They Now?" And there have been sloppy errors like the Web site posting of gold at "$70 a barrel." "Hackers" came out "hakers." And "billionaire bios" are being posted directly on the site, with no editing, often resulting in muddled prose and valuations that clearly haven't been calculated with the usual care and protocols.

In the winter of 2009, Steve and Tim made a secret trip to the Middle East to try to raise more capital. They came back empty-handed.

Forbes has also rehired Lewis D'Vorkin, who served as the magazine's executive editor early in the decade, to run all of editorial. His prior experience includes being Page One editor at *The Wall Street Journal,* an editor at *Newsweek* and *The New York Times,* plus a stint at AOL before founding his own digital news operation called True/Slant, which *Forbes* purchased in 2010 and has since closed down. D'Vorkin's title is chief product officer. Baldwin is now a columnist, writing smart, edgy investment pieces.

At Elevation's insistence, there is a new chief executive at 60 Fifth Avenue, and for the first time in nearly a century, his last name is not Forbes. After a search that took nearly a year, Michael Perlis, a perpetually tanned former Ziff Davis media executive who took "a deep dive into the digital world" as a venture capitalist for ten years, joined *Forbes* in the fall of 2010 as "the decider." Described by a fourth-grade classmate at Coleytown Elementary in Westport, Connecticut, as a "really, really nice kid" in a class where "not all the boys were," a now grown-up Perlis seems to have retained that characteristic and, at least initially, was well received, as he began his "listening tour" of the building.

Steve and Tim's formal corporate duties have been reduced to being board members. That the family is no longer involved in running the company on a day-to-day basis is profound. It reflects Elevation's belief not only that the brothers weren't up to the job, but also that a dramatic new direction was needed in order to rescue the franchise and any hope of Elevation's getting any of its money back.

Perlis's arrival has also been widely viewed as the Hail Mary, the last-ditch effort to lipstick the pig and repackage *Forbes* so it's attractive enough to sell. Venture capitalists are best known for building value rather than managing an enterprise over the long haul, a goal Perlis hinted at in a message to the staff his first day on the job: "With our traditional products and innovative digital media we're uniquely positioned to break new ground and *create amazing value.*" (Emphasis added.)

Whether Perlis and D'Vorkin can stop the bleeding is unclear. In their zeal to travel a new road, the brothers have unwittingly gutted the soul of what they wanted so desperately to save by selling off key assets that made *Forbes* special, unique, and distinctive. To be ordinary, fungible, or common is not what Malcolm was. And that is now what the brand is turning into, or some would say, has already become. Marketing guru Simon Sinek says that Steve took the torch that Malcolm passed to him and "buried it in the sand," wiping out that "clear sense of purpose, cause, and belief" that B.C. formulated and Malcolm so vividly personified—that capitalism is not on this earth to make millions, but to create happiness. *Forbes,* Sinek says, is now just simply another enterprise chasing dollars.

In 2009 Forbes Media lost $40 million on revenues of some $100 million, including $50 million from the magazine and slightly under $40 million from the Web site. That's down from $200 million in 2000. By one estimate from an insider in a position to know, revenues for 2010 were less than the prior year's, and there was another multimillion loss.

Two decades ago, the family almost certainly would have earned a spot on the *Forbes 400* list of richest Americans, had they allowed that number to be published. Today, with a cutoff of $1 billion to join that exclusive club, they wouldn't come close. When you add up the spoils the family has accrued from all the asset sales and the private equity cash infusion, it comes to well over $500 million.

To find out how it came to this, and what happened to all that money, we need to go back to the beginning. To Scotland.

BOOK II

10

ROOTS

NOT FAR FROM THE North Sea lies the little town of New Deer, a tidy gray stone village, set in a spare, misty valley about thirty miles northwest of Aberdeen. It has a branch of the Royal Bank of Scotland, a post office, a general store, and four essentials of any Scottish village: a kilt maker and three pubs. One of them, the Brucklay Arms on Main Street, will pour you a Macallan or perhaps a Bitter & Twisted beer. If you've had too many of either, they'll make something called an oatmeal posset: milk, Scottish heather honey, a little oatmeal, and whisky.

Known in the sixth century as Auchreddie, Gaelic for "place of the bog myrtle," New Deer was formed around a tiny chapel built by a monk who would eventually become St. Kane. For him is named the town's only functioning church, or kirk, whose grounds gently cradle the remains of Malcolm Forbes and those of Bertie Charles Forbes, born on May 14, 1880.

The church, built in 1839, replaced a smaller one from the seventeenth century, and sits in the center of town. If, at dusk, you climb one of the highest nearby hills, the Hill of Clush, close your eyes and inhale the heather-sweet air, it's possible to imagine, if only for a few moments, the simple, stark beauty of what it must have been like for someone, possibly a young B. C. Forbes, to look out from this hill in the late nineteenth century.

The land was filled with cornfields and heath, punctuated by granite outcroppings and coarse limestone. According to an account of the time:

> Moss covers an inconsiderable area, which yearly grows less and less, owing to planting, reclamation or consumption of fuel . . . The soil, with few exceptions, is light and shallow, and a great proportion of the land rests on an iron-bound pan from 6 inches to 2 feet thick. Remains in the mosses indicate the existence of a primeval forest, but now . . . the parish is rather poorly off for trees. Ancient Caledonian standing stone, a rocking stone, and stone circles, in various places, have nearly all been destroyed.

Further back in time, New Deer and the surrounding Highlands were home to the clan chiefs, who were romanticized by history, but also widely feared. Demanding fierce loyalty, they derived a part of their power from their reliance on unreasonably cheap labor. Historian and essayist Edward Burt noted that the clan chief's need for glory and dominance often came in direct opposition to the material good of his followers. If a clansman would have the nerve to protest directly to his chief about a pay cut, he'd have been "carried to the next rock, and precipitated."

Bertie Forbes (pronounced "For-bess" by the locals) was the sixth of ten children born to Robert Forbes, the village tailor, and Agnes Moir, the blacksmith's daughter. They lived in a little granite house called Cunnyknowe, on a hill above the ruins of Robert the Bruce's castle.

It was not an easy life. The elder Forbes sold beer and groceries out of the front room to help make ends meet. Young Bertie, a small boy who looked much younger than his age, hoarded pennies won at card games and earned a few shillings cleaning the mud off the boots of English hunters who came up to Scotland for shooting.

He'd get up at five o'clock, walk through the fields in darkness, and shine up to twenty pairs of shoes. But sometimes it was hard to keep what he'd earned. Eyeing his son's shillings one day, Robert Forbes sold him what looked like a gold watch, but it turned out to be only brass. That transaction took all of young Bertie's savings.

Leaving school after eighth grade, the fourteen-year-old set off for Peterhead, a fishing village twenty-five miles to the northeast, where he worked for a few months as an apprentice bookkeeper before applying for a job at the local paper. His headmaster at the Whitehill Public School back in New Deer, Gavin Greig, wrote articles for a newspaper in nearby Buchan, and led young Forbes to believe that he could be a writer one day, too, having often praised his school compositions.

The notes B.C. took in school were not just mere statements of fact. They were little narrative pieces, including pictures. Wrote headmaster Greig in a 1901 letter of recommendation: "He has developed good literary style—ready and picturesque."

Young B.C. was ambitious, but also naïve. Being totally unfamiliar with how newspapers worked and believing the word "compositor" had something to do with writing, he signed up for an apprenticeship at seventy-five cents a week in 1894 with the *Peterhead Sentinel*. Only after he began did he discover his job involved not reporting but *typesetting*, which he considered nothing less than "penal servitude."

Because shorthand was a requirement in Britain for any reporter's job, Bertie started taking classes, winning prizes for his speed, which eventually reached 120 words a minute. He finally wangled a junior reporting job, not in Peterhead but at the *Dundee Courier*'s Perth bureau, where he lived in the dingy garret of a tenement house, furnished only with a rusty iron bed and a couple of empty boxes.

In Perth, his competent but not terribly hardworking boss William Watson "berated me unmercifully several times a week, with or without cause. He made me feel that I might be dismissed any day, notwithstanding all the work I was doing."

Remember this. We'll see this kind of behavior from editors again.

On a visit to the newspaper's head office one day, Forbes was chatting with an editor, who began praising several "great descriptive" stories from the Perth bureau that the editor had assumed Watson had done. When seventeen-year-old Bertie said he was in fact the author, the editor replied, "You just put up with all you have to stand for a little while longer, and we'll soon give you a district of your own."

That came quickly. After only six months as a junior reporter, Forbes was the senior reporter in Brechin, where a cousin, Charlie Moir, would be his assistant. There he scored a major scoop one evening when a trainload of cattle crashed right through the station, creating general mayhem, killing most of the animals, and seriously injuring the train crew.

Bertie ran to the scene, took down the basic facts, called his paper to reserve space for a big story, then phoned in flashes to the London papers and the big press associations. His coverage earned him the job of being a correspondent for several London papers. Always taking on more than he was responsible for, Forbes began writing editorials for his paper as well. Rejected by a young lass from a nearby village, Forbes fell into "black, black woe," deciding the only thing to do was pack up and head for the remotest corner of the world he could think of—South Africa. There, as the Boer War wound down, he figured he'd find some excitement and opportunity. As it turned out, neither came soon. Insecure, with little money, and finding no work despite applying for more than twenty jobs, a much-discouraged Bertie went to work as a typist with the government railroad. After months of looking, Forbes finally landed a newspaper job at the *Natal Mercury*, where he quickly became the fill-in for the main editorial writer.

Forbes soon established himself as a deft, if somewhat flowery essayist, leaving the reader in no doubt as to what his point of view was. "Surely, a nobler document was never penned than that which lays bare the inmost soul of Cecil John Rhodes," Forbes wrote when Rhodes's will was made public. "Great was he in lifetime; greater still is he in death. He was not perfect; no man born of the earth ever was."

Renowned British journalist Edgar Wallace, whose big scoop for the London *Daily Mail* was reporting that the Boer War was about to end, gave Forbes his next big break. Wallace had just been named editor of the *Rand Daily Mail,* a new Johannesburg newspaper that years later would become known for its courageous anti-apartheid stance, uncovering conditions other news organizations refused to write about. Wallace wanted Forbes to come over and be one of his senior reporters. Bertie jumped at it.

One of the paper's main features was a daily signed article by Wallace. Filling in for him one evening, Forbes wrote about the tragic suicide of Hector MacDonald, a British hero of the Boer War. It was an opportunity for Bertie to let his love for the Highlands sear into the text of almost every paragraph:

> Only those who know the Highlands of Scotland and the clansmen who inhabit its mountains, moors and glens, can realize the loss which the Empire will suffer by the downfall of Hector MacDonald. What drew hundreds of young Highlanders from the sheep-runs to the battlefield? . . . What filled the ranks of the gallant old 92nd? The record of its Highland recruit, the later-day hero of Omdurman.

Forbes ended the article in his typically upbeat fashion: "I have tried to tell something of his rise. Let others write of his fall." The next morning the paper's financial editor complimented him on the piece and said the Stock Exchange "just about stopped for a time" while the traders discussed the story.

One day Forbes set out to interview a member of the Japanese royal family who was staying at a local hotel. Told to go to a certain room at an appointed hour, he knocked and was told to come in. Forbes was startled to find his interview subject standing in a tub, buck naked. His highness bowed, and insisted that Bertie conduct his interview while he finished taking his bath. Years later, Forbes would write that the encounter "caused me to reflect that, after all, there was little difference between the humblest and the highest, and that I would never thereafter hesitate to approach anyone, no matter how exalted."

But South Africa wasn't enough for an ambitious young man who believed Johannesburg to be "a mining town which, for all its wealth, had the narrow mentality of a suburban parish." Plus, something inside him told him he needed "to be bumped and buffeted about a whole lot more." That would soon come.

11

BIG HAT, NO CATTLE

WITH A FEW THOUSAND dollars in his pocket, twenty-three-year-old Bertie Forbes set sail for America in 1903. He went first class, on the theory that to be at the top, you had to be around people who were, a maxim he would later follow many times. His editors in Johannesburg were sorry to see him go, and sent him thirty-five pounds, "in appreciation for the excellent work done by you whilst on the staff . . . Whilst we are very loath to lose so valued a servant, we nevertheless feel that we cannot stand in your way . . ."

It didn't go well in New York at first. Dressed in loud, inappropriate job-hunting attire and carrying a gold-topped cane, the young Forbes looked like the rube just off the boat that he was, and failed to impress any editor with his clips or experience. Nobody cared about the *Rand Daily Mail*. And Bertie looked like a very short teenager. On the advice of a Scots journalist he met, he started showing up for interviews in pinstriped trousers and black morning coat, a uniform he'd continue to wear for years.

Then one weekend, waiting for a golf game in Brooklyn, a man with a Scottish burr mistook him for a caddy. On a whim, Bertie played along with the mistaken identity, and carried the man's clubs,

engaging him in conversation. When Bertie mentioned he was looking for a financial reporting job, the golfer said he'd introduce him
to his friend and fellow Scotsman John Doddsworth, the managing
editor of the *Journal of Commerce and Commercial Bulletin*.

As directed, Forbes showed up for an interview, and though he
volunteered to work for nothing, Doddsworth paid him fifteen dollars a week to cover dry goods, which Forbes felt were "well named."
The routine had been for the paper to publish, without question,
"current prices" of raw silk, supplied by importers. But the prices
were always above the real selling prices. Pointing to the published
numbers, the importers would tell customers, "For you, we'll make a
deal."

So Forbes published the *real* numbers, creating a furor in the
market. But buyers and sellers alike soon began to pay attention to
what he was reporting. B.C. gave the paper a new credibility for
being accurate—and innovative.

Forbes knew how important appearances were in the business
community. So adopting a "big hat, no cattle" strategy, he moved
from his ten-dollar-a-week boarding house in Brooklyn and took
a room in the old Waldorf-Astoria hotel, where financial bigwigs
hung out in the evenings. "To do what I aspired to do, it was essential that I gain their respect, their confidence and their friendship,"
he told a colleague.

B.C. soon became a fixture, working the lobby and the bar to
make contacts, taking names and numbers, and always making sure
he told the Wall Street types he lived at the hotel and held a very
important job at the *Journal of Commerce*. The Waldorf cost him
more than the fifteen dollars a week he was earning, so he saved
money by pocketing the carfare the paper gave him for reporting
trips around the city and walked instead.

What Forbes learned from all this schmoozing was that people
were often more interesting than the businesses they ran—a focus
that he'd exploit more and more as time went on. He leveraged a job
offer to become the *Rand Daily Mail*'s "London editor and cable
correspondent" into a promise from Doddsworth that he'd make

B.C. financial editor, first spending some time as the assistant editor. In addition to his regular work, he soon began writing a daily column, which he called "Fact and Comment." With Doddsworth's permission, Forbes also took on the freelance assignment of filling in for a man on sick leave at the *Commercial and Financial Chronicle* who did a weekly column on foreign exchange and money markets. Doddsworth and others marveled at B.C.'s apparent limitless capacity for taking on more work. He was a totally driven man.

It paid off. Two years later he got a message to call the editor-in-chief of the *New York American,* William Randolph Hearst's flagship New York paper. It seems Hearst wanted to improve the paper's financial pages, and figured hiring the prolific young columnist was the way to do it. As the new business editor of the *New York American,* B.C. now had more influence than ever before. With colorful, often embarrassingly flattering stories on how the wealthy and influential achieved their greatness—a theme he'd later bring to his own magazine—Forbes soon made the paper's financial section almost as popular as the sports pages. Even the production staff took note. One day a makeup man named Murray, whom B.C. described as "always tipsy but ever lovable," hit B.C. up for a ten-dollar loan while he was busy making up the next day's financial page. "Mr. Murray," B.C. replied, "I just write about money; I don't lend it."

Letters of praise, encouragement, and advice began to flow in from the high and mighty—the heads of the brokerage houses, stock exchanges, railroads, and manufacturers. There were even kudos from the competition. Wrote an editor at the *New York Evening Journal*: "Your stuff is so much the best that is written that there is no comparison in my opinion."

Forbes, who had changed his byline from Bertie C. Forbes to B. C. Forbes because an editor told him "it's simpler," was now a financial journalist to be reckoned with. But his life would soon change again, as a result of a 1914 Saturday night poker game in Brooklyn.

12

"ENOUGH SACRED COWS TO POPULATE ALL OF INDIA"

I T WAS IN BROOKLYN that he met Adelaide Stevenson, the stunning eighteen-year-old stepdaughter of a pharmacist who hosted regular card games at his home in the borough where Forbes now lived after finally moving out of the Waldorf. B.C., seventeen years her senior, was instantly smitten when he met the poised young woman, an auburn-haired beauty. In what for the time was something of a whirlwind courtship, they married a year later, in the sacristy of Our Lady of Angels church in Bay Ridge. They couldn't be married at the main altar, since Forbes was a die-hard Presbyterian, and Adelaide a fervent Catholic—a critical difference that would later dominate and ultimately help destroy their marriage.

For a time, they were very happy. She was beautiful, he was a famous columnist who had unprecedented access to the movers and shakers of American business and finance. They lived in a large house on Fountain Road in Englewood, New Jersey, where they would eventually raise five sons, starting with Bruce, born in 1916. A year later would come another birth, B.C.'s own magazine.

Forbes wanted to call it *Doers and Doings*, a biweekly that would highlight the successes of American businessmen by celebrating their achievements. Their stories would be told in a highly personal way that gave hope and inspiration to those on the way up. He wanted a publication that would "strive to inject more humanity, more joy and more satisfaction into business, and into life in general."

The magazine's title became an issue. B.C.'s business manager, whom he'd lured from *The Magazine of Wall Street*, was adamant that it be called simply *Forbes*. B.C. thought that implied "silly vanity," but after consulting with many of the big shots he'd gotten to know, he finally gave in. "They impressed upon me that it was only business gumption to capitalize on my name, since it had been pitched before the eyes of the public day in and day out all over the country for years." But first there was the little matter of seed money. Between his Hearst salary and the income from the writing he did for other publications, Forbes was easily making $10,000 a year, or the equivalent in 2010 dollars of about $170,000. For 1917, it was an enormous amount of money, and B.C. had stashed away enough of it to maintain an extremely comfortable standard of living. But he didn't want to touch any of it for start-up costs.

So he hit up for loans many of the prominent men that he'd gotten to know and had written about favorably over the years, most of whom he'd profiled in his book *Fifty Men Who Are Making America*. The book was a collection of uncritical profiles of men like Henry Clay Frick, the steel and coke magnate, banker Jacob Schiff, and John H. Patterson of National Cash Register.

None of these men, it would appear, had any flaws, weren't the least bit ruthless, treated their employees like family, and, sure as the Highlands have fog, were just swell, charitable guys.

So flattered, why would any high-profile executive not agree to loan money to a journalist who'd no doubt continue to throw lavish praise their way, a cozy relationship that would almost certainly be assured to continue if that executive advertised in the new magazine? That was the unspoken dialogue that would continue, on a very subtle level, between *Forbes* and some of its key advertisers for years. "There were so many sacred cows, you could populate all of India," recalls one former senior writer. Another ex–senior writer says he was ordered in the 1960s to do a "puff piece" on a favored advertiser, a big tire company. But the story never appeared.

When the reporter showed up at a Midtown hotel early one afternoon to interview a top executive, the son of the chairman, he couldn't get an answer to even a softball question: "So what's the company's strategy for next year?" The son (and his wife, who was also in the room) had clearly been overserved with room service liquor. "I don't know," the man wailed, almost on the verge of tears. "My father won't tell me anything." "He's right," the wife helpfully added. "He treats [my husband] like nothing." The reporter left with an empty notebook.

Appearing on September 15, 1917, the first issue of *Forbes* had a cover price of fifteen cents (It's now $5.99.) The dream had become a reality. B.C.'s beliefs were embodied in his magazine. Nobody reading it could possibly mistake what B.C. stood for. The all-type cover, framed by a pair of Greek columns, previewed upbeat topics like "Keys to Doors of Success" and what for the time was a forward-looking, but ultimately patronizing, feature department called Woman in Business.

Inside, next to the table of contents, and beneath yet another rubric ("Devoted to Investment Finance and the Human Side of Business"), was a prominent National Cash Register ad. Anchoring the editorial well was B.C.'s first Fact & Comment column, which included musings on how the head of National Cash Register had a "deep personal interest" in the happiness of his workers and "spent money freely" in furtherance of that.

And of course there were the aphorisms: How business was originated to produce happiness, not to pile up millions; how "Mere getting is not living"; and "With all thy getting get understanding." B.C. erroneously attributed the latter to Robert Burns, when in fact it was from Proverbs 4:7. And many more were to follow: "A shady business never yields a sunny life." "Better to be occasionally cheated than perpetually suspicious." "Difficulties should act as a tonic. They should spur us to great exertion." "Golf without bunkers and hazards would be tame and monotonous. So would life."

The Woman in Business department in the first issue was eight pages, and included a solicitation to readers for ideas, "a forum for advice" of sorts on how the "untrained woman," who "knows how to cook, wash, iron and sew and take care of her children but was otherwise unqualified for work," could get into the business world. Later issues would include tips on how to qualify as a secretary: have an "even temperament and control your feelings like a hostess."

The first issue also included columns that would become regular features: Stock Market Outlook, a Stock Guide, a Business Forecast, and something called Wall Street Pointers. An early issue, November 24, 1917, contained the first *Forbes* "list"—an alpha ranking of the fifty businessmen in B.C.'s *Men Who Are Making America*. That list was entitled "America's Most Foremost Leaders of Finance and Business." While there were outside contributors, B.C. wrote an enormous amount of the content himself, including a curious preemptive strike in the first issue to counter the impression his profiles were too puffy.

Citing what he said was a question to him by a "very prominent financier" who once asked, "Don't you sometimes make your character sketches a little bit too favorable?" Forbes wrote, "I have learned by experience when I have written a long article upon a man's career, including generous references to his philanthropy, that it has been followed by some very substantial charitable act on his part." In other words, convince readers that an executive is generous and unselfish, and he'll try to live up to that. What a relief to know that positive profiles are really intended to increase the level of charitable giving and have nothing to do with advertising.

The first few issues also contained clues as to what B.C.'s favorite punching bags would be. Government interference, for one. In the first issue, the former superintendent of New York State banking railed against investigations of all sorts and called for them to be curtailed. Citing recent probes into his own department, he complained that the investigators took away books and records needed for the department's daily work and that all this was terribly "annoying and crippling."

B.C.'s second Fact & Comment warned that *Forbes* would make a point of "scrutinizing and publishing very prominently the names of banks and trust companies harboring the accounts of shyster brokerages promoting concerns which are found guilty of having cheated the public by nefarious stock-jobbing operations." The "shyster" reference showed up again in November, when B.C. wrote, "Forbes Magazine doesn't want booze advertisements. Nor will we print advertisements of shyster promoters or brokers."

Was B.C. anti-Semitic? Almost certainly not. But he caught grief in 1945 from the ever-vigilant Anti-Defamation League for a paragraph in an article entitled "Are Strikers Murderers?", which assailed Sidney Hillman, a highly influential, left-leaning Lithuanian-born union leader who was close to President Franklin Roosevelt and was a strong advocate for organizing the auto, steel, and textile workers:

When the war ends I foresee that Sidney Hillman and all other *alien-minded immigrants* who have conspired to attain dictatorial positions in this country will encounter rough weather, that they will experience something of what they *and their kind* have experienced throughout the world, throughout all history. (Emphasis added.)

B.C. promptly replied to the ADL that the question of Semitism or anti-Semitism didn't enter into the matter at all. But:

I am convinced that Sidney Hillman's domineering attitude, seeking to become a political overlord—even dictating, according to report, who could or could not be named Vice President of the United States—is objectionable to all thinking Americans, and calculated to lead to unfortunate repercussions by and by when favored factions, notably self-seeking labor leaders, come to be dealt with by Congress. It will be a sad day for America if and when a Sidney Hillman becomes our political master.

A regular feature called High-Placed Misfits also appeared. Among the victims: the head of the New York subway system, one Theodore

P. Shonts, whom B.C. characterized as "rough-tongued, uncouth and morally disjointed," a man whose "evil influence" is "likely to contaminate" his entire workforce, "making the employees rude and boorish towards the public they are supposed to serve and by whom they are supported." And that was just the first paragraph.

Oh, and what right have *you* to a raise? This was the title of another early piece that said employees who felt entitled to a raise each year just because of their length of service were way out of line. "Motorists sacrifice long-service cars for new types that make more miles per gallon of gasoline. Unless your service-giving efficiency is remodeled yearly, you are in the old car class and headed toward the second hand lot." This particular gem seems to have been immortalized and passed down in whatever secret management handbook subsequent editors receive.

B.C. professed to be concerned about railroad workers, particularly those he believed were being forced to work long hours, sometimes seven days a week. Both in the magazine and in personal letters to railway executives, he expressed his displeasure about such practices. The responses were mixed. Wrote the head of the New York Central Railroad: "The goodwill of 'the boys' is treasured most highly by me, and no organization can function properly without it." But the president of the Erie Railroad evidently could care less about morale: "Stop being sentimental about the welfare of workmen, and stop blaming the railroad for the conduct of workmen. Whoever owns a share of railroad stock or a bond, should get down on their knees frequently and thank God."

It took a while for *Forbes* to gain traction in the market, but before long, letters of encouragement started to roll in. B.C. published them prominently under headlines like "Readers Like Magazine." There were contests, like what's the best company in America— employees were encouraged to write articles about how wonderful their companies were. There were articles by his executive friends, under the rubric "What Business Leaders Say." And there were stories explaining "How Forbes Gets Big Men to Talk," by recounting B.C.'s reporting efforts—lots of research on the person, talking to the executive's associates and friends, then making persistent requests for an in-person interview. By doing that, he got an audience with John D. Rockefeller, who rarely granted press interviews. Rockefeller enjoyed the visit so much, Forbes claims, that he invited B.C. to stay for lunch and to come up later to Pocantico Hills to play golf, "where he made good his threat to lick me."

It was a smart strategy. By relying on the trusted friendships he'd built up over the years in the business community, some of which went back to his networking days at the Waldorf, B.C. could tap a deep well of well-known names to write about, gather ideas, and get feedback as to how *Forbes* could better serve its readership. Long before the concept of "focus groups" came into vogue, B.C. was informally doing just that, day in and day out.

Was his relationship with sources too cozy? By today's standards, it certainly was. But back then, it served a purpose, helping to create some interesting, innovative journalism for the time, and in the end, nobody really seemed to care. On the other hand, the parade of generally fawning profiles did prompt a letter from Stutz Motor Company asking if it could pay for an article about *its* president. B.C. sent a quick reply saying articles weren't paid for.

But B.C. clearly snuggled up to companies he wanted to woo for advertising. He once submitted for review a prepublication copy of an article he'd written about Thomas Wilson, head of the Chicago meatpacking company. "I have gone over the article," Wilson wrote, "and have only made one or two slight changes. I am sure you will agree with me on them. Otherwise I feel that the article is fine."

After a visit to Detroit, B.C. wrote to a relative with news of an exciting "accomplishment." Seems the head of Dodge, Forest Akers, asked B.C. if he wouldn't want a new car. "I said I wouldn't have the nerve to ask for one. But there is one now on order for me—their best four-door sedan, which should be delivered very shortly."

B.C. brought his Conservative ideology into the community as well. Once a member of the Englewood Board of Education, he found a tempting target in the textbooks of Harold Rugg, a professor at Columbia University's Teacher's College. Believing that Rugg's textbooks, which were used in thousands of schools, were left-leaning screeds that poisoned children's minds against "our native land and those responsible for building it," Forbes made it a crusade to remove Rugg's textbooks from the Englewood district.

In board meetings, in *Forbes* itself, and in his Hearst columns, B.C. railed against Rugg, citing samples of what "Professor Rugg is teaching your children and mine": "The fathers of the Constitution feared too much democracy. They were afraid of what the mass of people, who did not possess property, would do to the few who did. The merchants, the landowners the manufacturers, the shippers and the bankers were given what they wanted."

"I would not want my own children contaminated by conversion to Communism," B.C. wrote in an August 15, 1939, Fact & Comment. "Therefore I consider it my duty to protect the children of others against such insidious contamination."

Forbes also singled out a teacher for making what he contended was an unpatriotic remark by telling her students that "there are several countries that have as good a government as the United States." Arguing before the board, Forbes said the point he was trying to make was simply that the only way to teach the Rugg text "was to disabuse the pupils' minds of the idea that we have the best type of government."

The teacher was ultimately exonerated of unpatriotic teachings. And in the larger battle against the textbooks, Forbes lost as well, ultimately leaving the board when it became clear that he couldn't prevail. That was basically the end of B.C.'s "public service" phase.

Subscribers who wrote to ask what stocks to buy were told by B.C. that he made it a practice not to tout specific stocks outside of his published materials, which now again included a syndicated column that went to most of the Hearst papers and over seventy others, including the *Portland Telegram* in Oregon, the *Watertown Standard* in New York, and the influential *Oil City Blizzard* in Pennsylvania.

B.C.'s syndicated column gave him more exposure and clout than *Forbes* itself. In a 1936 survey done by the McCann Erickson ad agency, B.C. came in second only to Damon Runyon in popularity of feature writers who appeared in New York newspapers. Close behind were Heywood Broun, Louella Parsons, Cholly Knicker-bocker, and Dorothy Dix.

One reader, and an apparent old friend, wrote in looking for a trading edge, despite the existence of insider trading rules (it was 1951). Utica, New York, attorney William Seavey was trolling for stock tips on the theory that "your organization has the ability to get in touch with the inside of companies." Then lawyer Seavey, apparently a distant relative of Gordon Gekko, went a bit further. "I have been fortunate," Seavey wrote, "in having some friends who were the heads of some of our largest corporations and they gave me advice as to what to do ahead of the time when something happened, either good or bad, to the company in which I held securities."

B.C. replied that he couldn't help, but sent along a copy of a recent weekly bulletin from the Investors Advisory Institute, a *Forbes* unit that published a pricey investing newsletter. Earlier that same year in a letter to a reader, B.C. noted that it was against his practice to give specific securities advice, but added, "I might say, confidentially, that I have been purchasing shares in Venezuela Syndicate, in the low-priced field. Good luck to you."

Over time, B.C.'s reputation as a giver of advice inspired subscribers to write in for guidance on all sorts of things, including career advice and even nutrition. Responding to a reader who inquired about B.C.'s eating habits, Forbes replied he ate only one meal a day—dinner—plus a "small glass of fruit or vegetable juice, and a cup of coffee with skimmed milk—no cream or sugar" at 8:00 A.M. each day. Inexplicably, B.C.'s girth continued to expand.

But the *Forbes* formula was by now firmly set: heavy doses of investment advice; stock market data and forecasts; inspirational stories; how to succeed (where others fail); lists of notable executives; finger-waving guidance on how to be more productive in your job; adoring profiles of the most favored; and nasty attacks on people or companies the editor-in-chief felt were unworthy. It was the template that succeeding editors would follow for years.

13

"WHO ORDERED A
$5.00 LOBSTER?"

To RESOLVE WHAT WAS becoming a formidable clash over religion, B.C. and Adelaide devised an odd formula for the bap-
tisms of their growing family: Bruce, born in 1916; Duncan in 1918;
Malcolm in 1919; Gordon in 1923; and Wallace in 1928. The first
child would be raised Catholic, the second Presbyterian, the third
Catholic, and so on. It worked pretty well until later on when B.C.
occasionally started insisting on "double headers" for Bruce and
Malcolm, hauling them to *his* church, First Presbyterian, after morning mass at St. Cecilia's with their mother. "And now I'd like *all* my
sons to go to church with *me*," he'd say. Those were Sundays Malcolm and Bruce dreaded most. Their father offered a dime to each
son who learned a new hymn each week, but to earn it they had to
sing it all the way through. Not a lot was paid out.

Of the brothers, Malcolm was the most shy, with a romantic
sense of adventure, which played out in his love for swashbuckling
films, reading, taking somewhat lonely refuge in his toy soldiers, and
"publishing" his own newspapers. One was called *Family Album*,
which reported on things like family trips to Scotland, during which
the boys were often shipboard terrors, causing all sorts of onboard

mischief, running around the ship and once even heaving beddings and linens out the portholes.

Though he'd later letter in gymnastics at Princeton, Malcolm wasn't that athletic, unlike Bruce, who was an outgoing, slap-on-the-back-type jock. Malcolm was somewhat of a loner, eager to please, and close to his mother. In group activities, he tended not to be happy unless he could be in charge.

B.C. was a daunting father. A strict Victorian disciplinarian, he constantly preached hard work and determination; while generous to his sons, he didn't have particularly close relationships with them. As Malcolm once explained it, "His time, his upbringing did not equip him for that moment when there was candor in an exchange of opinion with his children, where the thing shifts from being a parent to being a friend."

B.C. was smart enough to see the 1929 crash coming, warned his readers accordingly, and cashed out himself to save the family's nest egg, which continued to be augmented by his column income from Hearst. In a 1951 radio interview with Tex McCrary, he recalled that he started, as early as 1928, to "start shrieking our heads off" that the "worst, most catastrophic panic was coming." Forbes told Mc-Crary that right after the crash, he got a letter from Paul Hoffman, the chairman of Studebaker, who said that that "one sentence in your magazine saved me over a quarter of a million dollars." That sentence, in a 1928 article: "This is an ideal time to get out of debt."

What B.C. did not see coming was the Depression. Along with many others, Forbes started buying up bargain-basement stocks, only to see them evaporate once the Depression hit full force. Some of his followers were not pleased.

"We blame all our financial troubles on you. You, and you alone, started us on our downfall," wrote one outraged subscriber from California in September 1931. "Following the 1929 crash, when I saw your benign and honest face on the screen in our favorite Imperial Valley movie, and heard you solemnly announce the worst was over, I bought with both hands . . . I can see you yet, with your head slanted over to one side, saying convincingly: 'And make no mistake, it IS over.'" Oops. Or this unsigned love note, dated July 14, 1933, from Sacramento: "You silly ass. You are so consistently wrong that you are a joke. Your chatter is so biased that no one pays attention."

One of B.C.'s favorite themes was endorsing the gold standard, a stance that decades later would be vigorously upheld by his grandson, Steve. But not all *Forbes* readers agreed. One who wasn't particularly fond of Gold Bugs was Franklin Hopkins, a self-described "monetary ethicist," who wrote this wonderful letter to B.C. in 1928:

Dear Bertie, Old Thing, I used to think you had brains enough to be a hypocrite; now I know it's just ordinary dumbness. You see, to write the stuff you turn out proclaims either hypocrisy or ignorance . . . Don't you ever read history? Didn't anybody ever tell you that every nation WITHOUT EXCEPTION, which established [a gold standard] came to a bad end! . . . Can't you get the old cabeza working a bit? Maybe a ray of sunlight will get into you?

In a footnote, Hopkins added: "Bertie, Care of his own Cute Little Mag."

Along with economic hard times came new competition. *BusinessWeek* appeared in 1929, bringing a news-focused approach to coverage. *Fortune,* which featured long-form corporate profiles and elegant layouts, came along a year later. By the end of the 1930s, *Forbes* was mired firmly in third place in circulation, its conflicting nasty/fawning approach to business increasingly seen as quirky and out of step. *Fortune* was far ahead at 248,000, *BusinessWeek* at 192,000. *Forbes* trailed at 102,000. Increasingly, B.C. had to dip into his own pocket to keep the magazine going, thankful—for the moment—that he had the safety net of his Hearst column income to help pay household bills.

But for the Forbes family, the most tragic event of the Depression had nothing to do with money.

Duncan Forbes, age fifteen, was Malcolm's closet pal. Together they planned and executed all sorts of hijinks and mischief, including the infamous shipboard incident of throwing linens out the port-hole window.

One weekend in 1933, Duncan took a ride with Bruce in a used Model A convertible Bruce had received for his birthday. They decided to drive one hundred miles north for a surprise visit to their parents who were staying at an upstate New York resort. Coming around a corner, Bruce swerved to avoid hitting a car that had stopped in the right lane to assist another car that had a flat. The Model A flipped over. Thrown out of the car, Duncan died instantly from a broken neck.

It was a devastating event that plunged the whole family into anguish. Malcolm found his father sitting on the side of his bed, sobbing. But in a cold, insensitive effort to get the tragedy behind them, B.C. had Duncan buried the next day, much to the horror and fury of Adelaide. B.C. then packed everyone off on a trip to Scotland, a well-meaning but incongruous gesture to a family still in shock.

One bizarre result of Duncan's death was that in order to keep the family's Catholic-Protestant ratio from getting out of control, Wally was raised Protestant instead of Catholic, which he would have been had Duncan lived. Wally would later say: "We all believed that our mother must have snuck us out to be baptized in the Catholic Church without my father knowing it. She would have thought we'd all end up in hell if she didn't."

B.C. mostly kept his grief inside. But he did often visit plot number 285 of the Mount Carmel Cemetery in Tenafly, New Jersey, to place a boutonniere on Duncan's grave, which lies about fourteen yards from an ancient maple tree that gives a comforting umbrella to Duncan and his mother. Duncan's inscription on the simple Forbes headstone reads, "Loveable, Loved, Loving."

Malcolm did his best to memorialize Duncan in a homespun newspaper called *The City of Dunc Weekly News,* that reported "news" out of a cardboard box city Malcolm and Gordon had built in their basement, complete with lights, toy automobiles, and toy soldiers. Malcolm's co-editor-in-chief was one George P. Shultz, an

Eagle Scout buddy of Malcolm's who'd later become secretary of the treasury and secretary of state.

Unfortunately, a basement flood almost completely destroyed the cardboard town. In the newspaper's last edition ("Since there is no city there is no use for a city paper"), Malcolm lamented, "All the homes and stores and factories became soggy with the water they sopped up and some collapsed from the weight . . . Several clay soldiers became soggy and mushy and had to be thrown out."

The Depression brought tough years to the family. Adelaide went into despair when Malcolm broke a tooth while roller-skating—not because her son was in pain but because it meant a trip to the dentist and another bill to pay. Only B.C.'s determination to forge ahead kept the magazine alive. Malcolm would later say, "There were times when he would have been better off letting the magazine fold." But B.C. simply wouldn't give up—the "stick-to-itiveness" that he preached to businessmen in his columns defined his own priorities—the magazine first, then himself.

In 1934, B.C. shipped Malcolm off to the Hackley School in Tarrytown, New York, an uprooting Malcolm resented because he wasn't involved in the decision and it meant leaving his mother. But with the help of a mimeograph machine his father had given him for Christmas, Malcolm started up the *Hackley Eagle,* in competition with the prep school's weekly paper.

Transferring to Lawrenceville (along with his mimeograph) Malcolm quickly launched the *Kennedy House Eagle,* so named for the dorm in which he lived. But his roommates complained about all the late-night "banging away." Solution? Malcolm wrote to Gertrude Weiner, his father's trusty assistant. He asked her to approach B.C. about buying him a noiseless Remington portable. Perhaps wisely, he didn't mention his late-night newspaper work, but said his English grades—and those of his roommates—would suffer without a noiseless portable. "Doubtless if you explain this to Dad he isn't liable to refuse my request."

On the home front, things were deteriorating. Adelaide continued to be upset over how B.C. had reacted to Duncan's death. And they constantly fought over money, a theme that had emerged very early in the marriage. "How can you spend so much?" he once demanded. "But I love to spend money," she replied.

Which prompted Malcolm years later to note his mother was "an early Keynesian," and how ironic it was that her philosophy "is considered more essential to our economic well-being than the abhorrence of spending oft expressed by the Founder of *Forbes*." If he weren't already dead, Malcolm added, "the very thought would have killed him. In fact, it could well be enough to resurrect him."

B.C. worried about money no matter who was spending it. Wally used his father's membership to entertain at the New York Athletic Club, and ran up what B.C. characterized as "enormous" food and liquor bills. "Who, for example, ordered a $5.00 lobster? I, personally, would never think of indulging in such extravagance," B.C. wrote in one letter. B.C. went on to tell, or rather order, Wally not to take anyone there for the rest of the year (this was in late October) since "you have already incurred much more than I have budgeted" for the club. B.C. later deducted thirty dollars from a check he wrote to Wally to cover unpaid dues at the Princeton Club.

B.C. expected to be obeyed, whether it was by his sons or his wife. He demanded that Adelaide play the classic role of dutiful spouse, housekeeper, and mother, while he hung out with his poker-playing buddies, who included an apparently oft-burned Wendell Willkie, who once wrote B.C. "the first time I get an opportunity I want to take some of your money . . ." There were other problems. The seventeen-year age difference began to matter, as the cigar-chomping, paunchy B.C. started to look much older than his younger wife, who continued to look stunning.

And there was the thorny issue of Miss Weiner, B.C.'s longtime secretary to whom he had given 5 percent of the company's shares. Was Gertrude just an assistant—or his mistress?

14

THE RISING SON

A winner must first know what losing's like.

—Malcolm Forbes

AT PRINCETON, MALCOLM TRIED out for *The Daily Prince-tonian,* but didn't make the cut. Undaunted, he started up his own magazine called the *Nassau Sovereign,* intended to "bring to the college campus the *Time/Life* sort of journalism that was then sweeping the country." B.C. didn't want him to do it, concerned it would distract him from his studies. But Malcolm, as he would do many times later in life, simply did what he wanted to do, no matter what others said. The *Sovereign,* which included campus polls prepared with some help from pollster George Gallup, who lived in town, finally won B.C. over, and he wound up giving Malcolm some financial support for the effort.

After Princeton, again with financial help from his father, Forbes bought a weekly newspaper in Ohio, on the theory that building a chain of papers in the state that produced more U.S. presidents than any other except Virginia would provide him with a solid political base. But he couldn't make a go of it, and shut the paper down after enlisting in the army, where he was badly injured by German machine gun fire while serving as an infantryman on the European front. B.C. had wanted Malcolm to become an officer, but Malcolm thought being an enlisted man would look better on his political résumé—and again did exactly what he wanted.

Malcolm returned home in 1945 on crutches along with a Bronze Star and Purple Heart, "anxious to get to work money-making in a big way." Looking spiffy in his beribboned tan uniform, with its creases ironed knife-sharp, Malcolm met nineteen-year-old Roberta Laidlaw at an Englewood cocktail party during his last week in the army. Stunning, blond and blue-eyed, she was the daughter of Robert Laidlaw, whose Wall Street firm, then known as Laidlaw & Co., dated back to 1854. In a classic love-at-first-sight moment, Malcolm proposed at the end of that first meeting. Married the following year, Malcolm and Roberta's euphoria inspired B.C. to put on a kilt and dance at the reception—a scene that unnerved the straitlaced Mrs. Laidlaw, who viewed B.C.'s antics with some alarm.

By then Malcolm had joined *Forbes* at $100 a week to focus on editorial matters. B.C. had moved Bruce back to New York from Detroit to handle the advertising side, bringing with him an invaluable Rolodex of contacts in the auto industry. Malcolm was brimming with ideas, not all of them wise. One of his first projects was launching an improbable magazine that was almost certain to fail—and did.

Nation's Heritage was an over-the-top, oversize, and overpriced (twenty-five dollars a copy) hardcover magazine that would come out six times a year. "Snooty, eh what?" B.C. sniffed in a letter to Gordon. It was filled with stunning photography intended to be inspirational and uplifting to the country that had just won World War II.

For its editor, Malcolm chose Robert Heimann, a Princeton friend, a talented writer and editor (he was chairman of *The Daily Princetonian*) who had a reputation for devilment and pranks. One of Heimann's achievements at Princeton was helping produce an "unofficial university catalog," an irreverent publication that evaluated courses and professors.

Nation's Heritage eventually won Malcolm a gold medal from the Freedom Foundation, presented by General Dwight Eisenhower, then president of Columbia University. It was an event that gave Malcolm more momentum for his own political ambitions.

Without any advertising, *Nation's Heritage* folded not long after the Freedom Foundation award. But Malcolm redeemed himself in his father's eyes by coming up with ideas that would eventually generate substantial new revenue streams.

The first issue of *Forbes* each January had always been miserably thin with barely any advertising. Malcolm thought it would be interesting—and fun—to rate corporate America's performance at the beginning of each year by assigning grades based on sales, profits, and return on equity. A report card for business.

There were predictable wails from companies that got low grades, but the overall reception was positive, and over the years, the "Jan One" issue became a huge commercial success, giving *Forbes* important credibility in the market for its numerate, analytical approach to assessing the winners and losers in business. It set the predicate for what editor Jim Michaels would later define as *Forbes*'s role as the "drama critic" of American business—who's doing well, who isn't, and why.

Malcolm's other idea was a simple extension of the magazine's stock-picking abilities: Why not sell a separate investing newsletter to *Forbes* subscribers from a new entity called the Investors Advisory Institute? It would include "exclusive" investing advice and information not contained in the regular magazine. At thirty-five dollars a year, it was a big hit, and was soon delivering nice profits to the *Forbes* bottom line.

Roberta began delivering Malcolm a family as well. Steve came along in 1947, Bob in 1949, Kip in 1950, Tim in 1953, and Moira in 1955. Timberfield quickly came alive with the chaos and organized bedlam of five young children. *Forbes* employees and friends would follow the family's expansion through annual Christmas cards picturing the kids at various *Forbes* venues—the ranch, the boat, Timberfield, and the Galleries.

15

"BULLY, EGOTIST, TYRANT, BOOR"

Back in Englewood, B.C. had been alone ever since the fall of 1943, when Adelaide moved out of the house on Fountain Road, no longer able to put up with what she felt were B.C.'s considerable shortcomings. She filed a thirteen-page affidavit in chancery court in Newark, suing for legal separation, support money, and custody of Wally, then fifteen. *The New York Times* reported her complaints of B.C.'s drunkenness and brutality and of his being a "bully, egotist, tyrant and a boor."

The affidavit said that Adelaide had been forced to act as B.C.'s "man-servant, tying his shoe laces, buttoning his shirt, drawing his bath and opening the door of his car." On one occasion in 1934, the affidavit alleged, B.C. had prevented her from visiting her mother who was "in danger of death."

B.C. had a different view of things. To a sister, he wrote that life at home was now much more harmonious with Adelaide no longer there, and that the split had to do not with his personal behavior, but with the long-simmering religious differences. "Adelaide suddenly went berserk one night," he said.

She had become so enamored of a supposedly extremely pious Catholic woman [who] convinced Ad that to live with a Protestant was to live in "sin." Outside of warning Ad against making a public fool of herself, I let her have her own way when she was misled into taking the matter to court and making a lot of diabolically false statements about me . . . It was soon brought home to her, after she left, that she had made a tragic mistake. But it will do her good to lie for awhile in the bed she has made for herself.

Adelaide was also suspicious of B.C.'s cozy relationship with his longtime secretary. Coming from a poor Jewish family in Brooklyn, Miss Weiner was an attractive young woman just out of secretarial school who got a typing job at *Forbes* through a want ad. B.C. admired her spunk, related to her impoverished background, and eventually made her his assistant.

At times, they certainly *acted* like a couple. Gertrude would nag him to stop writing personal letters when it was time to work on a column. "That's enough!" she'd say. He'd annoy her with off-color jokes and laugh uproariously at the punch line—to her stony silence. They'd play cards long after everyone else had left the office because he didn't want to go home. After the split from Adelaide, B.C. even took Gertrude on trips to Scotland, prompting raised eyebrows from relatives and friends alike.

B.C. clearly had an eye for the ladies, and there were various incidents of "B.C. the Fanny Patter," recalls one editor who personally observed the behavior. "His hand would slip and touch one of the girls as he padded around the office in his slippers," he says. When an attractive young lady friend visiting the offices one evening remarked how late everyone was working, B.C. pressed the elevator button with his cane, puffed his cigar, and said: "I pay them very well."

Did the relationship with Gertrude go beyond the platonic? A former senior editor at the magazine says it did. Another says it didn't. Gertrude once conceded to writer Arthur Jones that she had to "fight [B.C.] off once or twice." In an interesting clue and undoubtedly a surprise to his sons, B.C. appointed Gertrude as executrix of his estate, along with Chemical Bank. With that came for Gertrude the usual powers to buy or sell securities and other assets of the estate. She also got an outright bequest of $5,000, the largest amount given to anyone but his sons. Whatever the relationship, it made for the kind of gossip that's common, if not vital, to any office environment.

It's clear the sons relied upon Gertrude for all kinds of support. She'd buy and send them books, arrange for their travel, and perform other chores. Gordon once even considered hitting her up for money for a new business venture he was considering. B.C. waved him off. "You cannot look to Miss Weiner and certainly not to Malcolm for any financial assistance," he wrote. "They have troubles enough of their own!" B.C. apparently had misgivings about Malcolm and money anyway. Earlier, he had written Gordon that "Like yourself [Wally] has much more money sense than Bruce or Malcolm. *They're terrible.*" (Emphasis added.)

16

POLITICS 101

THOUGH TRYING TO FOCUS on the magazine, Malcolm soon became distracted by politics—a gravitational pull his eldest son would feel strongly, too, many years later. Malcolm spent a term as borough councilman in Bernardsville, New Jersey, played with a congressional run, and snagged a New Jersey state senate seat, a race in which he rang "18,000 doorbells, was bitten by 13 dogs and won with the largest margin ever recorded." So buoyed, Malcolm next set his sights on becoming governor of New Jersey, with an ultimate eye on the White House.

Meanwhile, B.C. had formulated a succession plan, and told his sons the business would be left to them, "absolutely free and clear," with no outsiders holding any shares or bonds. They'd inherit *Forbes,* he said, "without a penny of debt—except, of course, current bills." Bruce and Malcolm were each to inherit one-third of the stock; Gordon and Wally one-sixth each.

Pondering a letter from his father about the inheritance plans and Malcolm's growing political ambitions, Gordon wrote back to say that if Malcolm left *Forbes* to become a full-time politico, "you will have only one son" in the family business and [Bruce] cannot do it alone . . . I have my own ideas about what should be done with the magazine."

Gordon didn't want to see someone outside the family move in to run things, and volunteered to come back to New York from California, where he'd been working as a production chief at several film studios, starting out with an entry-level job at Republic Pictures right out of Yale. "We could make *Forbes* a business that would pay off handsomely and not be continually worried about just keeping our heads up above water."

B.C. shot back quickly. "For heaven's sake, don't take the slightest step towards giving up your high-salaried job. Your training does not fit you to step into Malcolm's shoes," he said. "Two sons are enough in the business."

B.C. made it a practice to go to Scotland every two years, to throw a big picnic for friends and relatives on his old school grounds, handing out shillings to the winners of sack races and tugs-of-war, candy for all the kids, and treating the oldsters to high tea. The next trip was supposed to be in 1954, but perhaps with an impending sense of his own mortality, B.C. moved the trip up to late fall 1953.

He used the occasion to donate a baptismal font to the church, in a ceremony that brought tears to nearly all in the congregation. B.C. then returned home for the holidays and, in early spring, began to plan a festive picnic for his family and all the *Forbes* staff at the Fountain Road house. It was to be held at the end of May, to celebrate the completion of sixty years of work.

But the celebration was not to be. On May 5, 1954, the *Forbes* elevator operator, whose job it was to make sure all the lights were out each night, stuck his head into B.C.'s office, found him dead, slumped on the floor. Malcolm became editor and publisher, Bruce president.

In addition to the distribution of *Forbes* stock each of the sons got $10,000 in life insurance proceeds. Bruce got watches and any other things with "B.C.F." engraved—those were Bruce's initials as well. Malcolm got books; Wally got paintings and photographs from his father's home and office. Gordon and Wally got B.C.'s cars, with Gordon getting first pick.

Any *Forbes* employee who'd been there for at least ten years got $500. Adelaide, to whom B.C. was still officially married, got the house on Fountain Road and some furniture. Two years before his death, on his penultimate visit to Scotland, B.C. set up a trust, funded with British government securities, to pay for an "annual Christmas tree and party for the children of the Whitehall Public School" in New Deer—a touching, final gesture to the place so close to his heart.

B.C. was first buried at Mount Carmel cemetery. Adelaide was buried there in 1973. But in 1988, Malcolm, Wally, and several other family members took B.C. back to New Deer now for the last time, to the kirk of St. Kane's.

In 1957, Malcolm won the Republican nomination for governor of New Jersey, but soon found himself fighting an uphill battle against the popular Democratic incumbent Robert Meyner, a former trial lawyer and state senator who had made a name for himself during his first term by uncovering a big scam in the state employment security division. Consistently upbeat about his chances right up until election day, Malcolm spent at least four days and nights a week ringing doorbells, giving speeches, and trying to drum up support for his no-income-tax, no-sales-tax platform.

Ironic in light of another campaign forty years later, one person fretting about the cost of Malcolm's campaign was young Steve, then only ten. He told a classmate at the exclusive Far Hills Country Day School he was afraid his father would "spend so much money there'll be nothing left for me and my brothers."

During the gubernatorial race, one of Malcolm's favorite photographs was one of his riding in a motorcade with Roberta and a "be-orchided Bergen County lady leader" who wore a decidedly unenthusiastic expression. There were no voters in sight on the street, and Malcolm assumed that his waving hand was aimed "at what must have been the only soul in sight—the photographer."

The photo proved to be prescient. On Election Day, Malcolm lost in a landslide. By coincidence, that very evening there was a *Forbes* staff event. Bruce and Malcolm, neither of whom particularly liked the other, both attended. While Malcolm was away running for governor, Bruce had been holding down the fort.

At one point during the evening, Malcolm grabbed the mike, and said, "Bruce, you've done a great job in my absence. Here's a watch for you!" It was meant as a joke, but it stunned everyone, Bruce in particular. And it merely underlined Malcolm's determination to get whatever he wanted, no matter what. After Bruce died in 1964 from cancer, Malcolm pressured his widow, then Gordon, Wally, and finally, Gertrude Weiner, to sell him their shares, thus assuring himself total and absolute control.

17

ROOTS II

H ARD BY THE SHORES of Lake Erie in upstate New York lies the gritty town of Buffalo, home to the most important editorial architect of *Forbes,* Jim Michaels.

In the 1920s, one of the local celebrities was George Dewey Michaels, owner, director, and producer extraordinaire of the Palace Burlesque Theatre, home to nameless strippers and forgettable standup comics. Dewey, as he preferred to be called—he hated the name George—was one of eight children of Levin Michaels, a German Jew who immigrated to Buffalo in the late 1880s from a region called Posen, in what's now known as Bavaria, near the Polish border. The elder Michaels ran movie theaters in town and got young Dewey, born in 1898, involved in the business when he dropped out of school after tenth grade because he couldn't pass his math exams.

Named for the admiral who won the Battle of Manila Bay during the Spanish-American War, Dewey quickly found he had a talent for show biz promotion and made such a success of the Palace that in 1937 he was able to build a five-bedroom brick home for his family on Dana Road in the fashionable North Buffalo area, moving them from a series of unfashionable two-story "flats" in a less trendy part of town. Profits from his various theaters' candy and popcorn concessions would ultimately send all three of his children to college (James, born in 1921, to Harvard; Harriett, born in 1925, to Wellesley; and Albert, born in 1937, to the University of Pennsylvania).

A Runyonesque figure who promoted fights and auditioned strippers, Dewey played the role of man about town—driving around in a chartreuse Cadillac and not spending a whole lot of time at home. He'd spend all day at the theater, come home for dinner, then go back to work, a routine he'd follow on Saturdays as well.

This left very little time for his children, particularly his sons. "He had absolutely no influence on Jimmy," says Albert Michaels, now a history professor at the State University at Buffalo. "Neither of us really had a father," Albert adds. "If anything, Jimmy was *my* father. He took me to Brooks Brothers to get my clothes [for college] and despite our age difference, we were extraordinarily close, talking almost every day, for the last 40 years [of his life]." (Jim Michaels died in 2007.)

But Jim Michaels did have an interesting family role model in Al Boasberg, his mother's brother, one of the most storied writers in Hollywood. Uncle Al was a "script doctor" and wrote skits and one-liners for the Three Stooges, Burns and Allen, Milton Berle, Jack Benny, and the Marx Brothers, among others. Boasberg, who dreamed up the hilarious stateroom scene in *A Night at the Opera* and invented the character Rochester as Benny's sidekick, preferred to work from home, sitting in a large bathtub and rattling off jokes into a Dictaphone.

But on Sunday nights, when the Benny show came on, he'd turn very serious, leaning forward into the radio so he could hear every joke, listening for what got a laugh and what didn't.

Here's one of his vaudeville classics, written for Bob Hope in 1927:

"My brother slapped Al Capone."

"Gee, I'd like to meet him and shake his hand!"

"No, we wouldn't want to dig him up just for that."

Boasberg later sent this skit via Western Union to Hope at the RKO Palace Theater in New York, where he was about to open after a gig in New Jersey: "WHEN GIRL MAKES HER FIRST APPEARANCE YOU SAY WHERE WERE YOU ALL LAST WEEK IN NEWARK AND SHE ANSWERS MR HOPE YOU TOLD ME NOT TO COME OUT UNTIL YOU GOT YOUR FIRST LAUGH STOP."

Boasberg's talent for tightly written sound bites may have been an inspiration for his talented young nephew. His success certainly had an impact on the family, which in typical immigrant fashion had an innate feisty, self-driven push to succeed, to be clever and the best in anything they set out to do. Which likely explains the Ivy-toned college credentials of Dewey's children, who were driven to excel— and possibly one-up—their smart but uneducated father, who was involved in a business vaguely embarrassing to them.

Dewey was not an outwardly warm person. But behind every gruff and grumpy Michaels, explains Michael Ellis, a fourth-generation cousin, lurks a warm—and yes, even generous personality. "It's hearing 'NO! NO! NO!' when you first ask a Michaels for something, and then, of course, they'll do it," he says. "As opposed to where the answer to every request is 'OF COURSE!' but then they never do it."

Just as B. C. Forbes couldn't wait to leave New Deer, there wasn't much in Buffalo to hold an inquisitive young James Walker Michaels. The middle name came from one of Dewey's older brothers who wanted to be a journalist but died at a young age from a blood infection. So the future editor of *Forbes* left home at age fifteen to attend military school, first at Valley Forge, then Culver (where his nickname was "The Brain" and where he excelled in debate). "He left it [Buffalo] all behind him," says his brother. "He did many things to distance himself from that part of his life."

Later in life, Michaels would talk broadly about his love for the music of Bach, Offenbach, Gilbert and Sullivan, history, classic French black-and-white films, politics, and colorful characters in business, or his passions for piano playing, gardening, badminton, riding, swimming, Indian cooking, or scuba diving, a sport he took up at the age of seventy-five. But rarely would he talk about his early days in Buffalo, sometimes not even to his children or grandchildren, and certainly never to colleagues at *Forbes*. "He just blocked it out," says his brother.

It's as if life for Jim Michaels began when he graduated from Harvard in 1942. And in a way, it did. After graduating in three years with honors in economics, Michaels tried to enlist in the army. But his eyesight wasn't good enough. Instead, he signed up as an ambulance driver for the American Field Service, attached to the British Fourteenth Army in Burma, driving around a somewhat battered Chevrolet.

It was a dangerous job. Japanese troops lurked everywhere. But his superiors didn't trust his eyesight enough to let Michaels carry a pistol. So he kept a bag of grenades next to him on the passenger's seat. Whenever he saw enemy troops (or what he *assumed* were enemy troops) he'd lob one or two out the window. *KABOOOM!*

It's unclear whether any innocent civilians—or British troops—fell victim to Michaels's curve balls. But grenade-lobbing would in fact become sort of a motif in his life, though the later grenades he'd throw would be all verbal—or written.

After the war, Michaels signed up with UPI to report from India, a place B. C. Forbes once characterized as a "filthy country." Working out of the New Delhi bureau, Michaels was the first newsman to write about the war in Kashmir, traveling on horseback to get behind Pakistani lines. In his dispatches, he described Pakistani military units marching up to the border in regimental regalia and changing into civilian clothes before crossing the border.

In June 1947, Michaels came back to Buffalo long enough to attend his sister's wedding (on the eighth) and get married himself (on the seventh) to Fran Cashman, the lively daughter of a Lerner's department store manager who was posted to Buffalo during the time Fran and Michaels were teenagers. Fran, a one-time dance instructor who enjoyed martinis (but never before 5:00 P.M.), was a spunky girl who'd hum and dance her way around the kitchen while cooking dinner. After the nuptials, Michaels took Fran back with him to India, where he'd score his biggest journalistic coup to date.

On January 30, 1948, Michaels filed the first detailed dispatch of Mahatma Gandhi's assassination. Here in his own words, as described in a private e-mail decades later, is the scoop behind his scoop:

> It's hard to visualize, but in those long-ago days there was little automotive traffic in New Delhi. It took me minutes to get to Birla House. I got there before the police had cordoned the property. There was immense confusion, of course, but I scribbled notes and rushed to file what, I believe, was the first detailed report to reach the outside world.
>
> In those days, pre-Internet, pre-mobile satellite phones, one had to file overseas from Delhi by cable from the CTO (Central Telegraph Office) at Eastern Court near Connaught Place. By the time I got there to file my first dispatch and returned to the scene, Birla House was cordoned off: No entry to anyone. I knew the place fairly well so I climbed a low stone wall in the back only to confront an astonished constable, who let me pass after I flashed a credential he could not read because he was illiterate. My agile trespass gave me a leg up on most other foreign journalists because they couldn't get inside for some time.

Michaels's reporting showed up the next day on the front pages of newspapers all over the world. Here's some of what he wrote, the spare elegance of his words previewing the kind of detailed, disciplined writing Michaels would years later demand of his own staff:

> Dressed as always in his homespun sack like dhoti, and leaning heavily on a staff of stout wood, Gandhi was only a few feet from the pagoda when the shots were fired. Gandhi crumpled instantly, putting his hand to his forehead in the Hindu gesture of forgiveness to his assassin. Three bullets penetrated his body at close range, one in the upper right thigh, one in the abdomen, and one in the

chest . . . The assassin had been standing beside the garden path, his hands folded, palms together before him in the Hindu gesture of greeting. But between his palms he had concealed a small-caliber revolver. After pumping three bullets into Gandhi at a range of a few feet, he fired a fourth shot in an attempt at suicide, but the bullet merely creased his scalp.

Then the following day, Michaels reported for all the world to read the details of Gandhi's funeral on the banks of the Yumana, one of the five sacred rivers of India:

The huge mass of humanity, wailing and weeping, packed around the newly bricked burning platform for as far as the eye could see . . . Gandhi's body was placed on the pyre with wood heaped below and around it. While the crowd raised a cry: "Gandhi! Gandhi! Gandhi!" Devadas [his eldest son] began the ceremony. First an unguent, a mixture of liquid butter and incense, was poured over the pyre. Then Devadas faced towards the sun, now lowering to the west, and began to chant the ancient verses of the Sanskrit Veda, holy book of the Hindus. The verses committed Gandhi to the gods who will be responsible for his next reincarnation. As the chanting ceased, Devadas took flame from the sacred lamp, which had burned all night beside Gandhi's body, and touched it to the pyre. The day was clear and warm. But a light wind arose and swirled up the dust hung over the whole eight-mile route of the cortege from Birla House to the banks of the sacred river. All of Delhi gathered at the pyre in final tribute to Gandhi. There were leprous beggars in the crowd and there were true nabobs with rubies as big as pigeon eggs gleaming in their feather-bedecked turbans . . . The multitude watched as the flames licked up through the sandalwood pyre, consuming Gandhi's earthly remains.

18

"I'M GOING TO FIRE
SOMEBODY TODAY!"

To be kind, *Forbes* up until the late 1950s was not much more than a quaint, second-tier stock tip sheet. It was type-heavy, gray, and often quite boring to read. During the twenties, "the old man's kind of hobnobbing with the tycoons was in. Then came the 1930s and the tycoons were in jail or hiding in Greece," Jim Michaels later told an interviewer.

With *Forbes* still in third place in the market, Malcolm needed some help to turn things around. His choice for *Forbes*'s first real hands-on editorial boss, who would carry the title of managing editor, was Bob Heimann, his Princeton friend who wound up editing the ill-fated *Nation's Heritage*. Heimann, a man of stately bearing who wore a trench coat and a homburg, was an important but little known engineer of *Forbes*'s transition to a real magazine.

To stand out from the rest of the crowd, Heimann believed *Forbes* had to be more pointed and edgy. But to be credible, Heimann knew *Forbes* couldn't just lash out at a company's performance without backing up the tirade with numbers. So when a young man named Ray Brady joined *Forbes* from the New York *Daily News*, where he'd been a copy boy, Heimann put him to work in a room with a stack of annual reports and an adding machine. Brady distilled lots of digits, and *Forbes* soon began supporting its thumbs-up or thumbs-down profiles with real analysis. "It was an entirely new model," Brady says.

Money was tight, and there was never enough to pay a high-priced photographer for a fancy shoot. So for a big story on Tropicana, Heimann, whose talents included being a pretty good photographer himself, volunteered a picture he'd once taken in California of a big truckload of what he assumed were oranges. But when the issue came out, Brady recalls, this letter arrived: "You guys don't know bags of onions when you see them!"

Heimann left in 1954 to join what was then American Tobacco, and eventually wound up being the tobacco giant's chief executive officer from 1977 to 1980, after it had changed its name to American Brands. He was succeeded at *Forbes* by Byron "Dave" Mack, who had worked at *Forbes* before as a writer but left for a stint in the business section of *Time* before returning to run the place. Mack was a talented but insecure editor who was forever fretting about losing his job and who might succeed him. He helped sharpen the edge of the *Forbes* knife, pushing writers to do tough stories—but not on favored advertisers. He was the first editor to bring in fact-checkers and give the magazine more credible heft. But with his staff, Mack fostered an atmosphere of sheer terror. He'd sit at his desk, and ponder aloud, "I'm going to fire someone today, and I'm just sitting here trying to figure out whom that will be." Invariably, somebody was fired.

When he heard a rumor that someone on the staff might be doing a book about *Forbes*—and him—he ordered everyone into his office. The lights were turned down. Mack sat there with a lead rule, the kind used in the old hot-type production process. He bent it slowly. "I hear someone's doing a book," he said, with a threatening tone. "Well, let me tell you nobody here is good enough to get a book published." End of meeting.

One of Mack's first and most prescient hires was Michaels, who had applied to *Forbes* after a stint doing intelligence work, reporting for a newspaper in Jamestown, New York, then spending a mysterious couple of months in Switzerland "getting analyzed," says his brother. Then, freshly in focus and presumably in touch with his feelings, Michaels set his sights on the publishing world in New York City.

Michaels's wife, Fran, had an uncle, Herb Matthews, a reporter for *The New York Times*. He'd gained notoriety during the Cuban Revolution by finding and interviewing Fidel Castro in the Sierra Maestra Mountains of Cuba after U.S.-backed president Fulgencio Batista had claimed he'd been killed. Matthews's reporting earned him the wrath of conservatives who claimed his coverage was colored by Communist sympathies, prompting the *National Review* to run a cartoon of Castro with the tagline "I got my job through the *New York Times*," a takeoff on the ad campaign the *Times* was then running about the effectiveness of its classified ads.

But even with that connection and his Gandhi coverage, Michaels was unable to get a job at the *Times*—or at *Fortune*. The latter rejection, coupled with some unflattering coverage years later of Steve Forbes, may have been part of the reason why Michaels so despised *Fortune* and any other Time Inc. publication. When *Forbes's* longtime auto writer, the late Jerry Flint, retired, Flint's wife, Kate McLeod, organized a party. Flint invited a friend and former competitor, Alex Taylor, who had covered Detroit for *Fortune*. Michaels was supposed to give a speech at the party. But when he found out Taylor would be there, he came in to shake Flint's hand, then left. "Had Jim discovered someone from *Fortune* was at his funeral," Flint says, "he would have broken out of the casket!"

A tiny birdlike man with large glasses and a raspy nasal voice, Michaels seemed harmless. But like a suddenly erupting volcano, he could frighten the bejeezus out of people with pyrotechnic fits of anger.

When Jason Zweig, a highly valued senior writer who specialized in mutual fund coverage, came into Michaels's office one afternoon to announce he was leaving for *Money*—a Time Inc. publication—Michaels's outrage was increased exponentially by the fact that Zweig's new boss would be Frank Lalli, a former assistant managing editor at *Forbes*. So it was a *double* betrayal: not only was Zweig leaving for the detested Time Inc., but he was also going to work for *someone else who had left* Forbes!

Turning to face Zweig from his standup desk, where he'd been editing a story, Michaels raged: "WHAT???? WHAT????? YOU'RE GOING WHERE???? YOU'RE GOING TO WORK FOR THAT STARFUCKER??????. GET OUT! GET OUT!! GET OUT!!!" As he yelled, Michaels jumped up and down—the first time, Zweig later told me, that he'd ever seen anyone *literally hopping mad*. Zweig backed out of the room, barely able to keep from laughing at the outburst.

Later, when Michaels heard that one of his more dazzling stars, Nina Munk, was going to *Fortune*, he sent his secretary up to Munk's office to put a yellow Post-It note on her door: "Get out! Now!— JWM." He'd written with such force that the pen almost broke through the paper. And one evening when he faced a dearth of copy for an impending deadline, he stormed into my office. Having patrolled the fourth floor, where most of the writers worked, only to find lots of empty desks, he snarled, "Where are your writers? Where are their stories????" After I explained that I'd already filed their stories, he'd edited all of them, and the writers had gone home (it was after 7:00 P.M.), Michaels said "Oh," then turned to go next door to confront another editor.

Perhaps it was their shared ability to frighten people that initially bonded Michaels and Dave Mack, but more likely it was Michaels's obvious brilliance and his ability to spot ideas and trends that others didn't see that convinced Mack to hire him in 1954. At an editors' meeting with executives of the Haloid Photographic Company, now known as Xerox, it was Michaels who instantly saw the commercial potential of an "electro-photographic" plain paper copier that could turn out limitless document copies.

One of Michaels's smartest moves was hiring Sheldon Zalaznick, the managing editor at *New York* magazine, to take the same title at *Forbes*. In a January 1985 interview with *Adweek*, Michaels noted *Forbes* had badly needed a makeover, to get away from the gray washed-out look and dreadful layouts that made the publication look stodgy and antique. Michaels wanted no part of a redesign effort, but it was a perfect assignment for Zalaznick, who proceeded to transform *Forbes* into what Michaels called a "more contemporary look." A new art director, Everett Halvorsen, worked with Zalaznick to create some memorable covers, including a year-end 1982 classic—Dracula, representing the bear market, beginning to cringe as the sun rises. Initially stumped as to what to do for the cover, Halvorsen and Zalaznick repaired to a nearby watering hole for two hours and came back inspired.

Being pompous around Michaels was not a good idea. Peter G. Peterson, now with the Blackstone Group, previously had an undistinguished stint as head of Bell & Howell and went on to become an aide to President Richard Nixon. The Washington bureau chief set up an interview with Peterson, and asked Michaels to come down for it. Early in the interview, Peterson made it clear he was talking to *Fortune* as well. Walking out of the White House, Michaels turned to his bureau chief and growled, "There's a son of a bitch who's looking for a job." So when *Forbes* soon did a piece on Bell & Howell, Michaels inserted a line saying, "the company is struggling today, trying to recover from the mis-administration of Peter G. Peterson."

Later, Michaels would be one of the first business editors to perceive the importance of the leveraged buyout, the telecom revolution, and the potential of the Internet: "Once the images are good enough to elicit real emotion, it's going to be huge." He also understood, before many others, the growing business role of entertainment, even though he banned the word "artist" when referring to singers or other performers.

But Michaels could be oddly clueless about popular culture. When writer Peter Newcomb proposed a cover story on the phenomenally successful Rolling Stones, Michaels professed not to know who they were. But when Newcomb and Lisa Gubernick later pitched a story on the "growth in country music" (that's all they said) Michaels slammed his fist down on his desk and declared "That's a cover!" Before anyone could ask "Why?" Michaels quickly added, "Because nobody would expect *Forbes* to do it!" The resulting story featuring Garth Brooks on the cover scooped all the national magazines, including *People, Time,* and *Newsweek,* in "discovering" the popular country-and-western singer.

Everyone needs an editor. Michaels was told to rewrite his first *Forbes* story by Richard Phalon, a talented business writer who was about to depart for a tour at the *New York Herald Tribune* and would later return to *Forbes.* As Phalon recalls it, "I made him rewrite on principle. The new kid on the block shouldn't get free tickets the first crack out of the box." Upon reflection, Phalon adds, "How *dearly* I paid for that, time after time, after time," his voice trailing off.

Michaels and Ray Brady became fast friends and regularly got into trouble together. After Brady's engagement party at the Overseas Press Club one night, Brady was giving Michaels and other revelers a ride to Grand Central. Michaels discovered a beach ball in the backseat. "Let's play football," he said. So Brady pulled over at a vacant lot, and the crew piled out. Feeling no pain from the party, Michaels tried to tackle someone a bit too enthusiastically, slipped, fell, and tore his trousers. Brady and Co. had to "pour him onto the train" to Port Chester. "And we're not sure whether he even woke up to get off," Brady says. "There were nights he didn't." One weekend, Brady, Michaels, and their wives were driving upstate and decided to stop at a restaurant Michaels knew had wonderful wines. But Fran Michaels was in no mood for Bordeaux. Or wine of any kind. At the restaurant, when Brady and Michaels had left the table to visit the restroom, Fran turned to Brady's wife and said, "Are we going to let that little son-of-a-bitch tell us what to drink?" Fran ordered a martini. Years later, after Jim and Fran split, Fran unexpectedly ran into Malcolm. "Take good care of him," he said. "He's doing a good job for me." Fran told a friend, "I didn't tell him we'd been divorced for over a year."

Occasionally, Michaels would complain about some of the tough things he had to do as editor. Telling Jerry Flint he fired a reporter with a wife and kids on Christmas Eve, he added, "Do you know why?" Before Michaels had a chance to explain it was so the guy could get his year-end bonus, Flint said, "Because you knew you might never get a chance to do something like that again!"

BOOK III

19

"I SEE RICH PEOPLE"

I F THERE WAS ONE thing that drove Malcolm Forbes nuts, it was the success of the *Fortune 500* list, a feature begun in 1955 that became part of the American business vocabulary. *Forbes* tried its best to compete with its own version based on a combined ranking based on assets, sales, profits, and market cap, but it never got the traction—either with readers or advertisers—that the *Fortune* list had. What to do?

Almost lost in history was the fact that B. C. Forbes ran a small list of rich Americans in 1919. But it was modest in scope, contained the obvious familiar names, and was a one-off effort. If B.C. thought of making it a part of the broader *Forbes* franchise, he kept it to himself.

Malcolm, of course, had a grander vision. "This magazine is about people," he said to a colleague. "Let's do a list of the richest people." *Forbes*, of course, was the logical publication in which to do this. For much of the twentieth century, a lot of what was written about great wealth reflected political and ideological opposition to it. Bloated plutocrats were unpopular, particularly during the Depression. Robber barons were vilified. Widely popular novelists burned lasting and highly critical images of wealth and capitalist values into their work. Sinclair Lewis's *Dodsworth* portrayed rich people as living pointless, empty lives. F. Scott Fitzgerald's *The Great Gatsby* told the tale of the pathetic character whose ornate parties, ostentatious car, and library full of books, all uncut, were nothing but shallow gestures to gain attention. In the view of many Americans, if you were very rich, you probably were a crook.

Malcolm wanted to temper that outlook with a listing of people that had nothing to do with birth, breeding, or background, but simply how much they were worth—assets minus debts. Period. It would be done not with a boring table, which *Fortune* twice used when it tried such a list, but with short bios done in a punchy telegraphic style. It would be called the *Forbes 400*, a name inspired by executive editor Jim Cook that conjured up Mrs. Astor's list of four hundred prominent New Yorkers, so called because it was the maximum number of people who could fit into the ballroom used for her swank annual invitation-only parties.

Malcolm was, of course, enthusiastic, but Jim Michaels didn't want to do it: too much trouble, too costly. Plus the numbers would be suspect since most would be hidden from public view—in trust agreements and other private documents locked up in law office safes or bank vaults. Managing editor Zalaznick weighed in with the fear that it would be a "hit list for kidnappers."

Malcolm dismissed all these concerns, especially Zalaznick's worry about possible abductions. "Oh, all these guys have security," Malcolm said. "I have security. It won't be a problem."

Malcolm said he'd throw whatever money and resources were needed into the project, and told a reluctant Michaels to get going with it.

Michaels first offered the assignment to Howard Rudnitsky, a quirky but talented staffer who once headed up the magazine's statistical department and who could dissect balance sheets as well as any CPA. But Rudnitsky's raw copy was almost always in need of a translation service, so convoluted and impenetrable were the words that served as connective tissue between his spot-on numbers.

Through an interpreter, Rudnitsky said no thanks. Michaels then turned to Harry Seneker, another talented but odd numbers guy who'd also spent time in the stats department.

Seneker had the assistance of a young researcher named Jonathan Greenberg who was adept at digging through newspaper clips and proxy statements. In some preliminary work on the project before Seneker took over, Greenberg and another more senior staffer, Jim Flanigan, had run across a freelance writer from Philadelphia named Dan Rottenberg, who had done a couple of stories in the "rich list" genre for *Town & Country*. Rottenberg was ready to move on to another career phase and was willing to sell his files to *Forbes* for $5,000, a deal Flanigan negotiated. The files consisted of two filing cabinets of clips on wealthy Texans and Philadelphians. But more valuable than the files was extracting from Rottenberg his methodology. How did he get all this stuff?

Lots of legwork and time on the phone: Go to a city and find the people who'd know who the really rich people in town are, newspaper editors, major bankers, real estate brokers, fund-raisers, lawyers, philanthropic organizations, socialites, and politicos. But that was just the start. To meet *Forbes*'s exacting standards, Seneker knew they'd have to get documentation from public filings, when available. And to estimate the revenues of private companies, they'd need to find people in town who knew the firms very well.

It wasn't easy. What Seneker, Greenberg, and another young researcher, Jay Gissen, thought would take a few months turned out to be a year, during which a still skeptical Zalaznick told Seneker, "We're letting you have all the rope you want to hang yourself!" Gee, thanks.

But when the first "rich list" debuted in September 1982, it became an almost instant institution. The cover looked like an elegant invitation, with the names of all four hundred rich listers "engraved" in a script font. At Grand Central, the newsstands sold out the issue within fifteen minutes. An excited radio reporter for WINS in New York said, "If you're not on the cover of the current *Forbes* magazine, you're an also ran." At its peak in the 1990s, the rich list issue would sell in excess of a hundred thousand copies on the news-stand, more than three times the normal newsstand sales. The "buzz effect" was phenomenal, and *Forbes* had a new, very appropriate franchise—measuring wealth.

The first list, with a minimum cutoff of $95 million, contained the usual suspects like the Rockefellers, John Kluge, and Donald Trump. But there were also surprises, like Bob Hope, Meyer Lansky, and Yoko Ono.

Hope, listed in 1982 at $200 million, told reporter Richard Behar the following year, "If my estate is worth over $50 million, I'll kiss your ass. I mean that." Hope left the phone momentarily to find some financial records, humming "Thanks for the Memories" while do-ing so. Though he disagreed with his ranking, he had no problem working it into his routines: "If I had that kind of money, I wouldn't have *gone* to Vietnam. I would have *sent* for it." For 1983's list, *Forbes* spent $5,000 paying real estate experts to analyze and value all of Hope's real estate holdings, much of which was raw mountain land. Behar concluded Hope was worth $115 million, more than what Hope asserted but less than the $150 million cutoff for 1983. So Be-har wound up doing a two-page story on Hope, announcing he was off the official list, but noting "Leslie Townes Hope is not exactly poorhouse material either. You're off the list, Bob, but you're not off the hook. Isn't there something you owe us?"

The rich list had an interesting sociological impact. After it was first published, some of the richest bragged to their friends they were thrilled that *Forbes* had missed them. But after another year or two without being listed, their friends began to wonder—or they themselves worried that their friends would wonder—that perhaps they really didn't have that kind of wealth. "So you start hearing from centi-millionaires who now feel they have to come out of the closet to be included. That's the kind of power the list had in those early years," says Behar.

Even Michaels conceded it was a success. But Baldwin, particu-larly after he became editor, was never impressed with the list's ac-curacy. Noting one year that several of the rankings were the same—$1.1 billion, for example—he suggested tweaking some of the numbers so they'd be different and thus the ranking would seem more credible. "It's bullshit anyway," he told the issue's editor that year, "it's all made up."

People who appear on the list tend to have two reactions: those who'd rather not be on it at all or have their numbers lowered, and those who want to have their valuations pumped up so as to impress their bankers, among others. Carl Icahn and Donald Trump fall into the latter category and on an annual basis complain their published numbers aren't big enough. Frozen food magnate Jeno Paulucci, founder of ChunKing, called in to say: "I didn't work this hard all my life to be put on the pauper's end of your rich list." (Paulucci then sent in copies of financials that showed he was worth more.) Some like Herb Allen, of Allen & Company, the secretive investment company, write regularly to plead to be removed, saying that their valuation isn't accurate, while refusing to say what the correct number should be.

An early complainer was Phil Anschutz, another investor who didn't like publicity. From public documents filed with the Texas Railroad Commission, *Forbes* researchers calculated that from his oil-rich landholdings alone, Anschutz was a billionaire even back in 1982. His handlers tried to reach Malcolm to complain, but to no avail. They then tried to "talk down" Anschutz's wealth to the researchers, claiming his investments were in the toilet.

Extracting from a researcher the fact that the minimum to make the list that year was $100 million, Anschutz's PR people made a compelling argument that their boss was worth only $50 million. But right around the same time, a news item appeared reporting that Anschutz had just closed a sale of half of his ranch to Mobil Oil for $500 million. Oh.

During the reporting process, *Forbes* researchers were often yelled at and cursed, while recording some real gems. "Why don't you just publish my fucking address!!!!" screamed an irate member of the ever-so-proper Bancroft family, which at the time owned the majority of shares in Dow Jones, then the publisher of *The Wall*

Street Journal. Ivan Boesky said: "I really don't care about money."

The pestering from rich listers can be interminable. Former rich list reporter Randall Lane had to field weekly calls from Jerry J. Moore, the biggest strip mall builder in Texas. Moore was obsessed with his ranking and wanted to be listed as a billionaire. When Lane said that he was listing Moore at $500 million, Moore countered by offering the twenty-four-year-old, who was making $27,000 at the time, a $100,000-a-year PR job "with lots of golf." Lane declined but ultimately left *Forbes* to found his own "jealousy machine," *Trader Monthly,* which calculated the loot hot Wall Street traders raked in—such as the forty-year-old former army helicopter pilot who at Fortress Investment Group was hauling in $50 million a year, an amount, Lane notes, that was equal to half the GDP of the Falkland Islands.

There's an incredible voyeuristic appeal to seeing how much money other people make, and to see how you fit in. Whether they like it or not, *Forbes* rich listers are members of a very exclusive club, a fact *Forbes* has brilliantly exploited in its editorial content. Many of the inspirational—and aspirational—stories about successful entrepreneurs that appear throughout the year have this between-the-lines message: *Maybe one day you can be on this list, too, and we'll even give you some tips on how to do it.*

Never underestimate the lust-for-money factor in American business. A classic *Forbes* story that pushed the jealousy button hard began this way: "Don't read this story if you like golf and are bored with your middle management job. It'll make you mad." The story, of course, was about a guy completely fed up with his corporate job who quit to find happiness and success running his own company that made golf carts.

Malcolm was an inveterate meddler in the rich list process, often intervening on behalf of celebrity executives he knew well. "What's the minimum for this year's list?" he asked editor Peter Newcomb. "$125 million," was the response. "Put Armand Hammer in at $150 million," Malcolm said, ending the conversation.

For years, Estée Lauder's PR people had worked hard to keep the cosmetic queen's age a secret. So when Newcomb finally located her birth certificate and realized Lauder was seventy-nine in 1986, he was ebullient. Until a horrified Lauder called Malcolm after a fact-checker had called the company to verify her age. Malcolm picked up the phone and punched in Newcomb's extension. "You can't use it, Pete," he said. "But Malcolm, I spent the whole summer trying to get a copy of her birth certificate," Newcomb pleaded. No matter. In the issue, Lauder's age came out as "ageless."

The early research efforts were laborious, an "impossible difficult challenge," says Behar. "But it was in the public interest to have as clear a sense as possible who these richest people were, given the influence they wielded." Each rich lister or world billionaire today has an individual valuation file or "blue sheet," a name from pre-computer days referring to the color of the paper used for the calculations. Date of birth, the industry that's the source of wealth (finance, manufacturing, etc.), universities attended and degrees earned, places of residence, citizenship, and total net worth are entered in data fields stored in a secure, central hard drive, accessible only to a handful of staffers.

There's also a "notes area" in each file where reporters insert current news stories about the subject, source names and contact information, and summaries of their own reporting. The notes area is also where all the calculations of a subject's wealth are kept. The holdings are listed, the value of each is calculated, and then the total is tallied according to various metrics such as debt or asset discount. Calculations are always reviewed by an editor, whose comments and questions are inserted into the text of the notes. Editors with the proper access can pull up blue sheets going back several years. There are about nine thousand names on file, of which only about fifteen hundred are truly monitored, ranging from Anschutz to Zuckerberg.

The *Forbes 400* would eventually become the most visible and influential icon of the brand. Television, radio, and newspaper "pickups" of the list would increase annually, creating tremendous media leverage for the issue each year. Each of the overseas editions did its own regional rich lists, creating controversy—and valuable press attention each time.

Fuming at the success of the *Forbes 400, Fortune* managing editor Marshall Loeb decided in 1985 he needed to top it, so came up with the idea of doing a list of the world's billionaires, unaware that *Forbes* was about to do the same thing. Sure enough, during the research, *Forbes* reporters kept running into the footprints of *Fortune* researchers, who clearly had been at it longer. "Oh, yeah, a guy from *Fortune* just called a month ago about the same thing," a source told Seneker.

Malcolm ordered the project into ramming speed mode. Both rivals wound up publishing within days of each other, a virtual tie. Of course each publication wound up missing a few names the other had, but one big difference was that *Fortune* claimed that there were no Swiss billionaires, while *Forbes* listed a half dozen.

The best response to a wealth ranking came in May 2006, when under the heading of wealthy heads of state in the billionaires issue, *Forbes* listed Fidel Castro as being worth $900 million, from heading up some state-run companies and alleged kickbacks from cigars and rum. The Bearded One lashed out in one of his vintage tirades, declaring that *Forbes* was in a "dead-end alley, has fallen in its own trap, and scored a self-goal." He demanded *Forbes* prove its allegations, and challenged "President Bush, the CIA, all 33 US intelligence agencies and the thousands of banks in the world to prove those lies, and if they could find even one dollar in one account in his name he would resign."

Neither President Bush nor the CIA offered assistance. *Forbes* issued no retraction or explanation. Castro didn't resign. On the other hand, the *Forbes* PR department was delighted at the priceless exposure.

If *Forbes* were ever to be broken up and sold for parts, the rich list/billionaire database would be one of the most valuable assets, since it represents the brand's most popular and expandable franchise. How popular? Each year when *The World's Billionaires* list posts on the *Forbes* Web site, it brings in excess of 70 million hits from around the world—on just that first day.

Forbes publisher Rich Karlgaard has long mused about the potential of replicating the "sizzle and steak" rich list concept in local markets. "Let's suppose we see opportunity in local business news and want to challenge City Business Journals for readers and ad dollars," he told me. "The fastest way to announce our presence and get attention in cities like Phoenix, Minneapolis and Charlotte would be with a local rich list."

"And you know what? No one would challenge *Forbes'* authority to do so," Karlgaard added. "Dow Jones, CNBC, Condé Nast, *Fortune, BusinessWeek, The Economist,* the *FT,* Google and Yahoo have many weapons. They do not have this one." Sadly, the company no longer has the financial resources to staff up for such a venture.

Then came the spinoffs. One of the most successful became an annual listing of the most valuable pro sports franchises—baseball, football, basketball, and hockey. It seemed a natural fit within *Forbes.* U.S. pro sports franchises have made many owners—Jerry Jones of the Dallas Cowboys and the Steinbrenner family of the New York Yankees, for example—immensely wealthy. What sports fan hasn't dreamed of someday owning a team? Yet no mass appeal publication regularly covered sports as a business.

Baldwin, who doesn't follow sports, was less than enthusiastic when pitched the idea by Michael Ozanian, a sports fan who worked in the stats department and had done a similar list when he worked at *Financial World,* a publication that has since folded. "We have too many lists already," Baldwin told Ozanian.

Steve Kichen, Ozanian's boss, supported the editor's position, not necessarily because *he* didn't think it was a good idea, but because Baldwin didn't. Undeterred, Ozanian worked evenings and weekends producing a mockup that finally won Baldwin over, mainly because the pitch included an explanation of the methodology and some evidence that his numbers were correct: Ozanian had prospectuses from the recent sales of the Washington Redskins and the New England Patriots.

The first franchise rankings of four different sports—football, baseball, hockey, and basketball—ran in the December 1998 issue. The ad guys loved it and sold Dodge on sponsoring the lists, which would now be spread out across the year to coincide as much as possible with the sports' season openers. The lists brought *Forbes* important new buzz—with wire service and local paper pickups, plus sports talk radio programs, where listeners call in to argue about the numbers and debate the team rankings.

One frequent critic was baseball commissioner Bud Selig, who'd complain about the *Forbes* numbers, yet refused to provide what he said were the correct ones. The Yankees, however, loved the annual list, since it always placed the franchise at number one, most recently at a worth of $1.2 billion. Yankees president Randy Levine, a good friend of Steve Forbes, followed up by negotiating a deal to have Ozanian appear on pregame shows and some half-hour specials on the YES cable television network, of which the Yankees owned 34 percent.

Baldwin remained skeptical about the sports rankings, and would invariably say during meetings when the next list was pitched, "Didn't we just do one of those?" "Yes, Bill, but that was baseball," Ozanian would say. "This is football."

On several occasions the list morphed into a cover package, profiling a particularly successful franchise, like the Dallas Cowboys or the New England Patriots. Those invariably did well on the newsstands, as did a 2008 cover on University of Alabama football coach Nick Saban. The issue sold out all newsstands in the South, and *Forbes* had to do a supplemental run of a hundred thousand more copies to meet the demand. (Newsstand sales, except for special issues like the rich list, world billionaires, celebrities, and two investment guides each year, average around thirty thousand.) But as the magazine began to shrink in size, the sports list package was always one of the first things Baldwin wanted to trim.

20

"LET'S REALLY STIR UP THE ANIMALS!"

CUTTING STORIES BY AT least 15 percent without shedding any facts was a Michaels trademark—the key to making *Forbes* readable for busy executives overloaded with information. Said one of his former protégés: "Jim could edit the Lord's Prayer down to six words, and nobody would miss anything."

Nor would Michaels tolerate a story that read like a press release. "THIS ISN'T REPORTING, IT'S STENOGRAPHY! WHY IS THIS PERSON STILL ON STAFF????" he wrote on top of one particularly credulous piece. "WHY DON'T YOU JUST SEND THEM A VALENTINE!!!" was another favorite skewer.

Relentlessly, he'd push writers to move a story to "absolute truth" from "highly likely." Better to say, "this is a fraud" rather than just "it's shady." An assertion or a superficial statement simply wouldn't do. "How do you know that?" he'd ask. When Tania Pouschine turned in a story saying the numbers for the film company Cannon Group, a Wall Street darling at the time, looked funny, Michaels said, "I believe you, but you don't have the smoking gun." So Pouschine went back and created a chart showing every single film the company had ever produced, listing its cost, box office, video and foreign revenues, and calculated how much should have been amortized under accepted accounting rules. Those numbers provided what Michaels was looking for; the company later settled a Securities and Exchange Commission inquiry that questioned the company's financial results.

In Michaels's view of *Forbes* as the drama critic of American business, hard numbers were necessary to support the argument, but he knew, as B.C. did, that the people who ran the companies were the most interesting things on stage—human beings with virtues and flaws who created both triumphs and tragedies for their shareholders. And like Barney Kilgore, the visionary who had turned *The Wall Street Journal* from a sleepy financial paper into a powerful national brand that Rupert Murdoch felt was worth $5 billion, Michaels knew the key for readers was insight for the future, rather than rehashing what they already knew.

The more contrarian the story, the better. Michaels loved to take down big companies riding high on Wall Street and being gushed over by the competition. In 1973 a young reporter with a newly minted Harvard MBA turned in a negative story on Avon, a company with a spectacular growth rate and a high-flying stock. The writer, Subrata Chakravarty, said the growth rate was a sham and that the company had been built by exploiting women. It was counter to what everyone else thought. Passing the draft to other editors, Michaels got nothing but sneers back, and toned the story down, much to Chakravarty's dismay.

Not realizing that rewriting Jim Michaels was the equivalent of a death sentence, Chakravarty went back to his typewriter and reedited Michaels's edit. Not a good idea. Less than an hour after resubmitting the draft, Chakravarty's phone rang. A gravelly voice barked, "Subrata, who is the editor of this magazine?"

"You are, sir."

"That's right, and I'll thank you to remember that when I edit a story, it stays edited." Michaels slammed down the phone.

Hurrying to Michaels's office, Chakravarty found him slumped in his chair, glowering darkly. "Don't come in here now, I'm too mad to talk to you."

"But Mr. Michaels, I did exactly what you told me."

Michaels shot up in his chair, glaring. "I NEVER told you to rewrite me."

"Yes, you did," Chakravarty insisted, recounting an earlier lunch conversation when Michaels said that if a writer disagreed with something he'd done, it could be fixed and then discussed. Michaels relaxed and even managed a tiny smile. "Well, I misspoke. I meant we would talk about what you could change. Now you've added 150 lines to a cover story, and it's already laid out. So get out of here so I can fit it again."

Convinced by Chakravarty's arguments and facts, Michaels cut the story by knifing out many of the caveats he'd earlier included. After the story ran, on July 1, 1973, Avon's stock fell to $17 from $130 as its results bore out Chakravarty's analysis. It was an amazing support of a young reporter, in the face of opposition from others. But rewriting Jim Michaels was a mistake, Chakravarty recalls, "a rookie can make only once."

Later, Michaels would cite the Avon piece as a classic *Forbes*ian tale. "When everyone was saying that Avon was the final answer to what the model of a great corporation should be, we said that's a lot of crap. It's a lot of women with nothing else to do, unloading stuff on their neighbors."

The Avon cover was only one of several that made waves and got *Forbes* some badly needed attention in the marketplace. A piece by Jim Flanigan on Litton Industries, illustrated by the company name in front of a piece of shattered mirror, poked holes in the earnings reports of the diversified defense contractor that had run up an unprecedented streak of constantly improving quarterly earnings reports. Litton was a Wall Street darling, but Flanigan didn't like the way the balance sheet looked. Michaels encouraged Flanigan, not letting on that he'd heard from Paul Cabot at State Street Investment in Boston, who had similar concerns. Michaels flew out to Los Angeles to join Flanigan in the interview with "Tex" Thornton, Litton's chairman. Litton's PR people were excited that Michaels was coming along and gave him and Flanigan wide access. "We got the full run," Flanigan recalls. Flanigan's "the emperor has no clothes" story appeared December 1, 1969. It was the classic *Forbes* spin: Take something that appeared to be working well and turn it over, so the message to readers was "the damn thing isn't working at all." Not long after the story ran, Litton failed to improve its quarterly earnings for the first time in a long while. The stock reacted accordingly.

Midway through an early January 1992 story meeting when editors were still recovering from being overserved during the holidays, Michaels woke them up by blurting out: "It's time for a really *nasty* story. *Let's really stir up the animals!*"

The result was a piece by Richard Stern on William Agee and his wife, Mary Cunningham. Depicted in a "stop them before they kill again" June 8, 1992, cover as Louis XIV and Marie Antoinette, the story said they helped run Morrison-Knudsen into the ground. Morrison was a proud old construction firm that had built the Hoover Dam and the San Francisco Bay Bridge. The board subsequently fired Agee, citing alleged financial improprieties and accounting irregularities.

Another killer piece by Stern was on First Jersey Securities, a brokerage house that carpet bombed the country during the early nineties with TV ads featuring its chief, Robert E. Brennan, stepping out of his helicopter urging investors to "come grow with us." The company was posting astounding results. Staff writer Richard Stern thought it all sounded fishy and told Michaels so. His eyes lit up. Nothing got his juices flowing faster than the prospect of a story that would put a large spike through a big balloon, particularly that of an executive who flew around in a helicopter.

Stern had some history covering First Jersey Securities. In the eighties, he'd done a "follow the money" piece showing how First Jersey brokers in one office were selling customers out of a stock while on the same day, brokers in another office were selling customers into the stock at higher prices. But the reporting turned out to be easier than getting the story into print. Brennan had been putting intense pressure on Malcolm to kill the story. It finally ran, but without the disclosure that Stern had caught Brennan on federal election fraud. He'd been reimbursing his managers for contributions they'd made to Millicent Fenwick, a New Jersey congresswoman who was running for the Senate. Turns out she was being backed by the Forbes family.

Stern's October 26, 1992, cover story identified the investment firm as a house of cards that would soon collapse. Brennan was later nailed on stock fraud charges by the state of New Jersey and was ruled by a federal judge to have masterminded a "massive and continuing fraud" on his customers.

Stern briefly got into hot water with Malcolm over a headline on a story involving Bernie Cornfeld, the cheeky financier whose Investors Overseas Services mutual fund had the famous pitch "Do You Sincerely Want to Be Rich?"

Stern had gone to Cornfeld's mansion in Beverly Hills, which was replete with lots of gorgeous women and nightly parties, to report a piece on how Cornfeld wanted to organize a new company around housewives selling health foods door-to-door. Asked why he was so interested in health foods, Cornfeld replied that he wanted to be able to have sex when he was eighty-five. So for the headline, Michaels came up with "Do You Sincerely Want to Get Laid?" When Malcolm stormed into Stern's office ("How dare you put that headline in my magazine!"), Stern bravely put the blame on Michaels, who soon got a Malcolm visit of his own. The headline came out: "Do You Sincerely Want to Make Out?"

One of Michaels's favorite staff writers was Joe Queenan, a self-proclaimed "sneering churl" who loved to do "fiendishly nasty stories" on shameless self-promoters. Queenan's self-described "off-handed malice" comes across in a caustic but outrageously funny style that skewers all his subjects without mercy. Outside the orb of business, Queenan's favorite targets included Jimmy Carter, Susan Sarandon, Sting, Bono, Alec Baldwin, Tori Spelling, Andrew Lloyd Webber, Deepak Chopra, and the particularly despised Geraldo Rivera. All these people seemed to Queenan incapable of "scooping up a piece of litter or giving a blind dwarf a nickel without issuing a 12-page press release" about their generosity.

At *Forbes*, Queenan feasted on outfits like Ben & Jerry's, the hippie-tinged Vermont ice cream guys who peddle "sugar-laden, cholesterolly toxic products" that "could keep heart surgeons and dentists busy for the next millennium." The upscale products, with such "yuppie porn" flavors as Rainforest Crunch, are popular, Queenan noted, "with far more men in red suspenders than Ben or Jerry would like to believe. Inner-city residents would need a bridge loan to take home a pint."

Queenan's flamethrower also made a crispy critter out of the Vancouver Stock Exchange, a Wild West market that flogged flaky penny stocks, rig jobs, and outright scams. Though its members and supporters contended the VSE was a vital source of seed money for "intrepid investors seeking to transform their brainchildren into the next Xerox," Queenan concluded, "the brainchildren are born brain dead, and the next Xerox turns out to be the last Hydrodouche." Michaels salivated at a story that took on an entire institution. "We don't want to rape," he told Queenan, "we want to gang rape!"

But one of Queenan's stories got unwanted attention. The June 26, 1989, issue analyzed the views of Michael Fumento's book, *The Myth of Heterosexual AIDS*, which argued that there wouldn't be a major AIDS epidemic among heterosexual couples because most of the cases involved either gay males or people who shared infected needles. "Most heterosexuals will continue to have more to fear from bathtub drowning than from AIDS," Fumento wrote. In other words, the Lilly Pulitzer–bedecked wives who lunched at the Greenwich Country Club could relax, despite the hysterical warnings of Oprah and others. Michaels wanted Queenan to do the piece and gave it prominent play in the front of the book. But the gay community, fearing the article could have the effect of cutting government spending on AIDS research, was irate. ACT UP members picketed the *Forbes* building, carrying signs like "Don't Touch Malcolm's Tool!" All this prompted Malcolm, in a personally awkward position given his sexual proclivities, to print a mea culpa saying he wouldn't have allowed the article to appear had he not been on vacation.

Queenan, citing medical literature that later supported Fumento's position, says that though the article was factually correct, *Forbes* shouldn't have run it, because it "was a bad time to publish it. It doesn't matter if you're right if it's the wrong time."

As a teacher, Michaels was rigorous in pushing his writers to drill down for the specific detail and evidence that would make a good story into a great story. He once chastised a writer who turned in a story about Perrier for not spending the money to go to France, since the on-the-ground reporting would have provided additional rich color. And for a story on the world's great economists, some of whom were dead, he wanted to know, specifically, how tall each of them was. This put the writer, Tania Pouschine, in the odd position of calling the descendants of David Ricardo to find one of the economist's old suits, so it could be measured. "Then we estimated how much to add for his head and feet," says Pouschine. "This sounds like make work, but it wasn't," she says. "The questions Jim asked invariably made the stories and the people come to life."

Michaels knew how to pick people, and didn't mind their idiosyncrasies. Robert Lenzner was one of those hires. A large man with an overbearing presence and booming voice, he wanders the halls talking to himself, snatches a handful of grapes from the cafeteria (without paying), and often bursts into song or a loud self-pep-talk when working on a story: "GO, BOBBY, GO, YOU CAN DO IT!"

Editors often pretended to be on the phone when they heard Lenzner approaching, fearful he'd pop in, Kramer-like, and finish a monologue already begun in the hall about some "big story" usually involving "a guy from Goldman," an epic that invariably would never materialize. Lenzner would then leave, usually still talking.

Lenzner's greatest resource was the seemingly endless list of people he knew. Starting his career at Goldman Sachs, the Harvard-trained writer arguably had more sources on the Street and Washington (where his brother Terry is a powerful insider) than all *Forbes* staffers put together. It enabled him to lure people like George Soros and Martin Sosnoff onto his Forbes.com Street Talk video segment and interview legends like Albert Gordon, one of the founders of Kidder, Peabody & Co., the banker who lived to be 105 and did the original underwriting of AT&T.

Connections helped him gain access to Viacom's Sumner Redstone, who opened up to Lenzner and researcher Devon Pendleton for a 2007 cover piece called "Family Feud." It revealed the rifts between Redstone and his daughter Shari and set the scene for a coming battle for control of the giant media company.

Lenzner, a warm teddy bear inside his gruff exterior, was sometimes too close to his sources and reluctant to be too harsh. He regularly fretted about what might happen after a story appeared—particularly one that had been toughened up by an editor. "Sumner will *never* speak to me again, *never*!" Lenzner worried during a taxi ride home the night the Viacom story was about to go to press. "I'll have to resign! Maybe I'll go into acting."

Central to Michaels's management style was a compartmentalization that kept many staffers in the dark about what was going on. While most writers reported to an assistant managing editor, Michaels had his own group who worked directly with him, including, for a time, Allan Sloan, Lenzner, Susan Lee, Joe Queenan, and Peter Brimelow, a writer known for inserting his anti-immigration views into his stories. It wouldn't be unusual for a long piece, possibly even a cover story, by one of these writers to materialize late in the publishing cycle without any advance notice, sending the art department, copy desk, and the fact-checking crew into total panic. Michaels didn't care. He'd often arrive back from vacation near the very end of the two-week cycle and rewrite or kill several stories that had already been sent to the printing plant. Once disapproving of a cover story Laury Minard had top-edited and already been sent to the plant, Michaels called several reporters into his office late at night, sent them back to their desks to do additional reporting, and then rewrote the entire piece. And, of course, it turned out better.

One of the most intriguing *Forbes* stories was one that never

ran. Written by Jim Norman, an accomplished investigative reporter who had a distinguished career in newspapers and at *Business Week* before joining *Forbes* in 1990 as a senior editor, the story
looked behind what was really behind the July 1993 suicide of White
House Deputy Vincent Foster, a former law partner of Hillary Clinton at the Rose Law Firm in Little Rock, Arkansas. Officially, Foster's death was linked to a deep depression, driven, among other
things, by a series of negative references to him on *The Wall Street
Journal* editorial page, including one of the first public references
linking Foster to the "Travelgate" scandal, in which the White House
Travel Office staff was fired and replaced by a travel agency in Little
Rock with links to the Clintons.

Reading all the coverage in the national press, Norman wasn't
convinced that a few editorial zingers from the *Journal*'s Bob Bart-
ley were enough to cause a tough lawyer to put a gun in his mouth
at Fort Marcy Park in McLean, Virginia, a national park and site of
a fort built in 1862 as a Civil War defense to protect the approach to
Washington, D.C. This is where Foster drove his light gray Honda
Accord, still with its Arkansas plates, from the White House on the
afternoon of July 20. Foster's body, minus his dark blue suit jacket
and tie, which were neatly hung over the car's front seat, was found
about ten feet from one of the fort's old cannons. His White House
pager was turned off.

Norman puzzled over troubling questions: Why wasn't there
more blood on the ground, why were there no bone fragments or
brain tissue? Why were there rug fibers all over the clothes? Why no
dust on his shoes despite the long dirt path from his car to his body?
Was Vince Foster murdered?

So Norman started digging, contacting his sources in the intelligence community. After weeks of research, during which Michaels
started grumbling about Norman's lack of productivity on "regular
stories," Norman turned in a manuscript that said Foster, who had
made periodic one-day trips to Switzerland, was under investigation for leaking high-security U.S. secrets to Israel, in exchange for
money deposited to a coded bank account at the Banca della

Svizzera Italiana in Chiasso, Switzerland. According to Norman, Foster became alarmed when he checked his account to discover that the $2.7 million on deposit had been moved to a holding account at the U.S. Treasury. The $2.7 million was just part of some $2 billion in illicit funds, Norman says, that had been swept out of offshore bank accounts of people connected with the government.

The story, an early draft of which even included the allegation that another *Forbes* senior editor was a CIA operative, said the funds were removed by something called the Fifth Column, a small group of rogue CIA computer hackers who located Foster's account by tracking money flows from various Israeli government accounts. They allegedly discovered Foster's name while secretly scanning the electronic files of Israel's own spook operation, Mossad. Through an intricate "connect-the-dots" grid of documents, interviews, and off-the-record conversations with shadowy intelligence agents, Norman stitched together a convoluted tale that linked Foster to the world of secret surveillance of international banking transactions, espionage, and money laundering.

By any measure, "Fostergate" was an explosive story. Was it all true, or had Norman been conned by CIA disinformation operatives? But that was just part of it. There was to be even more drama involved, material that deeply troubled Jim Michaels.

Norman's reporting had also turned up information that Caspar Weinberger, the former secretary of defense and then the chairman of *Forbes*, allegedly had his own Swiss bank account (Union Bank in Berne) and that the Fifth Column successfully removed $2.3 million from that. In a subsequent private memo to Michaels, Norman said the "clear implication" of his reporting was that "Caspar Weinberger, while Sec. of Defense, was taking kickbacks on . . . arms sales."

Concerned that Norman was falling deeper and deeper into a vortex of whacky conspiracy theories, Michaels asked Baldwin to take a look at the story. Concluding "Fostergate" was the journalistic equivalent of a third rail, Michaels finally decided not to run it, later telling *The Baltimore Sun* that he was concerned over some of

Norman's sources. Norman, of course, was furious, convinced that it was Weinberger who had the story killed.

In his private memo to Michaels, he argued, "we are sitting on the most important story of the past 50 years. And one way or another it's going to come out in a massive way. I wish *Forbes* would stand up and do its journalistic duty, no matter what bogus claims of national security may be invoked. This is corruption of the highest order."

Norman went on to urge Michaels to reconsider and "to do what is right." This enterprise, Norman said, "has come face-to-face with a crucial ethical problem. How it handles it will reflect for a long time not just on *Forbes Magazine,* but also on the man whose name is on the cover." Michaels admired writers who stood up to him and pushed back. But he did not appreciate ultimatums of any sort, no matter how logically presented.

Acknowledging Norman's talent and being genuinely eager to keep him on staff, Michaels gave him permission to get the piece published elsewhere and suggested that he take an unpaid leave "to do a book on this" and then come back. But dismayed over what he believed to be an unforgivable cave-in to pressure, Norman felt he could no longer work at *Forbes* and resigned. "Fostergate" appeared in the August 1995 edition of *Media Bypass,* a magazine whose audience and contributors tended to be conspiracy theorists. Norman did a number of radio interviews about his story and Representative Bob Dornan, then head of the House Intelligence Committee, promised to read the story into the Congressional Record. But the mainstream media ignored it. Apart from some Internet chatter, "Fostergate" remained one of those stories that would continue for years to be an "exclusive." Norman went on to continue his career, working again at McGraw-Hill as a writer for Platt's Oilgram. He's now editing a group of oil publications for a privately owned Houston company.

Michaels was seen by many of his writers as relentlessly harsh and cruel. Arthur Jones says it sometimes came across like James Joyce's view of Ireland as the "mother sow that eats her farrow."

But in Michaels's case, it was "the mother of genius who eats her farrow." While Michaels's brilliant but difficult personality defined the "*Forbes* experience" for editorial staffers, few of them knew much about what Michaels was like outside the office. So it was revelatory for those who attended his funeral to hear stories from his two sons about what a wonderful, loving, and devoted father he was. In fact, most staffers didn't even know that Michaels *had* children—two sons and a daughter. Jim Jr. is an accomplished journalist and author in his own right; Rob works in health care, and with his second wife, has adopted four young daughters from India. Ann and her husband live in New Haven, Connecticut, in a condo her father bought for them, near Chapel Haven, a school for kids with special needs from which they both graduated.

Unlike Dewey Michaels, who had little influence on his children, Jim Michaels was immensely supportive of and involved with his. "He was smart enough not to be demanding," says his son Jim. "He was encouraging, particularly if you had an idea that was out of the ordinary. He was automatically supportive, would tell you all the reasons it was a good idea, reinforcing your logic so in the end you felt perfectly comfortable doing it." For Jim Jr. the contrarian idea was joining the Marines, for Rob, it was heading off to Australia before going to college. His father even helped get him a job on a ranch. And there was always the brilliant mind at work. "He'd be interested in anything that was going on, you could see him processing," Jim says. "His recall was frightening. Everything was in context."

Michaels liked people who pushed back, and kicked those who were willing to be kicked. He admired people who stood up to him, staffers like Susan Lee, who called him "Jimbo" to his face and often engaged in lively debates. Lee, in fact, gave me the best advice of anyone about how to deal with Michaels, even before he offered me a job. "You'll think you've agreed with him on salary and title, and then, at the last minute, before you shake on it, he'll say, 'Let's review the bidding,' and everything will be different." It's a *test*. Sure enough, over oatmeal at the Cosmos diner on East Twenty-third Street near

Gramercy Park one Thursday morning, Michaels, dressed in a knit shirt and khakis, said to me, "Let's review the bidding . . ."

"But Jim, that's *not* what we agreed to."

"WHAT???? Oh, I must have got that wrong."

Michaels was casually dressed because he was on his way to Rhinebeck to continue editing the issue from home. That was always the routine, to go up on Thursday and return Tuesday morning. Some years later, I learned the reason for that. Michaels had been claiming Rhinebeck as his legal residence, which got him off the hook for New York City taxes. This "avoidance" finally caught up with him, and since there's no statute of limitations on owed back taxes, he not only had to pay a hefty tax bill, but also had to make sure he spent enough time each year out of the city. "That's what all those are about," he told me, pointing to a stack of document boxes in the corner of his office.

Michaels and Fran, the children's mother, would ultimately divorce. Then on June 30, 1985, *Forbes* edit staffers were stunned to pick up the Sunday *New York Times* to learn the boss had married one of their own: Jean Briggs, a proper, demure woman from upstate New York who had joined *Forbes* in 1972 as a fact-checker. Some twenty years younger than Michaels, Briggs was immediately dubbed "the child bride" by the copy desk. Newsroom liaisons are notoriously hard to keep under wraps, but Michaels and Briggs somehow had kept their romance a secret.

Michaels didn't treat Briggs any differently from any other editor. He'd frequently storm into her office, waving a copy of a story she'd just passed along: "For God's sake, Jean, doesn't [*fill in any writer's name*] know what a *Forbes* story is? *This is a piece of CRAP!*"

Briggs's writers were fiercely loyal to her, and still credit her with helping their careers, being encouraging, and teaching them the basics of fact-checking and how to structure a story. To those chosen few and to any *Forbes* staffer she met socially, she was charming, gracious, and always interested in how wives, husbands, or children were doing. But others resented the amount of time she took off, how little hands-on editing she really seemed to do, and the sometimes haughty way she dealt with office space allocation and expense accounts, two important "control" responsibilities she took *very* seriously. And she could be cold and insensitive. One day senior editor Dana Wechsler Linden, one of the magazine's brightest and most prolific writers, came in to tell Briggs she was pregnant. Briggs replied "Oh, that's *terrible!*" Perhaps she meant to say it was too bad the magazine would be without Linden's imaginative stories during her maternity leave. But it didn't come out that way.

In a moment of uncharacteristic candor, and for him, a complete lapse into even *thinking* about staff morale, Michaels once confided to me that promoting his wife to an assistant managing editor's job may not have been the smartest thing to do politically. But of course he couldn't undo it. To do so would have risked being met at the door of their Gramercy Park apartment or home in Rhinebeck by a cast-iron frying pan much larger than he.

To the extent that Michaels needed a gatekeeper, it was a central casting role played to perfection by the saintly but formidable Harriett Miller, a delightfully eccentric middle-aged woman who wore large owlish eyeglasses, short skirts, high heels, and wildly colored stockings. Not to be trifled with, Harriett fiercely protected "Mr. Michaels" (she *never* referred to him as "Jim") from unwanted intruders and phone calls, deftly deflecting with good-natured humor the boss's outbursts. Including the time he picked up his new and deeply hated IBM Selectric and threw it out of his office, demanding the return of his beloved manual. Ms. Miller made sure it was promptly retrieved.

One of Harriett's key roles was that of weather person. It was never wise to enter the lair without first determining if it were stormy or sunny inside. Unless the matter at hand were urgent—such as to report a machine-gun massacre by one of the fourth-floor inmates—an answer of "He's not in a good mood today" clearly argued for an "I'll be back" response. Maybe in a week or so.

Michaels's biggest star—and ultimately his biggest loss—was Gretchen Morgenson, a glamorous, tough-as-nails writer who worked the phones constantly, turning up dirt and conflict on Wall Street.

Her coverage of the anti-investor practices on the NASDAQ market for *Forbes* was shortly followed by Justice Department and SEC investigations.

Morgenson, a former stockbroker and financial columnist for *Vogue,* had two stints at *Forbes,* one from 1986 to 1993, then from 1996 to 1998. In between she was an executive editor at *Worth* and spent six months as Steve Forbes's press secretary during his first presidential campaign.

Upon her return, Michaels promised an assistant managing editor's title, but that didn't happen for months. Morgenson was particularly discouraged when Baldwin was named managing editor, a sign he'd likely replace Michaels whenever he retired.

Morgenson asked Michaels if she could report to him and not Baldwin, a manager she considered, along with many, ill equipped to do the top job, with few people skills and what was perceived to be a narrow vision of what *Forbes* was and could be. But Michaels, respecting the chain of command, said no. Confiding to me that she felt "the wheels are coming off here," Morgenson started looking around, interviewing at the *Journal* and the *Times.* The *Journal,* in a then-common practice that frustrated many job applicants, no matter how senior, dragged its feet with its bureaucratic hiring process. The *Times* pounced.

Morgenson left *Forbes* in May 1998 to cover world financial markets for the *Times* and ultimately won the Pulitzer Prize in 2002 for her "trenchant and incisive" Wall Street coverage.

Magazines don't compete for Pulitzers. But had Morgenson stayed at *Forbes,* or, in the dreams of many writers and executives, had she succeeded Michaels as editor, she almost certainly would have brought new recognition—and buzz—to *Forbes.* How could the family have let this talent go? Later, when asked whether she'd consider coming back to *Forbes* to run it, Morgenson said, "Why, to pull a sheet over it?"

Morgenson's departure thoroughly demoralized a staff already unhappy with what was perceived as foot-dragging by the family in making it clear what the succession plan was to be. By that time,

Michaels had become increasingly cranky and more difficult to deal with (if that were possible), dismissing some of the stories the tech writers were pitching as just pieces about "gadgets," an attitude that often crept into his editing. That made the job of the writers—and *Forbes* sales people—in Silicon Valley more difficult, a situation often exacerbated by the work of freelance columnist Steve Manes, who reviewed new tech products. Unlike Walt Mossberg of the *Journal* or David Pogue of the *Times*, Manes was rarely enthusiastic about anything, making the *Forbes* staff's efforts to maintain cordial relationships with the tech companies a constant struggle. The standing joke at editorial meetings was that the headline "Something Else That Doesn't Work" could be placed on any Manes column.

The generally gloomy mood also triggered something of a miniexodus, including Carolyn Geer, a talented young writer and Morgenson protégée who'd made her career at *Forbes* out of volunteering to cover insurance, a yawner of a beat to most writers, but one important to the money and investing coverage. *Fortune* had offered Geer her own column.

Others left, too, and the cumulative effect of losing talented, seasoned writers was beginning to have an impact on quality. It wasn't just the dwindling number of writers. It was the absence of distinctive voices—veterans like Morgenson, Allan Sloan, Susan Lee, Lisa Gubernick, and Joe Queenan—and their enthusiasm for doing stories younger staffers were often afraid to tackle, that made the difference.

With morale low, and fears of more defections in the air, Tim Forbes asked me to lunch at Il Cantinori, a neighborhood Tuscan haunt made famous by *Sex in the City*. The boss wanted a pulse check on what was happening on the third and fourth floors, where the reporters, writers, and editors worked.

After a few minutes of debating whether the exodus was simply cyclical turnover or a *Forbes*-specific phenomenon, I brought up the issue of succession and why the staff was getting restless. Forbes put down his fork and cupped and uncupped his fingers in the classic "tell me more" gesture.

21

"FUCK! WE'RE GOING
TO DINNER!"

Dennis Kneale, a talented editor recruited from the *Journal*, yearned to be sitting in Michaels's office, and once declared in front of two writers "I'd like to go in there and put a pillow over his head." But another editor who'd been toiling away for much longer than Kneale had ached for the corner office, too. Laury Minard, the longtime managing editor who'd never worked anywhere else, had clawed his way up to the number-two slot by writing DBI (dull but important) stories on Rust Belt companies and even a story that featured a dead man on the cover.

Joseph Schumpeter was an Austrian School economist who introduced and popularized the concept of creative destruction, in which entrepreneurial innovation may destroy the value of established companies in the short term, but will ultimately result in stronger long-term economic growth. The story was a snooze to readers and most of the writers on staff, but it was the kind of piece that made Steve Forbes's pulse race. He jumped on it as an example of the kind of reporting that went to the core of the *Forbes* mission, and cited it continually for years.

But Minard was earning no kudos from his own staff. With

Michaels as his only role model, Minard assumed the road to the top ran through Nasty Town. While Michaels became enraged at the *words* people wrote, Minard often made it personal, and came across as being brutish and petty. Closing nights at the magazine used to be invariably late, running well past midnight. One evening about 7 00 P.M., Minard had his topcoat on. We were about to go out to dinner. In walked Paul Klebnikov, an exceedingly bright, if somewhat aloof writer fluent in Russian who did tough stories on Russian businessmen, including Boris Berezovsky, a thuggish man once close to Vladimir Putin.

With Klebnikov that night was Kasia Wandycz, the fact-checker assigned to review the piece that Klebnikov had done for the issue. They had come to Minard's office to "put on changes," so the story could move through the final production process before being electronically transmitted to the printing plant. But Minard was hungry, and that was more important than spending the ten minutes that would allow the writer, checker, copy desk, and production people to get home at a decent hour.

"Fuck!" he said. "We're going to dinner. Come back in two hours!" Exasperated, Klebnikov and Wandycz retreated, unable to do anything for most of the rest of the evening. Minard, in typical fashion, never came back, having loaded up on martinis and steak, telling me to deal with the Klebnikov story.

For many years, Minard assumed he'd be the one to succeed Michaels when he retired, whenever that would be. "If there's any fairness in the world, you and I will be running this place someday," he once said to me. But like the Maytag repairman, his phone never rang. (Mine did, but the line went dead after only a few months.)

As it is anywhere in corporate America, taking a promotion for granted is the kiss of death. Michaels was always leery of editors who tried to take too much responsibility or had a sense of entitlement. And he was nervous when talented people were around, whether or not they seemed to be after his job. "Jimmy never had a good night's sleep when Norm was here," says Michaels's close friend and colleague Ray Brady, who went on to small-screen fame as a business reporter for CBS News. Brady was referring to Norman Pearlstine, who spent two years as executive editor before leaving to return to the *Journal*, where he'd eventually become managing editor.

Years earlier, Michaels had made it very clear to Sheldon Zalaznick, who was managing editor for several years, that he wouldn't succeed him. The former managing editor of *New York* magazine, Zalaznick had been a wise and kindly counterpoint to Michaels, mostly treating the reporters, writers, and copy desk hands with respect. As an editor, he had an elegant touch. Nattily dressed and always courteous, Zalaznick was an effective balance to Michaels's nastiness and would get his points across not with intimidation but with low-key humor. "Be reasonable." He'd smile. "Do it my way."

Michaels dispensed with Minard by Chinese water torture, including dismissive notes on tops of stories Minard had edited for all the staff to see on the electronic editing system. Example: "I SEE YOUR INITIALS ON THIS STORY SO I ASSUME YOU UNDERSTAND IT. I DON'T. FIX IT."

It was painful to watch Minard being slowly flayed. And Michaels made it clear he had a new favorite: Bill Baldwin. Sometimes during editorial meetings, as Minard was trying to explain a story idea, Michaels would swivel in his chair, turn his back to Minard, then start chatting amiably with Baldwin about something else, an admiring smile on his face.

The sustained public humiliation, difficult for Minard to swallow and awkward for the rest of us to watch, came to an end on September 22, 1997, when Minard was named editor of *Forbes Global*, a new publication to be launched the following year, intended to cover the business news of the world. It was to rely heavily on stringers and a tiny New York staff of reporters and editors who'd do their own stories and rework the tops of domestic *Forbes* stories to give them a more international spin.

For Minard, it was a bittersweet assignment. Though passed over, he was finally out from under Michaels and was running his own show, which involved working closely with Bob Forbes and the business staff. He'd travel frequently to London, and for a time, seemed to be enjoying himself. At that point he was also newly separated, out from under a marriage he'd long characterized to friends as difficult.

But subscribers to the "real" *Forbes* in Europe and Asia quickly complained, to no avail, about what they were now getting in the mail. Here was a much thinner publication that covered global business news, but it wasn't edited abroad—either in London or Hong Kong. And before the days of Forbes.com, which would post the complete domestic issue of *Forbes* every two weeks, a common reader complaint was that *Global* didn't have much coverage of U.S. companies—a major reason, some said, that they subscribed to *Forbes* to begin with.

Forbes was simply tipping its hat to the well-tested editorial formula of one of its main rivals—the *Journal*. Though initially relying heavily on content from the domestic edition, editors of both the *Journal*'s European and Asian editions quickly discovered that what foreign readers really wanted was not a warmed-over version of what U.S. readers saw every day but content specific to the region, reported and edited with the local audience in mind.

In the pre-Internet era, most publishers, including *Time, Newsweek, Fortune, Forbes,* the *Journal*, and even *USA Today,* tried to create pan-European and pan-Asian editions that would appeal to what was actually an artificial regional/global ad market. The idea was to convince global outfits like IBM and the big banks to advertise regionally, paying a 5 percent to 10 percent increment above U.S. rates to reach some extra high-end eyeballs.

The key was a survey measuring business readership in the regions every other year so that all publications could generate their CPMs, the cost to reach one thousand readers. Editorially, the Asian *Journal* filled a need by giving its readers unbiased views of local economies and politics that the local media in places like Malaysia, Singapore, and China couldn't be trusted to provide.

In Europe, it was somewhat different. There was no distrust of local media, but *The Wall Street Journal Europe* and the *Interna-*

tional Herald Tribune (then co-owned by the *Times* and *The Washington Post*, now wholly owned by the *Times*) covered Europe as an emerging region, while providing a digestible amount of U.S. news.

But *Forbes Global* proved that attracting a global advertising audience could be extremely tricky. Equally important, unlike the *WSJ/E, The Economist*, and the *IHT, Forbes Global* never achieved the status of a credible pan-European editorial player, in part because it didn't have boots on the ground to monitor important trends. Its tiny staff was New York–based, not on the scene to develop a source network. By contrast, the *WSJ/E*, with a European staff of fifty, basked in prestigious Overseas Press Club awards for coverage of Eastern Europe emerging from Soviet domination and how Europe came together to create the euro.

Forbes Global folded in July 2005, replaced by *Forbes Asia*, a more focused publication that now has more readers in Asia than its competitors combined. It's edited out of New York by Tim Ferguson, a thoughtful, meticulous man whose code name ("Fergie") is shared by his niece, she of Black Eyed Peas fame. Thanks to the exuberant efforts of Will Adamopoulos, a burly veteran of the Asian advertising wars, first with Dow Jones and now with *Forbes,* the Asian operations have a hammerlock on the region through *Forbes Asia* and foreign editions in China, India, Korea, and Indonesia. Its signature annual CEO conference, held in places like Hong Kong, Singapore, Kuala Lampur, and Sydney, draws an international audience of some four hundred executives. It's been a consistent moneymaker for the company.

But Laury Minard would not be around to see that success. He died of a heart attack in August 2001 while climbing Mount Rainier, not far from his hometown of Seattle, where his father drove a streetcar. His daughter Julia, then sixteen, was with him when it happened. Tragically, Julia was murdered four years later while on a trip to Belize.

On October 7, 1998, Harriett Miller, Jim Michaels's long-time secretary, sent out word that the New York editorial staff should assemble at 10:00 A.M. around the spiral staircase connecting the third and fourth floors of 60 Fifth, traditionally the assembly point for major announcements to the edit staff. On the staircase were Michaels and Baldwin, along with Steve Forbes. Only Forbes spoke. In just a few moments, with little fanfare, it was all over: Michaels would "move up" to a corporate job, supervising television and book development. Managing editor Baldwin would succeed him as editor. From that day on, in more ways than one, *Forbes* would never be the same.

Imagine Apple without Steve Jobs *and* Steve Wozniak. Malcolm, the visionary, the man who so embodied the brand, had been gone for nearly a decade. Now Michaels, who brought the magazine to its level of editorial excellence, the one who made it happen, was no longer a factor. For a time, *Forbes* continued to thrive on Malcolm's momentum, as long as the indicia of Malcolm remained: the ranch, the plane, the boat, all the toys that made him special and made the *Forbes*ian vision of the world almost a social movement.

"Great second or third CEOs don't take the helm to implement their own vision of the future," says marketing guru Simon Sinek in his book *Start with Why*. "They pick up the original banner and lead the company into the next generation. That's why we call it succession, not replacement." But Steve Forbes, Sinek told me, "was not in lockstep with the original cause around which the company was founded." So in Sinek's view, Steve did not succeed his father. He replaced him. Similarly, Bill Baldwin didn't really succeed Jim Michaels. He merely replaced him.

Though privately bitter about what he felt was his abrupt removal as editor, Michaels conceded to Joe Queenan over lunch one day at the Players Club that it was probably time to move on. "Nothing's being done to save the general interest magazines," he said, adding, "there's no talent (out there) and when you get it, you lose it."

Besides, he was now throwing himself into television, having come up with the idea for *Forbes on Fox,* a weekly business show consisting of *Forbes* writers and editors mud wrestling with each other for a half hour, trading barbs and snide remarks on the economy, politics, and stock picks. The host, David Asman, whose role is more referee than anchor, tries as best he can to keep order.

Much to the surprise of the show's producers, Michaels became the show's star, ranting about various topics. During a debate over the legalization of prostitution, Michaels came out in favor of it. "Unlike politicians, at least prostitutes let you know you're going to get screwed when you give them your money." During the Iraq invasion, Michaels explained why he'd just put the words "Congress" and "Saddam Hussein" in the same sentence: "Well, they're both terrorists." The only thing missing was a waving cane to emphasize his points.

For years, Michaels had been jealous of his close friend Ray Brady, who spent many years at CBS News after leaving *Forbes*. Whenever they'd walk into a restaurant—and it didn't seem to matter which one—the hostess or a waitress would invariably fawn. "Oh, Mr. Brady, so good to see you!"

"What the hell's all that about?" Michaels would growl.

"TV, Jimmy. People recognize you."

After *Forbes on Fox* had gained some traction, Michaels and Brady walked into an Italian joint one night. Michaels, Brady says, "went crazy" when recognized by the staff and had his picture taken draped by two very attractive young waitresses.

Forbes on Fox also presented the opportunity for Michaels to have a near brawl with Dennis Kneale, who was supposed to show up one day at a specified time for a run-through taping. Kneale got delayed editing a cover story and missed Michaels's deadline by maybe fifteen minutes. Since it was a run-through, Kneale, who knew quite a bit about the TV business himself, figured it didn't matter. But Michaels pounced on Kneale as soon as he walked into the midtown Fox studio. Tapping a gnarly finger on his watch case, he snarled, *"You're laaate! You're laaate!"*

Kneale, whose six-foot-two frame towered over Michaels, tried to explain, citing the cover story. Didn't matter. "Listen," Michaels said, "you report to *me* on this, and when I tell you to be somewhere, I expect you to be there on time."

"No, Jim, I report to Bill Baldwin and Tim Forbes. Don't try to push me around the way you did your staff."

"WHAAT? Well, fuck you!"

"No, FUCK YOU," Kneale said.

He's going to knee me in the balls! Kneale thought, *but I don't think he can reach them . . .*

Fox staffers intervened to prevent an escalation. From the sound-proof control room, Tim Forbes watched the silent movie play out— both in horror and amusement. After initially being separated, Michaels skittered toward Kneale again, only to be restrained once more.

None of which did anything to make Michaels less cranky that day. No doubt what he needed was a martini. But his doctors once told him to limit his intake of those to one a day.

Except when dealing with Miguel Forbes.

22

"BUT WHAT IF SOMEONE *REALLY GOOD* COMES ALONG?"

To say no when yes is in order is to cause disorder.

—Malcolm Forbes

L ET'S HAVE A FISTFIGHT," is how Joe Queenan once described to me the story sense of Jim Michaels, a man who knew what would turn heads. By contrast, Bill Baldwin was cautious and risk averse. Staffers got an early taste of that when he made his first cover decision.

One option was a sexy, gauzy photo of the young singer Fiona Apple, who was quickly gaining traction on the charts; it was also a solid business story, with lots of numbers and analysis. Option two was a cartoon of two ugly-looking babies in diapers duking it out, depicting the market brawl between two big diaper makers, Kimberly-Clark and Procter & Gamble.

Nearly everyone pushed for the Fiona Apple cover: It would be a classic *Forbes* surprise, draw eyeballs at the newsstand and help lure younger readers. But Baldwin opted for diapers, in part because it featured two big publicly held companies. To nobody's surprise, it sank on the newsstands, selling far fewer than the average thirty thousand.

For a time, Baldwin ran on the fumes of Michaels's legacy, continuing to showcase the work of the magazine's most talented writers: Neil Weinberg (Wall Street), Bob Langreth (science and medicine), Elizabeth Corcoran and Quentin Hardy (Silicon Valley), Scott Woolley (telecom), Janet Novack (taxes), Monte Burke (sports), and Nathan Vardi (investigative).

Tech got a big spin, even after the dot-com collapse. The Silicon Valley bureau produced two annual specials that distinguished the magazine and became must-reading for the Valley's "big idea" people: The E-Gang feature in late summers profiled the executives, entrepreneurs, and inventors working on the most exciting new tech concepts. The 1999 issue featured a lavishly produced, $50,000-cover spread of a dozen tech luminaries—including Meg Whitman, Mary Meeker, William Hambrecht, and Linus Torvalds—all standing on a custom-built set in a San Francisco warehouse with fancy lighting illuminating the executives from below. The Midas List, published early in the year, ranked the top venture capital firms and what they were investing in.

Under the enthusiastic word crafting of Dennis Kneale, the editor poached from the *Journal,* covers took on more of a "saga" feel, narrative dramas with actors and conflict. "Tension points," "putting the company in peril," and "dismount" (a quick finish) quickly became parts of the *Forbes* virtual stylebook. One spot-on piece was May 23, 2003, Quentin Hardy's "All Eyes on Google," which chronicled the company's rise and potential, correctly predicting it would soon go public and create renewed excitement in tech stocks. Scott Woolley's September 28, 2006, "The YouTube Revolution," with a cover image of the YouTube CEO wearing dark glasses reflecting a Google logo, appeared just a week before Google bought the firm for $1.6 billion. A YouTube executive later confided to Kneale that Woolley's cover clinched the deal and probably resulted in sweetening it by $100 million.

But over Baldwin's tenure, there were fewer of the jarring, spit-in-the-soup covers that Michaels had so championed and gave *Forbes* its edge. One investment guide seemed to be a parody of Time Inc.'s *Money* and featured a "typical" family and how it was dealing with its finances. The October 1, 2007, cover on Bank of America's chairman Kenneth Lewis, "Money for the Masses," hailed him as one of the country's most visionary bankers. But only a few months later, shareholders stripped him of his chairman's title in the wake of staggering loan losses and Lewis's overpayment for Merrill Lynch, which forced the bank to seek a second Washington bailout.

Over martinis and broiled snapper one night at Midtown's fashionable Oceana restaurant, Kneale struggled for the perfect word to characterize Baldwin's story sense. "Narrow" was an early possibility, but then, holding his forehead in his open right palm, Kneale said, "No, no, it's more subtle than that. He's almost . . . *Amish* in how he views things." But Kneale has nothing but respect for Baldwin's brain and his insight into people. Trying to woo Kneale from the *Journal*, Baldwin pounced on Kneale's ambition to become Page One editor, a position he'd already been passed over for once. "Lemme see. So if you stick around and perform well, you'll get to be Page One editor by the time you're . . . SIXTY! Is that about right?" Kneale was forty-one at the time. Kneale, who bears a striking separated-at-birth resemblance to former White House press secretary Robert Gibbs (minus several pounds), says, "He put his finger right on the bruise."

The two men often sparred in edit meetings, always with surface jocularity, but with an increasing sense of underlying mutual disdain. Kneale particularly demeaned Baldwin's habit of poo-poohing ideas on companies *Forbes* had written about years ago even though circumstances had changed dramatically: "Come on, Bill!!!" To be fair, Baldwin's reluctance to revisit any topic was because he wanted to make sure no reader thought he was reading something he'd seen before, anywhere.

Years ago when Michaels was on vacation, Baldwin, then executive editor, had to deal with two different writers who'd done stories on the same company, one bullish, the other highly skeptical. (Communication among writers was never a priority when Michaels was in charge.)

Baldwin kept sending the author of the skeptical story back for more reporting, asking new questions nearly every day. That reporting wound up being reduced to a single paragraph raising "some cautionary red flags" in the published, generally positive, story. The final insult was that Baldwin asked the writer to fact-check it—to which the normally polite staffer replied: "Fuck you." The *Journal* capped off the embarrassment by running a skeptical Page One piece with much of the same material in the *Forbes* bearish version.

Baldwin also killed a tough story on Tyco, a troubled company about to implode because of the shenanigans of CEO Dennis Kozlowski, he of the $6,000-shower-curtain fame. Within weeks, the Kozlowski scandal broke wide open, with the *Journal* carrying much of the financial detail the unpublished *Forbes* story had.

Kneale realized that he'd never replace Baldwin, a fact formally underscored in an awkward meeting one day with Tim Forbes. To a certain extent, it was a classic case of the host rejecting the skin graft. An outsider, talented though he may have been, tried to bring in too much change too fast, something that the family wasn't comfortable with. Kneale departed in October 2007 for the world of cable TV—three years at CNBC and then to the Fox Business Channel.

One reason Baldwin wasn't that sad to see Kneale depart was that while he admired his editing skills, he didn't much care for his attitude or behavior. "Dennis is just fine as long as there's always an adult around to supervise him," Baldwin would say. Kneale once lapsed into a rap routine at a *Forbes* CEO conference while introducing three prominent black entrepreneurs, who were not amused.

Kneale also had a reputation for being sort of the white man's version of the old Tim Meadows's "Ladies Man" character, Leon Phelps, on *Saturday Night Live*. From the *Journal*, Kneale brought along a large jar of blue jellybeans labeled "Viagra," a joke gift from the paper's news staff when he left. One day I suggested that while amusing, it might not be appropriate to display it so prominently. "Oh, you want it for *your* desk?" he asked.

Having been subjected to similar rumors over the course of my career, I declined. The jar disappeared, but soon an innocent event in the backseat of a taxi involving the attractive young wife of a *Forbes* staffer got Kneale mentioned, albeit anonymously, in a Page Six item in the *New York Post*. One of those sly, nasty "Which editor . . . ?" references, it was mortifying to Kneale, who knew it wasn't written for the general public but for the small group of insiders who'd instantly recognize who it was. Though Kneale didn't realize it at the time, he came very close to being fired.

Later, Forbes assigned a "watcher" to make sure Kneale behaved himself at subsequent annual sales conferences in Palm Beach, always attended by a bevy of attractive young sales women. Faced with the ultimate temptation one year, Kneale was briefly considered for an informal medal of honor for *not* joining a group of giggly young girls who'd stripped to panties and bras and jumped into the Breakers swimming pool in the wee hours—a cascading event initially inspired by a senior female executive who thought "it would just be a good idea" to jump in and swim a lap fully clothed. The aquatics also included "chicken fights," with panty-clad girls on men's shoulders.

By routine, Kneale sat to Baldwin's left at editorial meetings. One morning he was a few minutes late, so Baldwin told Larry Reibstein, editor of the Outfront section, to take his place. As if on cue, Kneale walked in. "What are you dong in my chair?" he demanded.

"You're late," Baldwin snapped. Kneale looked around, saw no empty seats, and stormed out in a huff, slamming the door behind him. Raucous laughter all around.

While Kneale was a swashbuckler who often joked he didn't like to let facts get in the way of a good yarn (some writers didn't think the "joke" was amusing), Baldwin was obsessed with accuracy and micromanagement. He once called in two members of the statistics department for what would be a long, Excedrin-inducing meeting. Baldwin wanted to review a page of graphics showing market caps for companies in different industries. The graphics were colored circles, sized proportionately to reflect the market value of each company. But Baldwin didn't think they looked right. So he took out a metric ruler and measured each of the circles, asking the eye-rolling staffers to resize some by minute amounts until he was satisfied.

Baldwin's brilliance sometimes dazzled. Kneale tells the story of how Baldwin once took issue with a piece on a software program that scheduled things like lawn-mowing crews. It said ten crews with ten jobs had a possible combination of one hundred different assignment setups. That number had been fact-checked with a Ph.D. mathematician at Princeton. Baldwin looked at it and instantly said the right answer wasn't one hundred—it was a one followed by a hundred zeros, a *googol*. He told the fact-checker to go back to the Princeton whiz and challenge him. Chagrined, the mathematician conceded that Baldwin was right.

Baldwin's disdain of jargon and clichés was as intense as Michaels's, but Baldwin actually *codified* it by compiling a long list of "banned" words, which were *never* to appear in the magazine. Just some of them: aggressive, bandwagon, jump-start, low-hanging fruit, mission-critical, poster child, ramp up, results-oriented, role model, shell-shocked, warp speed, wave of the future. By contrast, Michaels handled the same topic in a simple, one-page note to the staff on September 7, 1994, that became known as the "Orwell Memo."

Ladies & Gentlemen:

George Orwell was a man of tremendous intellectual honesty, whose hard, clear prose reflected his character. I commend to your attention a set of six rules he laid down for clear writing that avoids ambiguity and says what it means. Here are the rules:

1. Never use a metaphor, simile, or other figure of speech which you are used to seeing in print.
2. Never use a long word where a short one will do.
3. If it is possible to cut a word out, always cut it out.
4. Never use the passive where you can use the active.
5. Never use a foreign phrase, a scientific word, or a jargon word if you can think of an everyday English equivalent.
6. Break any of these rules sooner than say anything outright barbarous.

Please display these rules in a prominent place hard by your machines. Absorb them. Before handing copy to an editor, vet your manuscript for violations and eliminate them. Doing so will not only make life easier for the editors, it will make you a better writer and a more accurate journalist.

For those who want more than these simple rules, read the essay that contains them. It is entitled "Politics and the English Language" and can be found in an in-print paperback, "The Orwell Reader," published by Harcourt Brace. The essay has a lot to say about concreteness—something lacking in much of the copy that reaches my desk—and about cliches—which too often replace specificity in the copy I see.

I admired Baldwin tremendously for the way he handled problematic stories. He made no secret of the fact he disapproved of the harsh way Michaels treated writers. Instead of firing off a nasty note the whole staff could read, Baldwin would wander into a writer's office and say, "I really like your piece, but there are three things that would make it even better." The collective Zoloft and Zantac bill for the edit staff almost certainly plummeted to a postwar low. Using a sports analogy, it was like how former New York Knicks coach Red Holzman used to handle discipline. Phil Jackson, who played for Holzman and until recently coached the Los Angeles Lakers, recalled for *The New York Times* that when Holzman needed to upbraid a player, he preferred to do so in the privacy of his office—the bathroom adjoining the locker room—rather than in front of the team. "All those things that honor the game," Jackson said, "which is to build people up, not tear them down."

But Baldwin was uncomfortable dealing with personnel issues of any sort. Confrontation was clearly stress-inducing for him. During one of the several rounds of layoffs following the dot-com collapse, Baldwin asked the edit department's business manager to prepare paperwork for the removal of twelve of the thirteen people he'd picked to thin out. On the Day of the Ax, only then did Baldwin reveal the name of the mystery thirteenth person: the business manager. Irate at Baldwin's insensitivity, she departed with a handful of Elite limo vouchers and used them for Midtown shopping sprees and other personal trips.

One day Larry Reibstein, the editor who dared to sit in Kneale's chair, came in to make a reasoned argument as to why he should be an assistant managing editor. Baldwin, who was viscerally opposed to title inflation of any sort, listened carefully, then replied, "But what if someone *really good* comes along?" So motivated to work harder and rendered momentarily speechless, Reibstein got up and walked out. (Update: He's now an executive editor.)

Similarly, Baldwin once promised me the executive editor's title after he'd promoted Kneale to managing editor. "But I can't do it right away," he said. "I need to wait a month."

"Why?"

"I'm trying to hire Alison Leigh Cowan from the *Times,* and that's the title I may have to give to her, so you may have to share it."

"I could live with that."

A month later, I revisited the issue with Baldwin. "I can't do it," Baldwin explained. "Cowan won't come here unless she's the *only* executive editor."

"So let me get this straight. I've been here over ten years, yet someone at the *Times* is dictating what my title should be just because she *says* she wants to come here?"

"That's the way it works," Baldwin said.

Cowan wound up staying at the *Times,* but the executive editor title went unfilled. I was, however, later in that summer of 2006 promoted to deputy managing editor, and managing editor in the fall of 2008. Then in late March 2009, I presented Baldwin with a cost-cutting plan I'd been working on—budget cuts of $600,000 in salaries and benefits, plus some other numbers he'd asked me to get, in preparation for another round of layoffs everyone knew was coming the following week. Baldwin looked at it and said it was a "good list," but that it was "just a fraction" of what he had to cut next Tuesday.

Only half-joking, I asked, "So am *I* going to have a job after next Tuesday?"

Baldwin thought for a few moments, face frozen in death-mask stare. Finally he said, "Do you want an honest answer, or do you just want to wait until next week?"

"Well, I guess that's my answer then," I said. Baldwin then began the boilerplate HR speech, a script I'd read to others before, about how tough times were and how he had to eliminate high-paid jobs in order to retain the low-cost ones that actually produced the content. I told him he didn't have to finish it.

Then he added, "You can't tell your wife," who also worked at *Forbes*.

"Why???"

"She'll just tell Bob Mansfield [her boss in the art department] and it'll be all over the building."

"And your problem with that would be . . ."

"If word gets out that you're being let go, *nobody* will feel safe."

"That sounds about right," I replied, getting up and heading toward the door without shaking his hand. At the last minute, I turned and added, "It's been a privilege to work here," then walked out. I did what Baldwin asked of me. Sort of. Instead of calling my wife, who was in Pennsylvania visiting her family, I went right into Mansfield's office, pointed at the clock (it was 4:15 P.M.) and said, "Gotham. Martinis. Right now." I told my wife that evening. My departure was gussied up as a resignation, and I wound up staying around another month. But a building full of reporters quickly found out the real story. I hold no ill will towards Bill. He's a good and decent person, with a wonderful wife and two great kids. He just can't help acting the way he does.

When it came to budgets and spending, Baldwin was a B.C. clone, the polar opposite of Kneale and me. Dennis and I approved each other's expenses and at one point appeared to be in a contest to see who could win the "Expense Account of the Month" traveling trophy. Though I spent a lot traveling overseas and helped keep the Gotham Bar and Grill in business with frequent drinks and business meals, I threw in the towel the day Dennis turned in a *$6,000* dinner chit from Esther Dyson's now-defunct PC Forum in Scottsdale, Arizona. Granted, it was for twenty-five people, but it was still a stunning amount, one I never came close to matching. It reminded me of the George Clooney line from the movie *The Peacemaker* in which Clooney's character, an army colonel, is being asked during a Senate hearing about a $5,200 tab for four people from a Moscow disco called Nightcrawler: "Well, we had dinner, and I bought a couple of rounds . . ."

While staying at the Beverly Hilton, the Georgian, or the Beverly Hills Hotel, Kneale would take taxis around Los Angeles rather than renting a car. Baldwin almost never traveled to bureaus or took editors or writers out to lunch for pulse checks. While Michaels had a car and driver to take him to his apartment (about ten blocks away) or a hundred miles north to his home in Rhinebeck, New York, Baldwin took the subway to and from the Upper West Side, wearing full Unabomber gear: ski jacket, backpack, and knit cap. The joke was he'd need a map to find the Gotham, less than a block away on East Twelfth Street. Baldwin once even told me (in *mid-May*) to *cancel* the annual editorial Christmas party after being told of a dip in advertising pages. As they always do, ad pages turned up in the fall, and the staff party went ahead. But any prolonged ad drought would always prompt the question: "Do we have too many writers?" It was question dear to the hearts of the finance people, who would always respond to a request for a new hire by saying the number of edit staffers hadn't dropped as much as the number of pages in the magazine. Which, of course, was true.

Though Baldwin would make special appeals to the bean counters if a valued staffer was being wooed by a competitor, basic *Forbes* salaries lagged behind the competitive market. Entry-level reporting jobs at *Forbes* in 2007 began at $42,000. That was below the $50,000 the *Journal* offered at the time for a lifestyle writer with two to three years' experience, the $65,000 to $100,000 for experienced beat reporters, $125,000 for "divas," and $150,000 for "experienced divas."

In 2007, the average salary for *Forbes* senior editors, the title given to the most experienced and talented writers, was $123,000. *Bloomberg News* trumped *Forbes* by snatching away a young writer from the *San Francisco Chronicle* by doubling her salary to $120,000. Condé Nast's ill-fated *Portfolio* magazine later did the same, raiding Forbes.com for two of its most talented lifestyle writers. By the fall 2007, the number of senior editors on staff had dropped to sixteen from twenty-six in 2000. Editors began to complain they weren't getting enough good ideas.

Summing it up, Gretchen Morgenson told *The Nation* that "Jim Michaels had a knack for taking a small story and making it big. Bill Baldwin has a knack for making a big story small." To which Baldwin replied, "*Forbes* has always been brusque in judgment and tough on people, and if you dish it out, you have to learn to take it."

23

THE DEATH STAR

*F*ORBES'S SENIOR TECHNOLOGY EDITOR David Churbuck, who'd won several national awards for his reporting, had become increasingly intrigued about the Internet—the huge network of networks that connects millions of computers worldwide. He'd written several pieces about it during the early nineties, and his internal tech seismograph sensed a tremor the day managing editor Laury Minard passed along a John Markoff clip from the *Times*. Markoff's piece was about the potential of the World Wide Web—the powerful information-sharing model built on top of the Internet that allows for the search and exchange of information.

Churbuck, a tall, ruggedly handsome Yale graduate who'd rowed at New Haven, started doing some research, and drove one day from his home on the Cape into Cambridge to look at a Web demonstration in the offices of Mitch Kapor, founder of Lotus and the Electronic Frontier Foundation.

Having seen various iterations of videotext such as Time Inc.'s ill-fated Teletext experiment go down in flames, Churbuck immediately saw publishing potential in the Web. Excited, he wrote a memo to Steve Forbes urging the company to open its own Web site.

But Forbes never got back to him.

So Churbuck registered the Forbes.com domain name himself, learned HTML coding and built a beta model of Forbes.com. He put it on an Iomega Zip drive and brought it down to New York.

Once more, yawns from the brothers.

Why would we want to do something like that?

Sounds expensive.

It was a reaction that would characterize many of the brothers' business decisions. In an age where events develop super-fast, change at *Forbes* came glacially.

But Churbuck kept arguing. Finally, in 1995, after managing *Forbes*'s short-lived presence on CompuServe, he got the green light to go ahead with a pilot Web project. Working with a staff of two in a tiny corner of the magazine's library on 60 Fifth's mezzanine, Churbuck began making the magazine's various lists more interactive and searchable. Now warming to the idea, Tim Forbes asked Churbuck and Greg Zorthian, the man in charge of new ventures, to come up with a business plan. The projections looked plausible. With magazine sales people flogging what Churbuck called "big, blunt weekly sponsorships," the new low-cost enterprise figured to be cash-flow positive quickly.

Forbes Digital Tool rolled out in May 1995 with a big party on the *Highlander.* Because Tim Forbes wanted it to be a separate operation, the newly assembled staff of nine moved to four thousand square feet of rented space just up Fifth Avenue at Nineteenth Street. There weren't even cubicles. It was basically just an open bullpen, with used desks, terminals, phones, and no privacy. The reporters covered everything from mutual funds to emerging Web business models like eBay, doing spot news items in the morning, then feature reporting in the afternoon.

Churbuck's editorial decisions were driven by the assumption that the specter of Jim Michaels was always lurking: carefully researched stories with a contrarian spin and some attitude. As at *Forbes, Forbes Digital Tool* writers got grief from irritated readers, which Churbuck viewed as positive since it meant people were actually *looking* at the site. Reporter Vicki Contavespi got regular "hate mail" complaints over her contention that the GSM standard for cell phones would eventually dominate the U.S. market because it had more potential for global use than the rival CDMA technology. (Contavespi turned out to be correct.)

But staff turnover was high, at about 33 percent. So much of Churbuck's job consisted of trying to convince people not to leave. The site's infrastructure was also shaky, because of a classic *Forbes*ian shortcoming: Scrooge-like underinvestment in the technology needed to keep the Web site humming. Not putting enough into servers and ad insertion licenses, for example, caused the site to completely vanish for three days in September 1999 after AOL featured the annual list of the richest four hundred Americans on its homepage and directed so much traffic to the site that it crashed.

A big spike in traffic and media buzz for Forbes.com, as it was now known, came when editor Kambiz Foroohar gave his new computer crime reporter Adam Penenberg a story to check out from *The New Republic*, a piece written by a twenty-five-year-old staffer named Stephen Glass. Penenberg had done some investigative reporting as a freelancer for *New York* magazine, and liked to look for dirt. Titled "Hack Heaven," the vivid, colorful *New Republic* piece told of a fifteen-year-old hacker who broke into the computer network of something called Junkt Micronics, which then allegedly hired him as a security consultant. Foroohar figured the story might provide Penenberg with some good sources and ideas.

But when Penenberg started calling around, he couldn't find *any* evidence that either the hacker or Junkt Micronics existed. The story turned out to be a total fabrication. A Junkt Micronics "executive" Glass urged his editor to call to verify information turned out to be Glass's brother, who was a student at Stanford, in the same Silicon Valley area code, 650, as the fake company. Forbes.com broke the scandal. Glass was fired. All the major players, including Penenberg, wound up being portrayed in the 2003 Lions Gate film *Shattered Glass*.

Foroohar leveraged the big win by taking a job at TheStreet.com and tried to bring Penenberg with him. But *Forbes* didn't want to lose its hot new star, and offered him a senior editor's title at the magazine with a substantial pay boost—fostering envy and scorn from his coworkers. But it didn't work out. Facing a demand from a law enforcement official to divulge a source on another story, Penenberg dismissed *Forbes*'s request to have it handled by Tennyson Schad, the magazine's highly acclaimed libel lawyer, who ran his own first amendment shop. Penenberg insisted on hiring his own counsel. Dennis Kneale got involved. Tempers flared. When Penenberg, a man not to shrink from drama and attention, leaked news of the dispute to a media Web site, Baldwin pulled the offer.

Caught up in the dot-com frenzy, in 2000 Tim Forbes wanted to take the digital unit public, which would potentially enrich the family even more and enhance employees' retirements with "share appreciation rights." To that end, he brought in some adult supervision in the form of Jeffrey Killeen, the former CEO of Barnes and Noble's online operation. But the timing was awful. *Forbes* had planned to file with the Securities and Exchange Commission in April 2000, the month NASDAQ began to unwind. The offering was ditched.

But by that time Churbuck was having start-up fatigue, finding it harder and harder to keep the wind in his sails each day. Beyond that, he was troubled by the business side's increasing push for traffic. Like many Web enterprises, Forbes.com was getting addicted to the crack cocaine of page views and impressions—quantity above everything else. "I didn't think there would be an emphasis on quality," he says. "The obsession was pretty clear."

Particularly disheartening to Churbuck was an experiment they tried, totally unrelated to journalistic merit, to see whether some software hijinks in a story's metadata could build traffic artificially. Metadata is information hidden on a Web page that contains basic information about the story (title, subject, etc.). It's the digital equivalent of an old library catalog card. Also embedded in the metadata can be certain tags, key words, or other hooks to help rank a story high in search engine results. Sometimes more important than a story's content is its potential for "search engine optimization"

(SEO), so that mass market sites like AOL, Yahoo!, and MSN pick up a story and enhance the opportunity for page views.

Churbuck's techies embedded the word "tit" in the metadata of a random and otherwise unremarkable technology piece. Search engines noted the word and ranked the story high in their results for searchers seeking pornography. The story quickly became the most popular on the Forbes.com site. Skin gets traffic—as when *New York* magazine ran nude photos of Lindsay Lohan and got 40 million page views on its Web site compared to 2 to 3 million normally. Even more troubling to Churbuck was the suggestion that Forbes.com break stories into multiple "jumps" to build page views and start using pop-up advertising.

Then there was the CueCat, an odd gizmo dreamed up by something called Digital Convergence, a tech outfit that came up with a scanning device meant to link print stories directly to the Web. At a time when there was very little broadband, the big issue was how slow the Internet was and how tedious it was to dig deep into a Web site. With the CueCat, which was supposed to look like a cat but more resembled a rat, the reader of a newspaper or magazine could scan a bar code on a print page and be directly connected through his computer to a Web site of an advertiser or a story subject. "People already had a mouse with their computers. Now they could have a cat, too," says Eric Rayman, an attorney and then executive vice president of Digital Convergence.

Editors now had to trim stories enough so that the bar code could fit at the end of each piece. It quickly became a nuisance with no apparent payback: the ad staff tried to sell against it, but the results were incremental at best. At the podium of the annual sales meeting, Chris Buckley got up and opened his shirt to reveal a CueCat T-shirt, bringing hoots and jeers from the audience. Made by RadioShack, the Cue-Cats were sent out to every *Forbes* subscriber, resulting in the predictable, "I didn't order this, how much are you charging me?" letters, technical glitches, and underwhelming usage by readers. The problem was solved in less than a year when Digital Convergence went out of business, unable to roll out a large enough base of customers.

The results of Churbuck's little experiment in porn were consistent with an evolving business strategy to develop "portal driven" content that would appeal to AOL, Yahoo!, and other high-traffic sites. So in a sense, though Forbes.com was headed for more growth, it wasn't necessarily organic growth. A sensational un-*Forbes*ian story (like a slide show of famous Victoria's Secret models) might be widely viewed on other sites, but would that reader then go back to Forbes.com in the future to read about mutual funds or rich people? Not necessarily.

So after thirteen years at *Forbes,* Churbuck left for McKinsey that summer and never looked back. A fancier of bow ties, he was amused and pleased to see many of his staffers wearing them the night of his farewell party at a trendy Midtown cigar bar.

During the dot-com bust when every other publisher was cutting back Web operations, Tim Forbes strongly supported his favorite new toy and kept the money flowing. As CEO, he hired Jim Spanfeller from Ziff Davis. Spanfeller, a sort of publisher's publisher whose neatly coiffed cap of salt-and-pepper hair seemed incapable of being disturbed even in a tornado, had mostly been a print executive.

But he also had good instincts for online publishing, and came with a very logical strategy for Forbes.com: As others deployed chainsaws, Forbes.com would aggressively build up its market share to a dominant position so when things did turn around, the site would be an established major player. By 2010, when Spanfeller left to form his own media company, he claimed Forbes.com monthly traffic was 20 million. Based on competitive September traffic figures reported by comScore, a major Web traffic measuring service, that number would have put Forbes.com behind Nytimes.com (33.2 million) and The Huffington Post (22.5 million) but well ahead of the Web sites for *The Washington Post* (16.1 million) and the *Journal* (12.2 million).

Just one problem: For that same month, comScore reported traffic for Forbes.com as 9.6 million. Adding in traffic from Forbesautos .com, a "companion" site, the total was 11.5 million. But by those "official" numbers, Forbes.com was still behind the *Journal,* whose Web site was hidden behind a pay wall. Skeptics both within *Forbes* and at competing media companies had long believed Spanfeller was fudging the numbers, a subject covered with great glee by the *Times* and various blogs.

Spanfeller argued that the "official" numbers badly undercounted visitors to the site who were doing so from their offices. ComScore and Nielsen/Net Data, the other major traffic-measuring firm, both rely on "panels" of millions of online users who have monitoring software installed in their computers. Adjusting the resulting data to make sure all demographic groups are represented, both firms then put the numbers in their respective Cuisinarts and project national monthly traffic levels for major Web sites.

But most corporations and government agencies don't allow monitoring software to be installed in their computers. So Spanfeller "adjusted" his numbers for that, arbitrarily calculating the supposed business-hour traffic, among other things, perhaps including an estimate of how many times each day *Forbes* employees passed the big-screen Forbes.com monitors in the lobby or the newsroom.

Along the way to 9.6 million (or whatever it is), Forbes.com got a lot of attention in August 2006, but it wasn't the kind the family really needed. Michael Noer, one of the Web site's brightest editors, known for his imaginative ideas for lists and multistory "packages," thought it would be fun to do a tongue-in-cheek piece about the pitfalls of men marrying high-powered career women. He based the piece in part on studies done by the research journals *Social Forces*, the *Journal of Marriage and Family*, the *American Journal of Sociology*, and the Institute for Social Research.

Noer concluded the more successful a wife is in her career, the more likely she is to grow unhappy with hubby, have an affair, and run off with a coworker, for the husband to fall ill, and for the house to wind up being dirty, among other things. Some of the obvious red flags signaling that the piece was supposed to be funny were removed in the editing, so the story came out looking much more like a serious piece of social science.

Headlined "Don't Marry Career Women," the story began: "Guys: a word of advice. Marry pretty women or ugly ones. Short ones or tall ones. Blondes or brunettes. Just, whatever you do, don't marry a woman with a career." Instant outrage, from readers and *Forbes* staffers. If people got beyond that first paragraph, it only got worse. Noer might just as well have written that Betty Friedan, Gloria Steinem, and even Susan B. Anthony were nothing but foaming-at-the-mouth bra-burning crypto-lesbian feminist nut jobs who didn't shave their armpits.

Though the article was on Forbes.com, the magazine got most of the hate mail (so much for product separation). The article was briefly pulled down but soon reappeared with a rebuttal by Elizabeth Corcoran, who worked in the *Forbes* Silicon Valley office and is married to George Anders, a former news editor at the *Journal* and author of several nonfiction business books. Theirs was a good marriage, Corcoran reported, despite the fact she earned a good salary and had a distinguished journalistic career at *Forbes* and, before that, at *The Washington Post*. In her rebuttal, titled "Don't Marry a Lazy Man," Corcoran called Noer's piece "downright frightening."

In general, Noer was unfairly vilified as a churlish, knuckle-dragging misogynist living in another century who clearly now wouldn't get laid for decades. *Forbes* devoted the biweekly Readers Say column to an entire page of angry letters. Editors of the column briefly considered politically incorrect headlines for each letter but decided that wouldn't be particularly useful.

Perhaps the best response to the flap came in an e-mail from none other than Gloria Steinem (who says women don't look at Forbes.com?):

> I'm deeply grateful to *Forbes* magazine for saving many women the trouble of dealing with men who can't tolerate equal partnerships, take care of their own health, clean up after themselves or have the sexual confidence to survive, other than a double standard of sexual behavior. Since a disproportionate number of such unconfident and boring guys apparently read *Forbes*, the magazine has performed a real service.

24

"WORLD WAR I WAS
A ROUGH ONE"

A T FORBES, WE DON'T preach nepotism, we practice it," Malcolm Forbes used to say. This was never truer than in the case of Miguel, the adopted son of Bob Forbes and head of the family's television and licensing ventures, and the one family member I interacted with the most. A perfectly pleasant and charming young man, Miguel sometimes wears the puzzled expression that suggests he'd have trouble understanding the complex plotlines of a Three Stooges movie and often perplexes staffers with conversation openers like, "How much do you have to be worth to make the billionaires list?"

Bob Forbes adopted Miguel not long after Malcolm decreed in his will that Miguel would be considered to be his descendant by birth, giving Miguel the same inheritance rights for the voting shares of any grandchild. Which gives pause to those on staff who live in fear of some horrific, cataclysmic event that would tragically vaporize the brothers and all other heirs to the family fortune, leaving Miguel as the sole owner and boss.

Extensive due diligence doesn't appear to be his strong suit. One day Miguel introduced me to two tough-looking representatives from *XXL,* a Ukraine "lifestyle" magazine whose racy photos made *Playboy* look like *House and Garden.* They said *XXL* wanted to be the Kiev-based licensee for *Forbes.* I said such a relationship probably wouldn't be appropriate, since the publisher had no experience in business journalism. The boys left, only to reappear a few months later.

This time the partner would not be the lifestyle magazine. Rather, the *XXL* owner had some kind of relationship with a chain of restaurants across Ukraine (all sorts: Mexican, Chinese, French, et cetera). The point was that initial circulation of a *Forbes Ukraine* would come from the database of regular dining customers. Perhaps not. (A new *Forbes Ukraine,* with a partner unrelated to racy photos or restaurants, is scheduled to debut in 2011.)

Forbes got involved in foreign editions long before Miguel came on the scene, including a short-lived Arabic edition in the 1970s and a Japanese version that started up in 1991 but was discontinued in 2009. In 1989, Malcolm wanted to enter the European market with a German-language magazine. What better way to get entrée to Europe than to do it through ties to royalty?

With the help of money manager Alexander Papamarkou, a skilled pamperer who advised many European royals, Malcolm got to know King Juan Carlos and Queen Sofía of Spain. At a black-tie dinner in Madrid one night, Forbes met with Dr. Hubert Burda, the head of the family-owned Burda Media group, one of Germany's most powerful publishers. Burda knew that Forbes was close to signing a deal with Ringier AG, a Zurich-based media firm that published several high-quality German-language magazines in Switzerland. Those involved say Burda told Forbes that Ringier was a fine company and that circulation would be great in Switzerland, but not in Germany. Forbes, who went by his gut rather than relying on staff-produced due diligence reports, liked Dr. Burda and what he had to say. So they sat down and did a napkin deal.

But it did not go well. The original editor was Mathias Nolte, a man with no business journalism background who'd previously edited the German-language *Penthouse.* Installed in Munich as a "quality control" man (read: spy) was Richard Morais, a *Forbes* staffer who grew up in Switzerland and spoke several languages, including German. What he began to see was not reassuring. There was no fact-checking and articles began to appear with an anti-American bent. Morais kept track of the errors and judgment lapses, reporting everything to New York. The feedback from German bankers, businessmen, and media was awful.

Nolte, who was replaced within the first year, ironically then landed a job at Ringier, where he edited the Swiss tabloid *Sonntags-Blick*. But he lasted only six months after accusing Thomas Borer, the Swiss ambassador in Berlin, of having an illicit affair. That cost Ringier over 1 million Swiss francs to settle.

The *Forbes* name was being tarnished in one of the most important markets in Europe. After several more changes of editors failed to rectify the situation, Steve Forbes pulled the license in 1995, saying that Burda had failed to maintain *Forbes* quality. Back in New York, Fritz Blumenberg, Burda's point man in the U.S. during the years that *Forbes von Burda* was published, was sentenced to two and a half years in prison in 2003 for embezzling $2 million from Burda. He used fake invoices from purported outside vendors, using the loot to buy clothing, antiques, jewelry, and a $20,000 vacation at the Canyon Ranch spa in Arizona, prosecutors argued.

Quality control is a very tricky matter with licensees—as opposed to joint ventures where two companies are both deeply involved in the product. For the *Forbes* foreign editions, the terms are fairly straightforward: *Forbes* gives the licensee the right to use the name and any copy from the domestic magazine, in return for an upfront fee, and an annual license fee, with a minimum amount, usually about $150,000, plus additional monies based on a percentage of magazine revenues and any other income streams, such as conferences. The licensees are encouraged to provide a hefty percentage of the content locally. But it's supposed to be a strictly hands-off deal, no direct editorial involvement, no vetting or editing of foreign-generated copy.

Forbes just sits back and cashes the checks. Too much involvement could lead a third party (i.e., a judge) to conclude the arrangement was a constructive joint venture and open *Forbes* U.S. to damages, if a libel suit against the licensee were ever filed. *Forbes* worked around the liability issue at first by having people on staff that spoke the language of the foreign edition review the published issue each month and report any nonsense.

But since there was no prepublication review, that left the door open for mischief. Like the sex column complete with a *Kama Sutra*–like illustration that suddenly appeared in *Forbes Korea*. Susan Kitchens, a New York–based writer who'd spent part of her childhood in Korea when her parents were there as medical missionaries, spotted the column as she was thumbing through the issue. Was *Forbes Korea* going *Penthouse*?

E-mails to the *Forbes Korea* edit staff were ignored, so it took a phone call from Will Adamopoulos, the head of *Forbes*'s Asian operations, to convince Joong Ang Ilbo, the Korean licensee, to drop the column. But not before a *second* one had appeared (with another illustration) as well as a "travel" article, replete with graphic photographs, about where Korean transvestites could go for vacation (Spain seemed to be the number-one choice). Local custom and practice aside, the Forbeses would prefer not to be associated with smut.

Without knowing for sure, my impression was that some of the deals appeared to have been agreed to quite hastily, possibly late at night over alcoholic beverages—with the *Forbes* legal department being told the next day to draw up a contract simply because the other party said it would pay the minimum fee each year.

The first partner for *Forbes Israel,* something called SBC, now defunct, turned out to be run by a crook. Meir David spent time in the slammer for fraud. The new licensee, Mirkaei Tikshoret Ltd., publishes the highly regarded *Jerusalem Post. Forbes Arabia* was initially run by DIT, a conglomerate owned by a Saudi government minister, who evidently thought it would be politically useful to be known as the publisher of a Middle Eastern *Forbes.* The publication died after only a few years from malnutrition. The licensee refused to commit significant money to marketing, distribution, or

editorial, which struggled to cover eighteen countries with four employees in Dubai and some stringers, some of whom specialized in
plagiarism and creative writing.

So bad was the raw copy that I assigned Zina Moukheiber, a San
Francisco–based biotech writer fluent in Arabic, to vet the ideas and
do lots of hand-holding, serving in effect as *Forbes Arabia*'s stealth
executive editor—a cozy relationship we went to great lengths to
keep from the in-house lawyers, who continued to fret about creep-
ing joint-venturism. But absent Moukheiber's involvement, the family could have been badly embarrassed.

Some of the business due diligence issues could have been avoided
if Miguel Forbes had simply allowed his licensing head, Jonathan
Latimer, to travel. Unlike Hearst, which has a whole department to
manage its overseas licensees and encourages face-to-face meetings,
particularly when assessing possible new deals, Latimer was forced
to manage the licensees by phone and e-mail. (Latimer's successor,
Tom Wolf, a Hearst veteran, is now allowed to travel, and as a result
of his extensive contacts, has opened several new editions.)

Out of the blue one year came a rogue publication, *Forbes Ar-
menia,* neither sanctioned nor even proposed to *Forbes.* It simply
appeared, complete with a planned launch party and a cover featuring photos of supposedly rich Armenians. Salivating over what they
knew would be a slam dunk, the *Forbes* legal department quickly
moved to put the bad guys out of business. For a moment they even
considered showing up at the launch party. (*Hi!*) Meanwhile, one
New York editor helpfully suggested, "Why don't we just let *Forbes
Turkey* handle it?"

Forbes Turkey had its own dramas. Editorially one of the brightest stars in the *Forbes* galaxy, its first licensee, Merkez, was owned
by Turgay Ciner, an unpredictable character who fired the *entire* marketing department the morning after the magazine's launch party in
Istanbul because he didn't like the venue or the food.

Apart from some bizarre entertainment, which at one point featured a frenzied, wild-eyed man endlessly beating a drum to death,
everyone from *Forbes* thought the Turkish launch was just dandy,

including Miguel, who was obviously impressed by the elegance of the former Ottoman Imperial Palace in which the festivities were held.

The next day, caught in the nightmare of Istanbul traffic, Miguel asked me about some Turkish history. "Uh, so how long did this Ottoman Empire last anyway?"

"Well, the Turks backed the wrong guys in World War I, and the republic was formed around 1923."

Miguel looked pensive. "World War I," he mused, looking out the window of the black Mercedes sedan. "That was a rough one, wasn't it?"

Yeah, that mustard gas was nasty stuff.

Ciner then got into tax trouble with the government, which took over the magazine briefly then held an auction, open to other publishers. A new outfit, Calik Holding A.S., is now in charge.

Officials of the first Chinese licensee, Morningside, consistently misled *Forbes* executives about its intentions to start a Web site, something not allowed under the contract. When confronted with advertising for something called Forbeschina.com and an edit staff realignment to create a team of Web editors, business-side officials insisted it was simply a device to "market" the magazine. A replacement, Fosun Group, is now publishing *Forbes China*.

Mirroring the country itself, Russia has brought triumph, tragedy, and frustration to *Forbes*. Working late into the night of July 9, 2004, at the Moscow offices of *Forbes Russia*, Paul Klebnikov, the newly installed editor of *Forbes*'s latest foreign-language edition, had been on the phone speaking with his wife, sister, and his brother Peter.

All seemed to be well. He sounded happy and in good spirits, but in retrospect, Peter thought it was strange that Paul had called him for only the second time since he'd moved to Moscow from New York five months before. "I've heard stories of people [who] suddenly call their loved ones before they die," he told CBS News. "Maybe this was such a case."

Following a routine he practiced practically every night, Klebnikov, the last to leave the *Forbes* office, took the elevator down from the sixth floor, walked out the front door, crossed the parking lot, and headed to the subway, about half a mile away.

It was shortly after 10:00 P.M. Though Klebnikov knew how dangerous it could be to work as an investigative journalist in Moscow, he had refused an offer from *Forbes*'s licensee in Russia, the German publisher Axel Springer, to have a bodyguard or any other kind of security. Stubborn, somewhat arrogant and feeling invulnerable, Klebnikov, a champion of the "new" Russia, simply believed nothing could possibly happen to him.

About two blocks from the office, a black car with darkened windows suddenly cut Klebnikov off. A gunman using a nine-millimeter Russian Makarov pistol leaned out the window and pumped out nine shots, four of which hit their target. The car then sped off, leaving Klebnikov mortally wounded but still alive. He managed to give a passerby the phone number for the Axel Springer offices. The stranger reached Alexander Gordeyev, an editor of the Russian edition of *Newsweek*—which shared office space with *Forbes*—who came running to Klebnikov's side. Asked why this might have happened, Klebnikov kept saying, "I don't know, I don't know," but was able to give a good description of the gunman.

A passing ambulance called in the shooting. Another ambulance showed up fifteen minutes later but carried no oxygen. Moscow's Hospital Number 20 was only a short distance away, but by the time the ambulance arrived, only a few grains of sand remained in the hourglass. Klebnikov died in a stalled hospital elevator.

Word of the murder quickly reached *Forbes*'s New York office. But oddly, there was no immediate announcement or internal bulletin to the staff. Most of the senior editors found out by word of mouth. Details of exactly what happened were hard to come by, and most employees had to wait for coverage in the *Times* and the *Journal*, both of which had Moscow bureaus and immediately jumped on the story. Klebnikov's wife, Musa, the daughter of John Train, the prominent investment adviser and author, was at her mother's villa in Italy with their three children. *Forbes Russia* at first had trouble reaching her.

The following Monday, Baldwin sent out a strange memo announcing the tragedy to the staff, but taking pains, no doubt at the insistence of lawyers concerned about liability, to distance *Forbes* from Klebnikov and *Forbes Russia*. Among other things, the memo noted Klebnikov was no longer employed by *Forbes* (he was being paid by the licensee) and that *Forbes Russia* wasn't published by *Forbes*. Though it made perfect sense from a corporate standpoint—tragic as it was, it involved the death of a former employee—it came across as being cold and insensitive.

The Klebnikov family was upset that *Forbes* was trying to "marginalize" Klebnikov's death and, in their opinion, was doing very little in the way of support. At the same time, *Forbes* officials were complaining about how demanding the Klebnikov family was. *Forbes* argued it was being extremely generous, including paying for the airfare of various family members to fly to Moscow from around Europe to attend the Moscow funeral.

All but one. The family had been lobbying for *Forbes* to pay for a first-class ticket for one European relative who wanted to attend the service. Why first class? The relative was apparently overweight and needed the extra room. In the midst of sometimes testy negotiations over such details, one senior *Forbes* executive finally lost it and said to a colleague: "Drop the fat one!" from the free ticket list.

The murder has never been solved. Two Chechens also suspected in the murder of a Chechen official two weeks earlier were arrested and tried, but were later acquitted of both murders. The best guess is that the hit was a result of any number of Klebnikov's investigative efforts. The second issue of *Forbes Russia* contained a list of Russia's hundred richest people, some of whom were not pleased to be on it. Though it was not the first time a Russian-language publication had ranked wealthy people, the *Forbes* brand drew unprecedented attention and coverage of the rankings.

A 2000 book, *Godfather of the Kremlin: The Life and Times of Boris Berezovsky*, certainly did nothing to endear Klebnikov to the scary Russian tycoon, who told a Russian news agency that Klebnikov was a victim of his own "lack of accuracy. Unfortunately his way of reporting the facts was very arbitrary. He invented much," Berezovsky said, adding: "It seems that he seriously upset someone." Nor did his 2003 *Conversation with a Barbarian: Interviews with a Chechen Field Commander on Banditry and Islam* make him popular with the Chechen mafia.

But the murder did not deter *Forbes Russia* from doing tough stories. Klebnikov's successor, his brilliant young deputy Maxim Kashulinsky, stepped right up and continued to fill the mold that Klebnikov had set: Don't shrink from doing controversial stories. Don't be intimidated. Just practice good *Forbes* journalism: Be contrarian, have some attitude, get your facts right.

The one difference was that at the insistence of Axel Springer, both Kashulinsky and *Forbes Russia*'s publisher now had twenty-four-hour bodyguards. Security at the building was tightened. IDs were now required at two different checkpoints in the lobby, where a metal detector was installed. A Frigidaire-sized guard one didn't want to look at the wrong way was now conspicuously in place in the sixth-floor vestibule outside the *Forbes* offices, to make a last identity check before buzzing a visitor in through a locked door.

When entering or leaving the building, Kashulinsky's driver would bring the car under a protected carport at the rear entrance. If Kashulinsky wanted to take a stroll after a business dinner, the car would follow slowly behind him. Even on routine trips from the office or a restaurant, the driver would often make sudden, unexpected turns, sometimes in the opposite direction of where he was headed, just to make sure nobody was following.

There was certainly no pullback from aggressive Russian reporting. Kashulinsky took on the oligarchs, the Mob, and powerful officials close to Putin. In a remarkable display of courage, *Forbes Russia* even dared to question how Elena Baturina, the wife of the mayor of Moscow, had amassed a business empire that made her the country's only female billionaire. The exhaustively researched article pointed to a number of real estate deals that seemed to have been facilitated by Baturina's connections to her husband, who controlled

Moscow's real estate sector like a fiefdom until he was pushed aside by Putin in the fall of 2010.

To promote the story, Russian *Newsweek*, also published by Axel Springer, printed the *Forbes* cover image ahead of the issue's release. Baturina's lawyers saw the ad and claimed that the cover line "I am guaranteed protection"—a shortened version of a Baturina quote in the article—was taken out of context.

The lawyers bullied Axel Springer into holding up distribution of the issue. Over one hundred thousand magazines wound up sitting in a Moscow warehouse. Outraged that Axel Springer had bowed to Baturina's demands, Kashulinsky submitted his resignation. When I briefed them on what was going on, Steve and Tim Forbes made the instant decision to issue a strong public demand that Axel Springer release the issue.

Also at stake was the renewal of the licensing contract with Axel Springer, which was about to expire. After some tense and unpleasant phone calls between New York and Berlin, Axel Springer finally released the issue. Following some delicate negotiations, Kashulinsky agreed to stay on. It was a great day for courage in the executive suite and for press freedom in Russia.

But because of possible retaliation ("We don't want another Russian editor dead," Terry O'Connor, *Forbes*'s general counsel, said to me), I told Kashulinsky that it would be wise for him to disappear for a while. I contacted the U.S. embassy in Moscow about issuing emergency visas for Kashulinsky and his wife, but they decided instead to go to an "undisclosed location" in the United Kingdom for a week since they both had unexpired British visas. Meanwhile, to no one's surprise, the issue quickly sold out. The incident caused an enormous flap in the European media, particularly in Germany, with Axel Springer getting a huge black eye for having caved to pressure. By contrast, *Forbes*'s decisive stance got kudos all around.

But it wouldn't be the last time *Forbes* would have bizarre dealings involving Russia. An August 2006 Moscow meeting between Russian president Vladimir Putin and Steve Forbes appeared to go well. A key part of the agenda was to obtain Putin's agreement and blessing for a major *Forbes* CEO conference in St. Petersburg the following summer. The idea was to attract a group of up to two hundred top European executives to attend a three-day session that would feature an array of expert-studded panels on things like energy policies, foreign investment, economics, and politics. Putin would appear, make a short speech, then schmooze with the delegates.

With any CEO conference, delegates attend not to hear what insightful nuggets the panelists have to impart, but to network and make deals. This session would be no different, and the challenge, as always, would be to get commitments from the bold-faced names as early as possible, since most CEO schedules are booked up to a year in advance.

The St. Petersburg venue, as opposed to, say, London or Paris, was doubly challenging because of the intricacies of obtaining a Russian visa, a daunting, time-consuming process only slightly less complicated than getting clearance to read top-secret White House memos. Procedures to answer the thirty-four-question form must be followed *precisely* "so that no hurry or hassle interferes into your trip to our beautiful country." Among the questions: "Do you have any special skills, training or experience related to firearms, explosives/nuclear matters, biological/chemical substance?" Think carefully before answering.

All of Steve Forbes's initial concerns about organizing the conference were met with a *"Nye bespokoytes"* (Don't worry) response from Vladimir. He would assign a trusted deputy to help with logistics, the venue, recruiting delegates, and lining up sponsors. *Done deal*, thought Forbes. Everyone thought that with the help of the Russians, it would be possible to raise the money needed to cover the event's cost and clear a nice profit to boot.

Well, not really. No major sponsors or commitments from big-name CEOs were on the books by the end of 2006. So in February 2007, with the meeting now only months away, a concerned group of *Forbes* staffers, including Raechel Mark (code name: Natasha), a sultry Russian-speaking member of the conference group, flew to Russia to find out what was happening.

Joining the New York contingent in Moscow were Robert Crozier, *Forbes*'s London-based managing director for Europe, and Marietta Corsini, a glamorous art collector who lived in Monaco and was well connected in Russia and the rest of Europe. A Kip Forbes friend, she was supposed to open doors for the conference effort. But as it turned out, she appeared to have left her keys back at the casino.

Not much had been going on in Russia after all, the group discovered. Putin's delegated "go-to" guy didn't have much to report, explaining it must have been a misunderstanding that he'd actually do any work to line up sponsors or delegates. "That's not what this office does," he said. *Oh, really?* "But the mayor's office in St. Petersburg will bring you up to date," he said. "They're on top of everything."

Off to St. Petersburg. The mayor was not available, but Fillip Fialkovsky, whose title is "chief expert" of the St. Petersburg Government Committee for External Relations, helpfully explained that neither the mayor's officer nor he had any knowledge whatsoever of a *Forbes* conference in June at the magnificent Grand Palace, Peter the Great's "Versailles," parts of which date back to 1721. Not good news. Moreover St. Petersburg officials expressed concern about a conflict with a government-sponsored conference to be held there that same month to which many executives were invited.

Perhaps the palace management would clear everything up. So, after a lunch at the appropriately named, Dostoyevsky-inspired *Idiot* restaurant on the Moyka Canal, the increasingly depressed delegation set off for the palace. After a tour of the facilities, the man in charge of reservations opened up his book to June but found nothing entered that month for a *Forbes* conference. Not even penciled in. "Ah, but the palace is still available for those dates," he added.

Back to Moscow for a meeting with Andrew Somers, the president of the American Chamber of Commerce in Russia, a man who knew the local managers of every big U.S. corporation. Somers's instant response: It would be lunacy to go ahead with a conference at this point with no major sponsors or delegates signed up.

Is this how they do things at Time Inc.?

Nonetheless, one more try for a big-fish sponsor: Moscow-based Unified Energy System of Russia, a giant power grid company 53 percent owned by the Russian government. The company's formidable head of foreign relations, Liudmila Lebedeva, dressed all in black and looking remarkably like Nikita Khrushchev in drag, was not smiling—even before anyone said anything.

Crozier, the delegation's big gun, a polished "presenter" dating back to his days running Time Inc.'s operations in Europe, cleared his throat and began his silken pitch: how important this conference would be for Russia, the value of assembling so many CEOs all in one place, the compelling topics to be discussed, and so on. Arms were still crossed on the other side of the table.

Crozier then went on to the fateful next step: explaining that for a $1 million sponsorship, the company's CEO would be able to have a private audience with President Putin.

It took a few minutes for Natasha to translate Crozier's remarks for Lebedeva. But with every emerging word, the Russian executive's frown morphed into a scowl of rage. Frantically still taking notes, Mark began to deliver Lebedva's reaction, which went something like this: "How dare *Forbes* come here to demand $1 million TO MEET WITH OUR OWN PRESIDENT!!!!! This is insult to our company and Russian people!"

Time to leave. On the way out, I whispered to Crozier, "Well, that went well." "We'll get the $1 million," he said.

At no point was the ad sales arm of *Forbes Russia* approached to pitch the conference to their clients. Nor did anyone think of asking Kashulinsky or his staff what Russian CEOs might be worth approaching about attending. There had been tension between *Forbes* and Axel Springer, and bureaucratic hassles with the Russian government over the sponsorship issue. At the time, those concerns trumped having knowledgeable boots on the ground in a profoundly complex, mysterious, and often forbidding foreign environment.

Complicating the sales effort just as the project seemed to be gathering some momentum was a major *Forbes* story critical of Gazprom, the giant ($42 billion in sales) Russian energy company, whose board and powerful geopolitical influence had Putin's fingerprints all over it. The story noted that Gazprom's "brief shutdown of natural gas to Ukraine last winter sent a shudder through Europe and later provoked Vice President Dick Cheney to say 'No legitimate interest is served when oil and gas become tools of intimidation or blackmail.'" The thoroughly documented, factual story was a commendable example of separation of church and state. But the article ticked off the Kremlin as well as the *Forbes* sales and conference departments, whose tasks were now even more formidable. With a mixture of disappointment and relief, *Forbes* mercifully canceled the St. Petersburg conference not long after the fact-finding mission returned to New York.

Axel Springer has proven to be *Forbes*'s most efficient and competent publishing licensee. With revenues of $2.5 billion euros and 150 newspapers and magazines in 30 countries, it knows the business well, and runs two of *Forbes*'s biggest money-makers—*Forbes Russia* and *Forbes Poland,* both of which have aggressively moved into special supplements and brand extensions.

Axel Springer also briefly considered editions in the Czech Republic and Spain, but pulled back launch plans for both over economic concerns. For Spain, Axel Springer even hired an editor, Sonia Franco, a talented business journalist with solid editing credentials. The decision not to proceed deprived the *Forbes* PR staff of a once-in-a-lifetime opportunity to put a "Franco to Edit *Forbes Spain*" story in the company newsletter.

But in a decision that left many staffers at 60 Fifth scratching their heads, the company announced plans in late 2010 to launch an English-language European edition of *Forbes,* to be based in London or Paris, with original, local content. This in the face of huge economic uncertainties in Europe, political unrest in the United Kingdom and France, flame-filled riots in Greece, and higher oil prices from the turmoil in Egypt and Libya. Steve Forbes told *The*

Daily Telegraph in London, "This is precisely the right time to move in. There is a recovery coming." The demonstrated lack of pan-European advertising was one of the key reasons the old *Forbes Global* folded; a former *Forbes* European sales executive says several former prominent financial advertisers he spoke with were "amazed" and "surprised" that *Forbes* would try another print edition in Europe, given the current economic outlook. And it's unclear what impact an English-language pan-European magazine would have on the company's licensing partners who put out their own magazines on the continent, with their own local content. "I rest my case," says a former senior *Forbes* executive, who believes the brothers to be operating in some kind of parallel universe.

The founding father: Bertie Charles Forbes, 1927 (Courtesy of Bettmann/Corbis)

The family, 1952: Kip, Tim, Steve, Roberta, Moira, Malcolm, and Bob (Courtesy of Sygma/Corbis)

The boat: Malcolm's beloved *Highlander*, New York harbor, circa 1986 (Courtesy of Dave G. Houser/Corbis)

The Harley balloon: aloft at Balloonfest, October 7, 1986, North Branch, New Jersey (Courtesy of Bettmann/Corbis)

The last playground: Château de Balleroy, built from 1626 to 1636 by architect François Mansart (Courtesy of AKG Photos/Newscom)

The Forbes brothers: Kip, Steve, Tim, and Bob (Courtesy of Frank Tapper/Sygma/Corbis)

"How do you know that?" Legendary Forbes editor Jim Michaels, photographed in his office, October 1998. (Courtesy of Chang Lee/*The New York Times*/Redux)

Faster than a taxi: Malcolm arrives for a celebrity dinner on his Harley, April 17, 1989. (Courtesy of Bettmann/Corbis)

Celebrity moment: Elizabeth Taylor and Malcolm Forbes, wearing matching leather jackets, Englishtown, New Jersey, September 20, 1987 (Courtesy of Ricki Rosen/Corbis Saba)

On the stump: Steve Forbes pushes his flat-tax program in New Hampshire, January 30, 1996. (Courtesy of Rick Maiman/Sygma/Corbis)

The boss at work: no doubt arm-twisting a CEO for an ad, 1987 (Courtesy of John A. Giordano/Corbis Saba)

25

STEPCHILDREN

Nepotism.
A very good thing on occasion.
Like if the occasion is you or me.

—Malcolm Forbes

B EYOND MIGUEL, THERE'VE BEEN other stepchildren in the Forbes family: a group of additional print efforts, only a couple of which have been successful. In addition to Malcolm's ill-fated *Nation's Heritage*, there was *Egg*, a glossy magazine that tried to capture the hip, urban New York nightlife scene. Edited by Hal Rubenstein, it was punchy and readable, but closed a year after Malcolm's death due to a pittance of advertising and media buzz. A weekly *Forbes Restaurant Guide* lasted only two years.

Forbes ASAP, a quarterly technology supplement launched in 1992, was notable for its thoughtful long-form "big idea" pieces by prominent technologists. But along with other media victims of the dot-com collapse, it disappeared in 2002.

American Heritage, a storied brand acquired in 1986, fizzled in *Forbes* hands. Jim Michaels once referred to it as the "poor sad corner of the company" that "could have been the History Channel." Used in part as a lure to get history buff Tim into the family business, running *Heritage* was the first job for Malcolm's youngest son at 60 Fifth after a stint as a documentary film producer. After some initial success, driven in part by the heady economic days of the nineties, growth in circulation and advertising stalled; an online version failed to jump-start the effort, which was finally closed in May 2007. Sold in 2008, both the magazine and Web site have since been revived by the new owners, American Heritage Publishing Co.

Under the radar as far as the general public is concerned is *The Social Register,* the 125-year-old blue blood phone and address book that *Forbes* has quietly published since the 1970s. By tradition, those wanting to be included must be "sponsored" by at least five people already in the book. The list is then reviewed by an advisory committee, which rejects 95 percent of the supplicants and proposes candidates of its own. About a dozen new names are added each year. There was a historical bias against Italian-Americans, Hispanics, Polish-Americans, blacks, Jews, and even Catholics—to the point where a Protestant whose family had been listed for many years could be suddenly axed for just *marrying* a Catholic. Regardless of ethnicity or religion, the president of the United States and the vice president are always included, along with their wives.

As a bar to the masses, there are confounding abbreviations following each name to denote which clubs they belong to and which universities they attended. Presumably only those who were members of Harvard's Porcellian Club, Princeton's Ivy Club, or Yale's Skull and Bones know how to translate the hieroglyphics.

Here, for instance, are the secret codes for Kip Forbes from the 1989 *Register*: K.C.B.Eh.Gr.StJ.Plg.P'72. Those in the know instantly recognize that Kipper was a member that year of the Knickerbocker, the Century Association, the Brook, Essex Hunt, Grolier, American Society of the Most Venerable Order of the Hospital of St. John of Jerusalem, and the Pilgrims. Oh, and that he graduated from Princeton in 1972.

Seeking to enter the lifestyle-luxury arena, in 1989 the family approached Bill Flanagan, who edited the *Forbes* Personal Affairs section, to draft a proposal and mock-up for a separate magazine. Flanagan did so and submitted it, only to be told the editorship of what would be launched in 1990 as *Forbes FYI* would go to author and humorist Christopher Buckley, son of the conservative commentator William F. Buckley Jr. Immediately putting his witty, understated stamp on the new publication, Buckley generated a stream of clever, celebratory stories about the good life of travel, hunting, golf, collecting, fast cars, good wine, and luxury goods of the kind that if you have to ask how much they cost, don't bother.

A man irresistibly drawn to mischief, Buckley deadpanned a 1991 article that said Soviet officials had decided to sell Lenin's embalmed body for at least $15 million. Taking the bait, ABC News anchor Peter Jennings reported the pending sale on the evening news, an item picked up the next day by *USA Today*.

Tight-lipped but grinning, Buckley kept mum until the Soviet Interior Ministry called the story "an impudent lie," exposing the piece as the hoax that it was. *Tass*, the Russian news agency, suggested a libel suit might be coming. But the resulting tut-tut buzz brought *Forbes FYI* a wealth of media exposure, including a public reprimand by the unpleased Jennings, who intoned, "I'll be encouraged in the future if *Forbes FYI* knows the difference between April Fool's Day and November 3." Buckley beamed. Proving once again that any publicity is good publicity as long as the names are spelled right.

Eventually, however, *Forbes* president Berrien tired of what he believed was too much of Buckley's towel-snapping humor, including a double-entendre cover shot of a bikini-clad blonde holding a large surfboard next to a classic "woody" station wagon. The large type headline read: "Got a Woody?" Perceived by some as being cynical and arrogant, the magazine started getting guffaws in the marketplace, according to a former sales executive.

Berrien decided a different kind of product was needed, so put Buckley squarely in his cross hairs. Berrien changed the title to *ForbesLife*, then dumped Buckley, replacing him with Gary Walther, a consumer magazine specialist Berrien had known at American Express where Walther was the first editor of *Departures*. Buckley was named "editor at large," a title that required no responsibilities whatsoever. Which merely freed him up to focus on what he wanted to do anyway: writing books and pieces for *The New Yorker* and *The Wall Street Journal*.

Walther, a smartly dressed man with a Tim Gunn swagger, got rid of most of Buckley's staff, ordered up an expensive bigger format for the magazine, and spent millions on a fancy new design, heavier weight paper, and drop-dead photography. It was a stunning redo, emphasizing fashion as well as the usual luxury topics. But the magazine continued to lose money, and within barely a year, Walther, too, suddenly disappeared from 60 Fifth. His replacement was Richard Nalley, a veteran editor and idea man who'd been with the magazine since 2001. Any other publishing company would have shut down *ForbesLife* long ago, but "they have to have something for these kids to do," says a former senior executive.

Moira, Steve's most favored daughter, got *Forbes Woman* to play with. *Forbes* has long contended that women make up an important part of its readership, 125,000 of its subscribers and an unknown percentage of its average 30,000 newsstand sales. Given the increasingly important role of women in management, the publication arguably should have been launched a decade ago. But *Forbes Executive Woman*, as it was first called, did not appear until 2007. Its first editor was Catherine Sabino, who'd previously done *Four Seasons Magazine* for the hotel chain, a custom publishing client at the time of Forbes Media.

But from the beginning, *Forbes Executive Woman* seemed to struggle for the right identity. Should it skew toward luxury, lifestyle, or women in business? Having little background in the latter, Sabino tilted toward lifestyle. Staff writers at *Forbes* were encouraged to pitch ideas, but nobody believed Baldwin when he said *FEW* stories would count toward their *Forbes* story quotas. Plus, Baldwin's stance was that if an important female executive was worth writing about—a Carly Fiorina, Meg Whitman, or Anne Mulcahy—then it should be done for *Forbes* and not a "supplement."

Unhappy with the magazine, Steve and Moira jumped at the chance to hire Carol Hymowitz, a veteran *Journal* editor and a recognized authority on women's leadership issues who'd just been inexplicably laid off in the latest round of Murdoch cost-cutting. Wowing *père et fille* with her ideas and vision, Hymowitz quickly came on board, and began a relaunch process, hiring *Forbes* veteran Mary Ellen Egan as her executive managing editor. Out went Sabino and her art director. After reviewing several portfolios, Hymowitz hired Alexa Mulvihill from *Martha Stewart Living* to be the art director. Two *Forbes* writers—Heidi Brown and Kiri Blakeley—were recruited to report Web stories.

Then reality hit. It quickly became clear that Tim Forbes, to whom Hymowitz reported on budgets and staffing, was skeptical of the print project. Extracting extra money for anything was an ordeal, and there were other obstacles. There was to be no separate sales staff for *Forbes Woman*; it would simply be an "add on" to the luxury sell of *ForbesLife*, always problematic for a start-up, but particularly so in a bad economy. No copy editors—the *Forbes* copy desk would handle that.

Plus, the marquee name in the venture, *FW* publisher Moira Forbes, turned out to be a disappointing advocate. Attractive, gracious, and charming, Forbes is earnest and hardworking. But she appeared genuinely uncomfortable asking people for money and seemed to bear the entire weight of the family legacy on her size 6 shoulders, often asking in near panic, "Do you think it'll work?" In the midst of its spring 2009 launch, after a dozen or so pages had already been sent to the printing plant, ready to go on press, Moira and another sales executive decided it was time to look at the proofs. They didn't like some of the design elements, even though mock-ups had been posted on the *FW* edit wall for days, if not weeks. The plant was told to kill those pages already sent. In a panic, Hymowitz picked up the phone and called *Forbes* art director Bob Mansfield. "You've got to help," she said.

Mansfield rushed over to 90 Fifth and began reviewing the layouts, making suggestions and tweaks agreed to after lengthy consultation. The whole magazine had to be laid out for a second time and put through the entire production process again.

Then, after only three issues, Tim Forbes, citing the poor economy and the resulting paucity of advertising, shut it down. He fired Hymowitz and said *Forbes Woman* would continue, but only online.

Never mind that the feedback on the print product was generally positive: Not only did women executives like the magazine, but they also wanted something to hold in their hands and pass along to their friends.

Then in a stunning example of micromanagement, Tim Forbes dictated by name the rest of the *FW* staff who should be laid off—the art director, the two Web writers, and three other staffers. Egan and another top editor, Francesca Donner, were spared. But they would both leave on their own just a few months later, even though they had no jobs to go to.

Bizarrely, *Forbes* was still telling anyone who would listen as late as the fall of 2010 that the print *Forbes Woman* was not dead, even though there was *no editor* and *no staff.* They're simply hoping for the right advertiser to come along and single-sponsor each issue, for about $100,000 a pop. Good luck with that in this market.

Equally odd is the fact that something called the Forbes Executive Women's Board, made up of some twenty executives, kept up their quarterly meetings, but as of fall 2010 had not been told that the magazine no longer existed. It's unclear exactly what they've been talking about. Or whether anyone asked where Carol Hymowitz was.

26

HEIRS AT ODDS:
STEVE VERSUS TIM

Those in the driver's seat should be required to know how.

—Malcolm Forbes

F ROM THE BEGINNING, MALCOLM groomed Steve to be his successor. But the pressures of knowing that he'd someday have to
step into his formidable father's shoes were daunting.

As was his own father, Malcolm was demanding of his sons, insisting they dress up in kilts and, when older, memorize the names
of executives who'd be on the "boat" for Saturday trips to West
Point football games. "If you and your siblings had to go to church
dressed in kilts, your friends snickering at the sight of you all in
skirts, you could begin to understand why all of us are close," Kip
once recalled. Above all, they had to learn the social skills of being
gracious, gentlemanly hosts. If B.C.'s boot camp was Victorian,
Malcolm's was pure WASP.

But behind any controlling, competitive personality usually lies
a lonely child wanting to be heard, seen, and understood. For Malcolm, this played out in his solitary games and fantasies, the cardboard city in the basement, the toy soldiers and boats, all of which
constituted a world he alone could build and control. Later in life,
he simply upped the scale, surrounding himself with much bigger,

more expensive toys in a fantasy world he controlled through the power of his money.

It was remarkable to me that each of the sons seemed to inherit an aspect of the father, as if a beam of light had passed through a prism and refracted four separate, distinct colors. Though shy and ill at ease with other people, Steve got Malcolm's strong will to succeed and control. Nobody can run for president once, let alone twice, without having a feeling of invulnerability and a fighting spirit that trumps a more objective, reasoned approach to life.

Like his father, Steve tended to be a loner in college, marching to a different drummer and living in a conservative bubble amidst a world of confrontation and tumult. Radicals dominated the political agenda of most American colleges in the late 1960s, and Princeton was no exception, despite its reputation then as being "the northernmost Southern school."

Spurred on by the left-wing Students for a Democratic Society, protesters staged marches and sit-ins, and even stormed Nassau Hall, the university's historic original building, which once temporarily served as the home of the Continental Congress. When the university's marching band formed a peace symbol during halftime of the 1969 Yale football game, harrumphing alumni, well oiled by flasks and fancy tailgate parties, booed so loudly nobody could hear the band. That same fall, the *Daily Princetonian* characterized the prevailing campus mood as an "ugly, brooding one."

Within this environment, Steve Forbes remained in curious isolation. He joined the Young Republicans Club and elected to take his meals at Woodrow Wilson, then the main social option for upperclassmen who didn't want to join one of the storied clubs on Prospect Avenue—or never got a bid from one to begin with.

Not for young Steve was there interest in or from, for example, Cannon Club, Princeton's equivalent of the Dartmouth fraternity that inspired *Animal House*. During Steve's sophomore year, Cannon consumed a record *52 kegs* of beer over Housparties Weekend. That figure is not as alarming as it sounds. A former club member once explained that "much, if not most, of that beer was not ingested, but tossed or used to create waves for surfing the long lino-leum Banzai Pipeline" between the legendary dual taprooms in the club's basement.

As his father did at Princeton, Steve started up his own maga-zine. *Business Today* was sort of a mini-*Forbes*, featuring interviews with executives, columns from people like William F. Buckley, Jr., and Ralph Nader and general advice to students thinking of a busi-ness career. Its stories touched on business in the ghetto and the military-industrial complex. Despite being voted "worst magazine" on campus Forbes's senior year, the publication still survives today with a national circulation of two hundred thousand, plus confer-ences and seminars.

While the SDS briefly ceased hostilities over spring break, Forbes championed the cause of elitism by treating the *Business Today* staff to a relaxing time in Bermuda, using the "capitalist rewards" from the venture.

Also oddly removed from the reality of the time was the subject Forbes chose for his senior thesis for the history department. Instead of tackling something involving Vietnam, the political resurrection of Richard Nixon, or a history of the protest movement in America, Forbes chose to focus instead on a much narrower event: "The Contest for the 1892 Democratic Presidential Nomination." The contenders were former president and gold-standard supporter Grover Cleve-land and Tammany Hall–backed Senator David Hill from New York. (Cleveland won and went on to defeat Benjamin Harrison.) A pre-scient observation in that work: "Politics is always full of ifs and it seems to take delight in spoiling any precise calculations."

Once ensconced at *Forbes* after college, Steve started out like any new edit hire and began life as a fact-checker. No matter that he was Malcolm's son, Steve got the Michaels treatment along with every-one else. Deflated to see one of his first stories cut within an inch of its life, Steve got no sympathy from Michaels. "You may not like it," he growled, "but the readers will." Steve went on to cover mutual funds, a favorite subject for Michaels, and eventually got praise from the mountaintop.

But there were other motivations at work beyond wanting to please the demanding editor. Deep down, Steve's ambitions were driven by something else: a desire to one-up the old man, once Steve was out from under his daunting shadow. It was an understandable goal, given the overbearing demands his father imposed on all his sons. It was constant pressure, a total immersion process, to succeed and carry the family banner forward. Which would have unfortunate results as time progressed.

It was on Steve's watch in 1995 that *Forbes* became number one in ad pages in the business category, finally surpassing *Fortune* and *Business Week*. Not only was it a big business win for Steve, but it was also a personal triumph in achieving something his father never had. Having done that, it was time to try for something else his father never attained—the gold ring of the presidency. Malcolm had had that goal on his radar for years. Only his wipeout in the run for governor of New Jersey got in the way of his ultimate dream. But Steve would not be denied, despite incredible odds to the contrary, putting on his blinders and pushing full-steam ahead, not realizing the financial impact of his hubris that would soon come.

Tim Forbes inherited his father's business sense, though some insiders, including Jim Michaels, argued that he didn't execute that role very well, pointing to his removal as chief operating officer in the fall of 2010 as evidence. "Everything he touched went bankrupt," Michaels once snarled in a moment of exaggeration. Moreover, Tim's more objective personality was destined to clash with Steve's more cerebral view of the world when it came to defining a strategy for the company going forward.

More detached than his brothers, Tim rarely showed emotion, always wanted to see both sides of a conflict, and never seemed to be affected by others' weaknesses or good qualities while analyzing a problem. At Brown, Tim sported below-the-shoulders hair and was the program chairman of the campus film society, resolving often contentious debates over which films would be shown each night, remaining calm in the midst of shouting matches. "He never got rattled and handled pressure well," says Elizabeth Carder, the former president of the society. Forbes made it clear to his film club friends that he saw his future in filmmaking, not magazine publishing, despite his famous last name. He'd thought it through and knew what he wanted to do, until family forces intervened.

To me, Tim seemed much more practical than his ideology-driven brother. Like Arthur Sulzberger, Jr., who has publicly conceded there will come a time when *The New York Times* will no longer be available in print, Tim Forbes has told colleagues he does not see print in *Forbes*'s future. If the mission now is simply to push data through cyberspace, who needs to shell out $5,000 a page for paper, ink, printing, and distribution for a dead-tree product?

At the same time, in a meeting with a senior editor, Tim had an odd answer to a logical question, "What do you want the Web site to do?" "Well, you know, the value of our brand is not really what it should be," he said. "We need the Web site to prove how much the brand is really worth." Nothing about a new frontier in journalism, or trying to be a leader in the next level of new media. No, Forbes.com is simply a *valuation tool*.

As the editor-in-chief, a strong believer in traditional journalism, and a political voice in need of a national platform, Steve has passionately argued for print to be part of *Forbes* going forward. It's the one part of his father's legacy he cannot emotionally accept dispensing with. Though they seem outwardly in sync and *never* disagree with each other in front of the staff, the print–no print split has led to at least one shouting match, overheard behind closed doors. It's like the old Yogi Berra line that Steve himself likes to quote: "When you come to a fork in the road, take it." In this case, Steve has gone one way, Tim the other.

Already emotionally detached from day-to-day operations are the other two brothers, who seem to be concerned with holding on to what family money is left rather than mud-wrestling over strategy. Neither is on the board. Kip was an art history major at Princeton and has an obsessive interest in Napoleon III. He presently lives with the baroness in Timberfield, where he laments the passing of his Victorian collection.

The most approachable and at-ease brother, Bob, got Malcolm's bon vivant gene. He majored in Italian at Chapel Hill, spent a year in Italy, bought an organic vineyard in Provence, and generally lives the good life, mostly in Palm Beach, but also in London and in California, where his wife's professional dancing partner lives. (Lydia Raurell, who competes nationally in all types of ballroom dancing, once told an interviewer she likes the Viennese waltz the best, cha-cha the least.)

Unfailingly generous when it comes to gratuities—as opposed to his father, who once tipped a cabbie twenty-five cents for a taxi ride to the Upper East Side from *Forbes*—Bob once handed me his corporate American Express card when he had to leave a London dinner early, saying, "Leave a nice tip." Those of us who remained briefly considered *what else* could be done with the card that night, but thought better of it.

The family is capable of great kindness—as well as sub-zero insensitivity. When the young daughter of marketing executive Kendall Crolius was diagnosed with kidney cancer in May 2001 and faced surgery, radiation, and chemo, each brother sent boxes of Godiva chocolates to the hospital on a regular basis, giving Martha encouragement and the nursing staff a windfall supply of goodies. Similarly, when I once wound up on a ventilator at a hospital upstate, *Forbes* offered to send a medevac helicopter to bring me back to the city, tubes and all, and was extremely generous in helping cover unreimbursed medical expenses. Bill Baldwin even called my wife to see if she needed him to pick up visitors from the train station (the Baldwins have a weekend home not far from our farm). It doesn't get more supportive than that.

On the other hand, when Steve's office was alerted that a laid-off staffer might be coming to the estate to appeal his fate, the cops were waiting. The former editor found himself splayed out on the hood of his car. Not long after he became editor-in-chief, Steve Forbes decided to fire his secretary of thirteen years, Anne Barton, just before her sixty-fifth birthday. Barton sued for age discrimination. Forbes settled out of court after a federal judge refused to grant the company's motion for summary judgment based on federal law. The court ruled "the trier of fact could reasonably conclude [statements by company officials] reflected 'age animus'" toward Barton. And when Bob Forbes by chance ran into a just-laid-off *ForbesLife* staffer on the street he said, "Hope you've put some money away!"

Paranoia and fretting about real or imagined conspiracies apparently take up a lot of time on the executive floor: keeping family myths alive and keeping *any* negative press out of the media are top priorities of the extremely effective public relations staff, which excels at diverting reporters from potentially damaging stories. Even with positive press reports, the brothers nitpick them to death, and seem never to be happy with any coverage. They meet each month with a lawyer to discuss the family business. Also often in attendance: a psychologist, to keep sibling rivalries under control and prevent any untoward decisions. They hope to avoid the fates of the Bancrofts and Binghams, iconic families where splits and rivalries ultimately forced the sale of their respective beloved media properties: *The Wall Street Journal* to Rupert Murdoch and the Louisville *Courier-Journal* to Gannett. But in today's swirl of changing media, with each brother having a different priority, how long can it all be held together? Maybe not that long. After the brothers had been in charge for a couple of years, then *Forbes* chairman Cap Weinberger was walking up the grand staircase of the Galleries one day, stopped at a picture of the sons, and reportedly said, "Give them ten years and they'll ruin the whole thing."

27

THE PRINCE OF DARKNESS
(PART I)

WALL STREET JOURNAL MANAGING editor (and *Forbes* alumnus) Norm Pearlstine liked to shake things up—planting dynamite in various places around the newsroom, then sitting back to watch the survivors crawl out of the rubble, dust themselves off, and scramble for food. But few of Norm's bombs exploded as loudly as when, in the summer of 1987, he announced he was replacing Glynn Mapes, the well-loved Page One editor, in charge of the paper's signature display page, with an outsider, Lewis D'Vorkin, a talented editor who'd done stints at the AP-Dow Jones wire service, the *Times,* and *Newsweek*. Top editing jobs at the paper traditionally went to in-house veterans.

Even though he'd join the paper soon, D'Vorkin wouldn't take over Page One until early the following year. Pearlstine characterized the long handover as necessary to give D'Vorkin time to learn the ropes of running the page and get to know the people. But it would be an awkward six months. In-house politicians like Al Hunt, the influential Washington bureau chief, and other editors to whom the paper's talented stable of writers reported would be lobbying to gain the favor of the man who'd soon decide which of their writers' stories would appear on the front page each day.

D'Vorkin is a thin, kind of scary-looking guy with dark, heavy-lidded eyes that seem to pierce right through you. Depending on the degree of facial hair, he could look uncannily like the late Osama Bin Laden. When he was editing the business section at *Newsweek,* sporting a dense black beard, one of the photo editors speculated he might be Middle Eastern. She told colleagues the phrase *"Habibi,"* which means "darling" or "loved one" in Arabic, would almost certainly render D'Vorkin helpless with homesickness and sentimental memories.

So every time D'Vorkin walked through the photo department, people would shout "Ciao Habibi!" to each other or into the phone. Other phrases tried were *"Baksheesh"* (bribe), *"Inshallah"* (if Allah wishes), and various references to camels, burkhas, and hashish. D'Vorkin paid it no mind. Undeterred, the photo editor once even tried to engage him in a discussion on rugs, about which he professed to have no knowledge.

With a laser instinct for what he believes is a good—or bad—story, D'Vorkin has no patience with people who don't agree with him and is brutally honest expressing his views. "He's an idiot" or "This really sucks" are some favorites. "That guy makes me nervous" is a sure sign that a writer may have a limited life expectancy. He is, by nature, not collaborative, tends to impose his own ideas, and doesn't want to be questioned as to the logic of his strategies.

"He was very forward-thinking, very outspoken," says Meredith White, now a deputy managing editor at the *San Francisco Chronicle* who worked with D'Vorkin at *Newsweek*. "He knew who the smart people were. He didn't suffer fools."

When listening to a writer trying to explain the meaning of a story not obvious from the written word, he'd often interrupt: "WRITE IT JUST LIKE THAT!" D'Vorkin always quickly sizes up a staff, bestows his blessing on those he favors, then basically ignores everyone else. An A list and Z list approach—a characterization he has often disputed. The fact is if you're in the circle of the chosen, you're golden. If not, you're just a base metal, incapable of alchemistic help.

D'Vorkin wastes no time dealing with those who can't help him attain his goals. Taking over control of all editorial at *Forbes* in 2010, he refused to meet with Carol Hymowitz, the veteran editor from the *Journal* who'd been recruited by Steve Forbes to relaunch and edit *Forbes Executive Woman*. Knowing Hymowitz's magazine was doomed because of a paucity of advertising, D'Vorkin saw no point meeting with someone who'd soon be gone. After a brief conversation with a Web art director about a new site design, D'Vorkin asked for all the files he had on it, and then walked out with them. The art guy was gone within weeks.

That he tends to polarize a staff into fans and detractors matters not to him. At the *Journal*, detractors outnumbered fans by a wide margin, including the entire Page One staff. D'Vorkin sent Paul Martin, a widely respected editor and keeper of the *Journal* stylebook, to the national news desk, and ditched Mike Marks, a clever rewrite man whose bemused in-a-fog personality belied his talents. Those who were left were concerned that accuracy and balance weren't high on D'Vorkin's priority list. "We felt his story sense drifted toward the simplistic or the sensationalistic," says a former rewrite man.

One evening, D'Vorkin changed a headline to "Nuts and Sluts" from "Trash TV" on the top of a Dennis Kneale story about chair-throwing TV shows like *Jerry Springer*. It may have been more punchy and eye-catching, but someone with higher authority saw it later that evening and changed it to "Titillating Channels," much to the pleasure of the editor who handled the story and who, along with the rest of the Page One staff, felt D'Vorkin was pushing traditional *Journal* standards of taste too far.

His editing approach was also foreign to the staff. He preferred beginning stories with long magazine-style leads, rather than the classic *Journal* anecdote that got you quickly into the narrative. In those pre-Murdoch days, the *Journal* was institutionally resistant to radical change, and the Page One staff was fiercely protective of the look and content of what was then genuinely believed—with justification—to be the paper's franchise page. He was seen as a foreign body to be rejected.

When an Atlanta reporter visited the New York office one day, she talked to Mack Solomon, the veteran Page One deputy editor, about various procedures for the page. Then she went in to see D'Vorkin. "Anything that Mack Solomon says, you can bet I believe the opposite," he told her. The reporter left looking perplexed. She reported the conversation to her bureau chief, who told Solomon, who just laughed.

There was also a certain amount of amusement over D'Vorkin's personal quirks—his very eighties all-black outfits, his totally clean desk (except for a collection of miniature toys), the pin collection on his wall (including "Who Hired All These Sleazy People?"), frequent calls from what turned out to be bill collectors and odd ones from his then-wife, who once asked the person who answered the phone to relay this message: "Tell him all of his stuff is out in the hall." D'Vorkin's tenure as Page One editor did not last long—three months and three weeks, to be exact. This was partly due to the aforementioned spouse, a very attractive but flighty Italian girl from Brooklyn with a Minnie Mouse voice, fancy clothes, and designer boots, who years before had worked at the paper as a news assistant. Charming and flirty, Maria once ran into reporter Tom Herman in the *Journal*'s cafeteria and asked what he covered. "Funds," he said. *"You cover fun?"* she replied with astonishment.

Maria also liked to shop, as did her husband. A convenient way to do so was for them to use his corporate American Express card. At the time, the practice at Dow Jones was to pay the AmEx bills as they came in; staffers were expected to account for business expenses and reimburse the company for anything personal.

The bills just kept coming: Brooks Brothers, Lord & Taylor, Saks Fifth Avenue, Tiffany's, fancy flower shops—thousands of dollars worth of merchandise, clearly not legitimate business charges. After returning from a particularly expensive (the rumor was $25,000) trip to San Francisco, D'Vorkin was warned about his spending, reportedly spurred in part by an alleged call from a Nevada casino during that trip asking if it was okay for D'Vorkin to use his corporate card to up his limit.

Then one day it was all over. "D'V Day," as a relieved Page One staff referred to it. Solomon, who would run the page on an interim basis—but only on the condition that Paul Martin return to the page—assembled the staff to say D'Vorkin was gone.

But he couldn't say why—because nobody in the managing editor's office would tell him. Of course, word quickly leaked out. The newsroom burst into applause a few weeks later when Pulitzer Prize–winning staff writer James B. Stewart was announced as the new Page One editor. D'Vorkin soon filed for bankruptcy, prompting a story in the *New York Post*; copies of the public filing quickly made the rounds of the *Journal* newsroom, creating glee for the detractors and sadness for the fans, whose ranks by that time had been seriously depleted. The bankruptcy filing showed thirty-four creditors, and total debts of $129,308, including an unpaid American Express bill of $45,000, a $12,000 Diners Club bill, and two MasterCard bills totaling $10,000.

Forbes had already been on D'Vorkin's radar, but it would take time to make it work. By his own account, in the mid-eighties, he "grabbed an orange grease pencil and vigorously marked up three issues, boldly suggesting ways to make a storied media brand even better," and sent off the package to Jim Michaels.

Michaels asked him in for a chat, mainly just listened, and then introduced him to managing editor Laury Minard. D'Vorkin quizzed him on what role a role a capitalist cheerleader like *Forbes* could now play since "the eighties are over and Malcolm is dead." Many months later, Michaels asked me for my impressions of D'Vorkin, since we'd overlapped at the *Journal*. What seemed to perk Michaels up more than anything was D'Vorkin's reputation for polarizing the staff. Michaels's grin said it all: *Just what I'm looking for.* Michaels may have wanted to throw chum in the water, but didn't do so until several years later with an out-of-the-blue "How'd you like to work here?" phone call.

D'Vorkin showed up at 60 Fifth, but didn't go on the masthead right away. He was holding out for a fancy title that Michaels wasn't yet ready to give him—one that would put him on a par with Kneale, who was no fan of D'Vorkin's when they were both at the *Journal*. D'Vorkin moved quickly to purge the art department—then his principal realm of oversight—of what he perceived as formulaic mediocrity. He replaced a long-time assistant art director and urged editors and art directors to come up with "multiple entry points" for stories.

By that he meant more emphasis on eye-catching layouts, smarter headlines, prominent pull-quotes, bigger font sizes, and snappier photo captions. "Whatever you can do to hook a reader," he said, "do it." D'Vorkin once chewed out a veteran wordsmith who'd written a caption for the contents page not up to his new standards. "That's not the way we do things now," he said in a curt phone call. "Look at the magazine!" Hanging up, he sighed "Oi, yoi, yoi, yoi, yoi!" loud enough to be heard out in the hallway.

D'Vorkin brought in a consultant to give *Forbes* a fresh, new look—more white space, bigger photos, colorful charts, and more "display type" such as large pull-quotes. Gregory Heisler, a renowned and very pricey photographer, was retained for several cover shoots. Heisler used a large format analogue camera that produced images of exceptional quality and clarity. His cover of Richard Branson, showing the iconic entrepreneur wrapped in a British flag in front of one of his Virgin Atlantic's 747s, was one of the most striking covers the magazine ever ran. "For the first time," said the photo editor, "someone really cared about photography."

Editing a story about the music business, D'Vorkin inserted the phrase "Ch-ch-ch-ch changes" high up in the story. But sensitive to Michaels's renowned lack of the pop culture scene, he wisely inserted a parenthetical note explaining the phrase referred to David Bowie's signature lyric in "Changes," a popular single from 1972. No doubt preventing a nasty ("WHAZZIS MEAN?????") comment that all could see.

28

POLITICS 102

Life is never as you think it was going to be.

—Malcolm Forbes

COMEDIAN VAUGHN MEADER'S CLASSIC 1962 album *The First Family* captured with uncanny accuracy the clipped Boston accent of President John F. Kennedy. In one skit, JFK and Jackie are spending a lonely Saturday night at the White House, uninvited to any parties that evening.

Fishing for an invitation, Kennedy picks up the phone and dials the number of Dean Rusk, his secretary of state. "They're *always* entertaining," Jackie breathily offers.

"Mr. Rusk, please." Pause.

"The president." Pause.

"OF THE UNITED STATES!!!"

Fast forward to the fall of 1995. Tim Forbes summons to his second-floor corner office one of his most trusted deputies. Invoking a metaphorical *Get Smart* "Cone of Silence," Forbes explained the conversation was highly confidential.

"I'm going to be taking over," Forbes said. "Steve wants to be president."

"But I thought he already *was* president."

THE FALL OF THE HOUSE OF FORBES

"Not of the United States!" Forbes replied, hardly believing himself what was about to happen next.

Thence down the rabbit hole to not one, but two bizarre runs for president—one in 1996 and the other in 2000—that mystified and amused *Forbes* staffers and a good chunk of the American electorate. The campaigns would also create fissures within the family and ultimately have significant financial consequences for the company.

To a curious and bemused audience at the National Press Club on September 22, 1995, Steve Forbes stepped to the podium to announce his candidacy. It was already a crowded field, including Senate majority leader Robert Dole, former Tennessee governor Lamar Alexander, conservative commentator Pat Buchanan, Senator Phil Gramm of Texas, Senator Arlen Specter of Pennsylvania, and California governor Pete Wilson.

It seemed to many to be a presumptively arrogant move—a rich man with no political experience trying to buy his way into the White House. Nobody other than Ross Perot in recent history had tried to use the U.S. presidency as an entry-level job into politics. "How deluded can you possibly be?" said one senior *Forbes* official at the time. At least Malcolm, who at one point had his eye on the same prize, got some practice as a state senator and running for governor of New Jersey. And then stopped.

With no prior elective experience, both Hillary Clinton and Robert Kennedy carpetbagged their way into U.S. Senate seats from New York. But the rage directed at those polarizing candidates was less from questioning their credentials than from the maddening reality from the very beginning that they *were probably going to win,* given who they were. The entitlement thing.

No such ire was directed at Forbes, from the right or the left. Nobody really disliked the man. How could they? Outside of the media world, he was largely an unknown. With some obvious head scratching, *Time* magazine said, "Forbes' political experience makes a relative novice like Pat Buchanan look like George Washington." Here's this nice, decent, sort of geeky-looking guy with some weird ideas who obviously won't win.

Forbes told his National Press Club audience, "I expect there are a few skeptics in the room."

So why did he do it? Some of the usual supply-side suspects like Jude Wanniski, a former editorial writer for *The Wall Street Journal*, urged Forbes to run after Jack Kemp said he wouldn't be entering the race in 1996. Sensing a weakness in the tax policies of front-runner Dole—Forbes accused the senator of "voting for 16 tax increases in the past 13 years"—Forbes hired Kemp's former chief of staff, William Dal Col, as his campaign manager to help craft his core flat-tax pitch.

Also on board were two veteran lieutenants of the campaign wars of North Carolina Senator Jesse Helms, Carter Wrenn and Tom Ellis. Both became infamous for exploiting racial issues in Helms's efforts over the years, though there wasn't a hint of racism in anything Forbes set forth. Quite to the contrary, Forbes spoke out in support of affirmative action and of Kemp's policies of establishing "enterprise zones" and getting tenants control of public housing as ways of tempering social problems. The only hint of divisiveness came during a radio interview in New Hampshire when Forbes advocated a federal version of a California measure being promoted by Governor Pete Wilson that would forbid illegal immigrants from receiving government benefits—a one-eighty from what he'd said only two years earlier in a Fact & Comment column, saying Wilson was "morally wrong" and equating the measure with interning Japanese-Americans during World War II.

Still, the Helms connection was not particularly helpful PR-wise, as when the press reported a Wrenn quote during Helms's 1990 campaign against a black candidate, which Wrenn managed: "What you have opposing Helms is another coalition of homosexuals and artists and pacifists and every other left-wing group." Or the fall 1995 report by *Time* that during a Senate hearing in 1983, then Senator Joe Biden suggested that Ellis, up for a government position, had promoted segregation when he was counsel to the North Carolina Advisory Commission on Education in the 1950s.

Ellis had written at the time that the goal of school integration was "racial intermarriage and disappearance of the Negro race by fusing it into the white." When pressed, Forbes downplayed the roles of both Ellis and Wrenn, saying Ellis "occasionally sends a note, maybe once a month" and that Wrenn was just an office administrator, making sure the fax machines worked.

One of the more amusing miniflaps of the campaign centered around the résumé-inflating boast in Forbes's biography that he was "the only writer to have won the *highly prestigious* [emphasis added] Crystal Owl Award four times," given by USX Corp. to the financial journalist "whose economic forecasts for the coming year proved to be the most accurate."

But the Crystal Owl Award is not exactly the equivalent of a Pulitzer Prize for a record of sustained brilliant commentary. It seems that USX, previously known as U.S. Steel, threw a big Christmas party in New York every year for financial journalists. After being well lubricated with holiday cheer, participants got a questionnaire asking for predictions on things like GDP, the Dow Jones industrial average, the price of USX stock, and "tiebreakers" like who'd win the Super Bowl or World Series. A year later, he who "forecasted" most accurately got the Owl. "Christ, it was just a guessing game," laughed George Hess, then a contributing editor of something called *33 Metalproducing*, a trade magazine, who was twice the lucky recipient of the party-game trophy.

Forbes's campaign's centerpiece was a flat 17 percent across-the-board tax on wages and salaries that would exempt *all* other income sources so that dividends, interest, pensions, Social Security, and capital gains from the sale of securities or other assets would be tax free. It was a tantalizing message, especially when Forbes was able to visualize its potential impact for voters by holding up a postcard-size tax return that could be filled out in just a few minutes as opposed to the average 28.5 hours a typical taxpayer spends sweating over a Form 1040. To Forbes, the benefits of a flat tax would be not only eliminating the "horrifically heavy, appallingly complex, corruption-inducing" nine-million-word federal tax code, but also "revitalizing the economy and changing our lives dramatically for the better," a "renaissance the likes of which has never been seen before."

But the naysayers quickly pounced, arguing that a flat tax would be a giveaway to the rich, hurt home ownership, and reduce federal tax revenues. Buchanan called the financial elite in the party who supported the flat tax the "chablis and brie" wing of the Republican Party. The December 1995 newsletter of the Center for Public Integrity quoted Donald Alexander, a former IRS commissioner under Nixon, Ford, and Carter, as saying the flat tax "is not fair. It will increase the divide between the rich and the poor in America. The rich will become vastly richer and the poor, poorer."

How would a flat tax affect Steve Forbes? The Center for Public Integrity, using data from the Federal Election Commission, calculated that Forbes would pay $149,440 in federal taxes for 1995 based on the flat tax, against $278,420 under the current tax system, a savings of 46 percent. He'd pay tax on his *Forbes* salary ($813,000), but not dividends and interest ($238,000), various honoraria ($96,000), rent from a New Jersey property ($30,000), and $5,000 in farm income.

Farm income? New Jersey gives a big tax break to farmers who own at least five acres and have at least $500 in annual revenue. Of the 520 acres Forbes owned in Bedminster, 450 were used for cattle breeding, mostly polled Herefords, and two Scottish breeds, Galloways and belted Galloways—the latter the amusing-looking "Oreo" cows that are black with a white stripe around their middles. The farmland was assessed at only $160,500 instead of the $8.9 million market value that could apply without the farm break. So while the 70 non-farm acre taxes were $50,000, the 450 cattle acres cost Farmer Steve only $2,215.

For a time, Forbes escaped harsh scrutiny in the press, as his candidacy was regarded as a sort of oddity. Predictably, rival *Fortune* weighed in with a snarky profile subtitled "The first close look at the Forbes record, including some shady land deals, editorial cravenness, and the looming shadow of his famous father."

Though cleverly written, there was nothing of substance that came even close to derailing the campaign. The piece chronicled what it deemed the unscrupulous sales effort of the family to peddle portions of its Colorado land holdings to investors through what's known as an "installment contract for deed." Rather than getting title right away, the buyer got it only after making regular payments for as much as ten years. If a payment was missed, deed-holder Forbes could cancel the contract and simply sell the parcel again.

A lawsuit against Forbes in federal court in 1992 demanding a refund on a contract that had been terminated after eight years was dismissed after Forbes agreed to pay refunds to the plaintiff—and 236 other defaulting "investors."

Fortune also gleefully reported several instances that it claimed demonstrated *Forbes*'s advertising executives would demand changes at the last minute in stories, changes that would effectively turn a negative piece into a positive one. Cited were a March 1993 negative story on Georgia Pacific and a downbeat piece on AT&T's video-phone business that miraculously became positive stories upon publication.

But apart from trying to convince the electorate to embrace a simplistic yet radical change in the tax system, which for many Americans could have unknown and unintended consequences, Forbes's main challenge was his inability to relate to the average voter. Like Sergeant Shriver's memorable attempt to bond with some blue-collar workers during his 1972 run for vice president by bellying up to a Detroit bar and ordering a Courvoisier, Forbes was often uncomfortable and self-conscious on the stump.

Time described him as maybe the "only man ever to run for President who behaves as if it's bad manners to introduce himself to strangers," extending a "delicate, manicured hand as though he's reaching for a wine glass. He doesn't plunge into crowds; he tiptoes through them, smiling apologetically, as if he doesn't want to be a nuisance."

At small-town campaign events, he'd often stand alone, self-consciously gobbling up doughnuts at a table off to the side, waiting for people to come to him rather than proactively reaching out.

"There seemed to be a gene missing," says one former campaign aide. Out of sight of the press, his built-in GPS would guide him directly to the local Starbucks or McDonald's, without which he could not survive.

Shortly after he announced for the first time, Forbes took a Metroliner to Washington from New York. I happened to be in the same car. Throughout the trip, the man who wanted to become president of the United States sat glued to his seat, hunched over a legal pad, reading and taking notes. What would Bill Clinton have done in the same situation? Probably worked the entire train, coming back to his seat with a pocket full of business cards, maybe some pledges of money and the names of the conductor's grandchildren. But that wouldn't have been Steve's style.

On the road, his speeches, at least at the beginning, were painful to watch. He often had a head-nodding goofy grin that made him look as if he'd just been jolted by some kind of mild electric shock. And his hand movements tended to be mechanical and puppetlike.

But with each stump speech, Forbes got better. At a hoped-for "victory" party at the New York Hilton for the '96 New York primary (which Forbes lost by a wide margin) he gave an inspiring, energetic address that had even some of the cynical *Forbes* journalists who attended it on their feet applauding. Pumped up by the TV lights, balloons, and a bleacher filled with placard-waving supporters, Forbes worked the rope line with enthusiasm and was clearly enjoying the moment. It was a whole new view of the boss, the same guy everyone dreaded to wind up in an elevator with. "Wow. Too bad he didn't come out of the gate like that," I said to a campaign aide, who nodded in agreement.

Alas, Malcolm's ghost was hovering, particularly over the '96 Iowa caucuses. An unidentified opponent, likely Dole or Buchanan—whose camps denied any involvement—launched a nasty telephone campaign accusing Forbes of supporting homoerotic art. Why? Because his father had a painting by the late Robert Mapplethorpe, a gay artist whose sexually explicit works fanned Conservative wrath. "What the calls conjured up were images of the Crucifixion in a jar of urine," says Ernest Tollerson, the *Times* reporter who covered the Forbes campaign. "But it was really just a seascape that Malcolm had on the boat."

"Owning a seascape is not an endorsement of pornography and it is outrageous to imply it is," fumed Steve Forbes. "Would you paint over the ceiling of the Sistine Chapel because you don't agree with all of Michelangelo's work?" Not the kind of distraction Forbes needed.

Forbes also helped drive the final nails into his own Iowa coffin by taking on the powerful Christian Coalition, which had lashed out at him for his nonsupport of an abortion ban. "The Christian Coalition does not speak for all Christians," Forbes huffed. "It speaks only for its members." Dole immediately jumped on that, saying "politicians like Steve Forbes and Bill Clinton are uncomfortable with religious conservatives. They think people of faith have no place in politics, but they're wrong."

Both independent and Forbes's own pollsters soon showed a sharp drop-off in his support from religious conservatives, who by some estimates made up as many as 40 percent of the Iowa caucus goers and 43 percent of the undecided votes. Once gaining ground on front-runner Dole, Forbes had slipped to a disappointing fourth place when the Iowa caucuses votes were finally tallied, coming in at only 10 percent. Forbes managed two primary victories in 1996—Delaware and Arizona, privately vowing never again to ignore the religious right.

To his brothers' deep dismay and much of the country's amusement, Forbes tried again in 2000, bridging the gap between campaigns with pronouncements and fund-raising from something called Americans for Hope, Growth, and Opportunity, a not-for-profit, thinly veiled continuation of his campaign effort. Dal Col served as president of the organization until he once again took over to manage the 2000 campaign. After his 1996 defeat, Forbes was also a "founding signatory" to the right-wing Project for the New American Century, a nonprofit Washington think tank that lasted from 1997 to 2006. Founded by neocons William Kristol and Robert

Kagan, the organization urged President Clinton in 1998 to remove Saddam Hussein by military force if necessary and said that going to war against Iraq would be justified by Hussein's threat to U.S. interests through what the organization believed to be Saddam's stockpile of weapons of mass destruction.

Forbes announced his 2000 campaign in March 1999 with a taped speech on the Internet, calling his effort "the beginning of a national crusade to restore Ronald Reagan's vision of hope and prosperity for all Americans."

While his 1996 effort focused almost entirely on economic issues, the 2000 push emphasized social issues, in an attempt to draw more of the Christian right into his tent. In 1996 he said he opposed a constitutional amendment to outlaw abortion. Four years later, that stance morphed into support for just such an amendment and a statement that he'd only appoint judges who disapproved of the procedure. And when his good friend from childhood, New Jersey governor Christine Todd Whitman, vetoed a partial-birth abortion ban, Forbes, who had been a key crafter of the tax-reduction platform Whitman used to defeat Governor Jim Florio, ran commercials urging the legislature to overturn the veto. Forbes also talked more about family values this time, coaxing his wife, Sabina, to join him on the campaign trail. The daughter of an Episcopal rector, Sabina is a private, unassuming woman *The Boston Globe* once described as "the silver haired one wearing sensible shoes and a slightly pained expression that pleaded for permission to re-board the bus."

But no reporter confronted Forbes with the rumors—commonly whispered within the company but hard to prove—that he'd had at least two long-term affairs, one with a staffer and another with a nonemployee. "I'm just waiting for him to run for something again," says an ex-*Forbes* sales executive who was given the boot and thus holds no particular affection for the family. "I'd be more than willing to out him. I know the names."

The hard-right turn didn't yield the hoped for results. One early poll that asked Republicans who they planned to vote for in 2000 showed him trailing George W. Bush by 56 percentage points—4 percent to 60 percent. The novelty of a Forbes candidacy had clearly worn off, yet he and his staff, blinders fully in place, were still convinced he'd pull it off. As his father once said, thinking to the very end that he'd win the governor's race in New Jersey: "For politicos, 'tis easy to succumb to self-deception."

Forbes wisely pulled out early this time, officially dropping his campaign in February 2000, after coming in third in New Hampshire and Delaware, a state that he'd won in 1996. He got only 13 percent in New Hampshire, far behind the winner John McCain, and George Bush, who came in second.

The cost of hubris was high. Forbes turned down matching funds in both races, and spent $75 million of his "own money" for the two efforts. To finance the campaigns, insiders say, Forbes borrowed money from the company and sold off some of his shares, but not the voting shares that would have diluted his 51 percent.

The expensive campaign would come back to haunt the company once the dot-com advertising collapse gathered momentum, only weeks after Forbes pulled out in 2000. More gnashing of teeth from the brothers, who were not happy. "Tim was very pissed off," says a former sales executive. Certainly $75 million would have come in handy in the summer of 2009, when at an off-site managers meeting, Tim Forbes asked for ideas on how to generate $60 million in additional revenues each year. Nobody had any ideas. While joint family ownership of a company sounds like a good idea in theory, when times are tough, it's a little like having to sit down to Thanksgiving dinner *every day*.

The fissures, which tended to increase with time, amounted to this: Bob and Kip, the least involved in the day-to-day management, were interested only in protecting their personal nest eggs, and did not take kindly to Steve's costly Quixotic adventures. Steve, more an ideologue than capitalist or savvy CEO, had been totally distracted by politics but now wanted back in as a management player, while Tim had taken full command and was intent on running the company *his* way. Unlike what his father had done to his own brother,

Steve didn't publicly present Tim with a watch and thank him for watching over the store. But the atmospherics of that earlier scenario were there, and it was uncomfortable for the brothers. Particularly later when Tim launched changes that would forever change the direction of *Forbes*.

BOOK IV

29

"IT'S ALWAYS 4:20 SOMEWHERE"

CHUBBY WOMBAT DOES LEAD vocals and plays guitar in a Grateful Dead–tinged band called Moonalice that specializes in drug-infused lyrics like "It's always four-twenty somewhere, it might as well be here." The band plays such venues as Kaplan's Barn in Millerton, New York, and the Ukrainian-American Cultural Center in Whippany, New Jersey.

Mrs. Wombat, known onstage as Blue Moonalice, does percussion, guitar, as well as vocals. Her real name is Ann McNamee. She has a PhD in music theory from Yale. Occasionally, Jack Cassidy of Jefferson Airplane sits in with the band as the featured bass player.

Mr. Wombat, who sports graying shoulder-length hair, is known in real life as Roger McNamee, the charismatic, quirky financial whiz who's one of the founders of Elevation Partners, the private equity group that bought 40 percent of Forbes for $250 million in 2006. At a recent concert, Wombat told the audience, "I don't know how many of you have a day job. But I do, and right now it sucks."

He was referring in part to the dismal results at *Forbes,* which helped plunge Elevation's total return to a minus 10 percent in the first quarter of 2010. These aren't the kind of numbers Elevation's own investors, known as "limited partners," want to see. Elevation's LPs, which committed a total of $1.9 billion in capital to the firm's debut fund, include big institutions and pension funds like the Colorado Public Employees Retirement Association and the Washington State Investment Board.

Big investors like these seek out successful private equity firms whose returns rank in the top quartile of the industry to pool their capital for investment in so-called portfolio companies that have unusual potential for growth. Since the transactions are "private," there's no oversight by the Securities and Exchange Commission or any disclosure requirements. So not only is it a huge ($832 billion) business, but it's also very secretive. Hardly a new concept, "private equity" from families like the Vanderbilts and the Harrimans funded most of the early U.S. railroads.

But today's version is a bit more complex than a robber baron writing a check. Private equity firms first have to convince investors they've got the savvy to produce higher than average returns. The money is then put into a fund, which typically has a finite life of about eight to ten years, after which the portfolio companies are "harvested" through outright sale, merger, or initial private offering. With any luck, the LPs get their money back plus a nice double-digit return.

Private equity funds, which typically don't collect all their money up front, but space the process out with "capital calls" for funds committed, make money two ways: by charging a management fee (averaging 2.5 percent of the fund's committed capital) and collecting what's known as the "carry," a percentage of the capital gains in the portfolio investment, anywhere from 15 percent to 25 percent.

Elevation didn't have a track record when it was formed in 2005, but it did have some star power in McNamee, the chief rainmaker who had a dazzling career as a trader at T. Rowe Price, and as a venture capitalist at Kleiner Perkins and later at Silver Lake Partners, where he was instrumental in relaunching Seagate Technology, now an $11 billion (in sales) maker of hard drives and storage mechanisms.

Other partners included Fred Anderson, the former chief financial officer of Apple Computer, Marc Bodnick, a founder of Silver Lake Partners, another private equity group, and Bret Pearlman, a former senior managing director at the Blackstone Group, where he worked on media and communications deals and invested the firm's third and fourth private equity funds. Bodnick has since left for Quora.

The big-name front man is U2's Bono, the annoyingly know-it-all and ubiquitous Irish rock star whose song "Elevation" was the inspiration for the firm's name. Though he's a brilliant marketer and extraordinary performer, Bono isn't particularly known for his knowledge of the magazine publishing business.

McNamee, who has advised the Grateful Dead on how to communicate with their fans on the Web, likes to rattle off his high-concept strategies at machine-gun speed from a thirty-thousand-foot perspective. He's a thoroughly believable preacher of the firm's gospel: finding media/tech companies with first-rate content and figuring out how to leverage that into new demographics and platforms.

Part of McNamee's passion and drive comes from having survived a scary stroke at the age of forty-five followed shortly by open-heart surgery to correct a birth defect doctors figured out was the cause of the stroke. It was one of those moments, he writes in his book *The New Normal*, where "it's time to figure out who and what you want to be and put yourself on the right path."

Trolling for media properties, Elevation briefly looked at the *Times* and the *Journal*, neither of which showed much interest. So Elevation focused on *Forbes* for its brand and its franchise of giving people sound financial advice. "We're at a critical moment in time," McNamee told a group of *Forbes* editors in the spring of 2008. "People are desperate for insights and you guys are the ones who have them." Elevation sees itself not as a micromanager of the companies it invests in, but rather a "force multiplier," asking lots of questions and suggesting some broad-stroke strategies.

Considering that both *Newsweek* and *BusinessWeek* each sold in 2010 for what amounted to a ham sandwich and some assumed debt, the Forbes brothers look real smart for grabbing $250 million from Elevation. They quoted a fat price for part of a famous bridge—and got it. But the transaction, at least from Elevation's standpoint, was doomed by what was in retrospect a flawed investment strategy and some poor execution by *Forbes*. Nobody anticipated the horrendous decline in ad volume and prices—triggered by the global economic collapse and new technology that was turning the traditional ad market upside down.

For years, media advertising was all about manipulating consumers' perceptions of buying needs based on a "reach and frequency" strategy. Clever and smart ad copy (think Doyle Dane's classic VW "bug" print ads or Lord, Geller's Charlie Chaplin IBM TV spots), seen enough times in as many places as possible, punched through consumer boredom and made the viewer or reader act on it, i.e., buy a Volkswagen or a new business system from IBM.

Advertising rates, whether for television or print, are based on audience "reach"—number of viewers of a particular show, calculated by Nielsen—or a guaranteed minimum average of paid subscriptions within a six-month period, measured by the Audit Bureau of Circulation. The bigger the audience, the more the advertiser has to pay—thus the $3 million for a thirty-second Super Bowl ad that reaches 100 million viewers. At a rate base of 900,000, *Forbes*'s average per-page charge to advertisers before the dot-com bubble burst was roughly $75,000, or a cost-per-thousand of $83.

Today that per-page rate is down to an average of about $27,000, or a CPM of $30. If you count "pass-along" reach of about four readers a copy, the total 3.6 million works out to a CPM of $7.50. But big agencies tend to reject the pass-along add-on because it's more of a "brand recognition" exercise, rather than a hard-number measure of people who actually read the magazine.

During the fall of 2008 financial meltdown, *Forbes* tried to maintain a $27,000-a-page "rate floor," but went below that many times, averaging $23,000 to $25,000. At the same time, the overall number of ad pages has dropped from over six thousand in the year 2000 to 1,640 last year (2010). For those in a doom and gloom mode, the math is obvious.

For a time (2006 to 2007) print and Web CPMs were about the

same, averaging $40. Forbes.com CEO Jim Spanfeller, as we've seen, for years claimed that printlike CPMs were justified by the reach of the brand to what Spanfeller consistently referred to as an audience of "50 million business leaders." Are there really 50 million business leaders in the world?

This figure presumably included Forbes.com Web traffic, the circulation of *Forbes, Forbes Asia,* all the foreign language editions, and an indeterminate number of janitors worldwide who glance at *Forbes* covers before throwing them into the trash.

The number was highly suspect, and there was growing unease in the *Forbes* executive suite about how solid the online traffic numbers were, exacerbated by the fact that there's no undisputed industry standard to measure traffic.

Then came the ad networks, nimble outfits like AOL's Advertising.com that help publishers monetize their "cheap tonnage" of unsold digital ad inventory using software algorithms that put supply and demand in sync while giving advertisers a low-risk way to buy ads on a performance basis—they pay only if someone clicked on their ad. This obviously called into question the value of branded advertising on the Web—the cornerstone to *Forbes*'s online strategy. Networks also drive down CPM costs for advertisers to as little as twenty-five cents. The idea is to get more than zero for unsold inventory, even if it's only pennies. Some 80 percent of ad volume through Google now comes through these networks, some of which are already $1 billion revenue companies in themselves.

But rather than invest in technology that would give the Web site the flexibility of an ad network and more sophisticated data extraction tools, *Forbes* decided instead to spend time flaming about how bad the ad networks were. "That's going to cost us money," Tim Forbes told a consultant who urged the company to spend a relatively modest $500,000 on a sophisticated "pricing and yield management system" that could have potentially increased revenues by 30 percent. "They don't understand the value of investment in technology," says the consultant.

Put another way, it's not that the Forbes brothers, in general, were presented with bad ideas. *They just were reluctant to spend money,* even on good ones. One repeatedly kicked around within senior editorial management was the idea to build some sustained, revenue-generating program to provide the particular kind of information owners of family businesses need—how to manage family dynamics to avoid conflicts, and why it's important to follow "best practices," such as requiring a child who wants to enter the business to spend at least two to three years at another company and get at least one promotion before returning. Memos were written as well as appeals to various executives, but no Forbes family member would take up the cause seriously. No irony, of course, involved in that.

Similarly, Forbes dismissed out of hand an idea by Matt Miller, who ran the rich list and billionaires issues and databases, to develop a line extension—a *Forbes* consultancy unit that would charge premium prices for bespoke due diligence intelligence on companies and executives, going far beyond information available publicly. Given the cold shoulder, Miller raised $1 million in seed money with some partners and left to start his own firm, Wealth-X.

Forbes now may regret not holding on to Miller. Not long after forming Wealth-X, Miller was lured to Bloomberg to start up that company's own billionaires list, in a direct assault on *Forbes*'s main franchise. With its *own* billionaire owner paying the bills at a company that's constantly upgrading its hardware and software, Bloomberg is poised to throw what Miller terms "tons of resources"—it has over two thousand reporters worldwide—into the new venture, sensing *Forbes*'s new vulnerabilities. Bloomberg is also revitalizing its new acquisition, *BusinessWeek*, having plucked Time Inc. rising star Josh Tyrangiel, thirty-seven, to be its new editor. Tyrangiel used to run *Time*'s Web operations and was widely considered to be the heir apparent to managing editor Richard Stengel. Beyond its billionaires venture, Bloomberg has clearly locked in *Forbes* as a major target.

Tim Forbes once expressed puzzlement to a high-ranking editor as to why Bloomberg "was hiring all these journalists." He's now finding out.

30

THELMA AND LOUISE

The moment you think you're doing
your company a favor by working for them,
quit. Before you're fired.

—Malcolm Forbes

T HE ROOTS OF THE split between the print and online sides of *Forbes,* which would ultimately be the brand's undoing, were evident early in the new millennium. The July 2003 sales meeting's highlight was a *Thelma and Louise* takeoff, featuring print sales head Jim Berrien and his digital counterpart Jim Spanfeller both dressed in drag, with full makeup. The 1991 road-trip film, starring Geena Davis and Susan Sarandon, told the tale of two unlikely soul mates setting out in a vintage, teal-colored Thunderbird convertible to escape their troubled, restricted lives. But through various acts of self-destructive behavior—robbery, murder, blowing up things, etc.—they quickly fell into a downward spiral.

Channeling the odd-couple renegades, Berrien and Spanfeller talked about all the ways they'd leave the past behind and cooperate in sales efforts over the next year. The skit included the film's most famous clip: Thelma and Louise driving their car over a cliff.

It was an apt image. Like the movie, the routine was pure Hollywood. Berrien and Spanfeller didn't particularly like each other and had distinctly different views of the world. Both consummate salesmen, they talked a good game in public. But everyone in the audience knew that once the dresses came off, it would be back to business as usual.

Which is to say that Spanfeller, the former print executive from Ziff Davis, had become totally converted to the digital world. "Spanny" *hated* the idea of blending the two sales staffs in any way, fearing it would blunt his staff's innovative, gunslinging mentality. Comingling with the dead-tree types who were frozen in a legacy process would eventually stunt the Web site's growth, he believed. "Whenever you put two things together, one always gets hurt," he would tell anyone who listened. So Spanfeller made it very clear his staff wasn't supposed to be bending over backward to work with the print side, whose attitude in the early days of Forbes.com was, "Hey, get out of here, it's *my* client."

Berrien, a tall, tightly wound man with close-cropped hair and ruddy complexion, was frustrated with Spanfeller's obstructionist tactics and by the fact that Spanny represented what was perceived as the new hot engine of growth—Forbes.com. Once at a touchy-feely *Forbes* meeting for print-side executives run by an outside "moderator," Berrien came close to exploding about the fiction of how print and Web were supposedly working together. "It's a farce," he said.

Examples? The magazine lost a hard-won advertiser who'd been sponsoring a regular section of the book. Why? The digital sales team sold a competitor a similar package on the Web. Knowing it was forbidden to work openly with the dot-com staff, print salesmen worked "under the radar" with their digital counterparts on joint approaches. To nail an important $3-million-a-year Dell account, print salesmen "manufactured" an integrated program that Berrien personally pitched to the client.

Bill Baldwin was furious to learn one day late in the magazine's two-week publishing cycle that a special advertising-supported insert on technology, dreamed up by the Web's marketing staff and poorly executed, in his view, by the Web's edit staff, was to appear in the next issue.

The magazine's sales staff was totally blindsided, as was the editorial department. Only a phone call from the production depart-

ment asking if edit was aware that a "dot-com insert" was coming
alerted the troops at 60 Fifth. It was "editorial" but read like an advertorial, raising no tough questions and appearing to be little more
than unfiltered puffery.

"So," Baldwin said, rising to leave a meeting where the content
of the insert was discussed, "I guess Bruce Rogers [then Forbes.com's
director of marketing] is now editing my magazine." Baldwin stormed
out, leaving the group staring at each other in silence.

Arriving at *Forbes* from American Express in 1999, Berrien moved
quickly to change the demographics of the sales staff, which he felt
was too old and stuck in its ways. Soon to go would be Bill Flatley, a
veteran tough-talking sales manager who immediately clashed with
Berrien and was dispatched to work at Forbes.com. London-based
Peter Schoff, who had been hired by Malcolm and mentored Kip, got
the boot over the phone, and thumbed his nose at Berrien by attending an Old Battersea House function that night, standing in the reception line saying, "Hi, how are you? I just got fired."

Berrien went for younger and cheaper, thinning out several other
male veterans and hiring some very attractive young women, who
had the immediate—and positive—effect of giving the sales staff a
touch of sexy glamour. But few of them knew how to "get to the
client"—as opposed to simply dealing with an agency—or, for that
matter, how to sell into a down market, something everyone would
soon have to deal with.

Berrien rubbed many people the wrong way, with catchy phrases
like "the beatings will stop when morale improves." With a quick
and scary temper, he at times seemed to be a great candidate for
anger management class. But over breakfast at the Yale Club with
Tim Forbes, their first meeting, all was calm. The breakfast lasted
nearly until lunch, and Forbes saw in Berrien a take-charge person
who could bring added luster to the brand, as he had done at American Express, where he was instrumental in starting up *Departures*.
Talks between Berrien and Forbes continued in secret for several
weeks until the announcement was finally made in the summer of
1999. Even Scott Masterson, the company's general manager, whose

consigliere role for Tim Forbes was like Tom Hagen's to Vito Corleone, was kept out of the loop.

Tim Forbes would listen patiently to the whines of the print sales side about the competitive nonsense with Forbes.com, but did nothing. This despite the fact the "entrepreneurial" internal competition was costing the company valuable ad revenues—and more importantly, giving the marketplace the impression that *Forbes* had *no idea* what it was doing. At one point a half dozen different sales people, each from a different print or digital Forbes product, were calling on Toyota and other major clients.

"There was never a joint goal," says a former senior executive. "It was always a tussle for the dollars, who was getting credit for what." Berrien made repeated appeals to Tim Forbes to create a team goal so that everyone was pulling in the same direction, but it fell on deaf ears. The attitude at the top was that competition was good, even if the competition was internal. Though Tim was more practical than Steve, he never came to grips with the fact that the company had squandered untold millions building up two separate, duplicative enterprises—each with its own IT, HR, finance, sales, and edit staffs—under the same corporate umbrella. "Tim acted as if he were 75 percent owner and 25 percent manager," says one top executive. "Of course, it should have been exactly the other way around." Elevation viewed Steve as a totally nonstrategic owner. A source close to Elevation quotes one of the principals as saying, "Steve says stuff I cannot fucking believe."

The silo mentality is not new to *Forbes*. Compartmentalization, in fact, has long been a core tenet in the family, one that Malcolm famously embraced, keeping corporate information in separate drawers so nobody could really connect all the dots and figure out what the real numbers were. That notion carried on to his sons. Not until Elevation insisted, for example, was there *ever* a senior management meeting between the print and Web units to talk about common goals.

Not only did the separate silos send the wrong signal to advertisers, but they also demoralized employees, who increasingly saw themselves being pulled in different directions without being given a compelling mission from the top for working together. *Forbes* and Forbes.com had different logos and ad campaigns. There was no single, overarching "brand" message. Forbes.com sales staffers rarely if ever took copies of the magazine along on calls. Before one of the first sales meetings attended by personnel from both units, a magazine sales executive approached Spanfeller about a presentation he was about to give. "What do you think your people want to know about the magazine?" he asked. The reply: "Nothing!" The general message from the digital side to print: "You're not important to us and we're not going to help you."

The silo mentality presided in other departments as well, particularly IT. While the magazine leased all its Apple computers and got standardized system-wide upgrades on a regular basis, the Forbes.com technology acquisition strategy seemed to be an open bazaar. Most of its PC terminals came through barter deals or appeared to have fallen off a truck somewhere near Secaucus, New Jersey. They all could have included instruction manuals with only two words: "Good luck!" The operating system seemed to be patched together with chewing gum and duct tape. Everyone at Forbes.com appeared to have pirated software, something that was strictly against corporate policy.

"Upgrades" were done on an as-needed basis one machine at a time, layering fix upon fix, resulting in a hodgepodge collection of equipment of varying ages that slowed down the posting of Web stories and drove staffers nuts, one time resulting in a complete meltdown of the Forbes.com server. "Don't you ever upgrade your hardware?" one corporate IT staffer asked. "No, we run it until it dies," was the response. The Forbes.com Web site was "hosted" from a cage in a server room obviously run by Gene Wilder, wearing a mad scientist's lab coat and hopelessly tangling a maze of cables and wires across a floor littered with discarded servers.

Forbes.com spent millions on developers and consultants, most of whom were hired to develop ground-up systems from scratch rather than upgrading the existing infrastructure or advising that

Forbes.com buy off-the-shelf products that would get automatic up-grades and service. "At times you wondered whether Forbes.com was a software development firm or a media company," says one IT staffer, who adds, "None of our people are good enough to work for Google. That's why they're working for us."

Subtle and not-so-subtle efforts to undermine each other's tech efforts were common. Learning that I planned to attend a conference in Amsterdam for publishers interested in software that would help them merge print and Web, Spanfeller picked up the phone and tried to stop me from going, even though he had no authority to do so. "I can save you a trip. Nobody has what you're looking for." "Oh really," I said. "So then why is Rupert Murdoch spending millions to install an [Italian-designed] system at the *Journal* that will allow reporters to file stories to either the Web site or the paper just by clicking on the proper [screen] icon?" "It won't do what you think," assured Spanfeller, who then conceded he actually hadn't heard of Eidos, the Italian company that had just signed the deal with the *Journal* and would later do the same with *The Washington Post*. "Oh, and besides," he said, "we're going to build our own system."

To nobody's surprise, Thelma and Louise have both departed. Kevin Gentzel, an ambitious young salesman nurtured by Berrien, is now *Forbes*'s "chief revenue officer," in charge of the finally inte-grated sales effort. Gentzel leveraged a job offer from Time Inc. that would have made him publisher of its business magazine group to win his current position, in the process maneuvering his longtime friend Avery Stirratt, the widely admired head of print and digital sales, out of the company. Gentzel had been running the CMO Prac-tice, referred to in-house as the "Steve Forbes Babysitting Service," which meant ushering the editor-in-chief around to meet chief mar-keting officers to influence advertising and get those executives to participate on the Web site's CMO network.

Officials say Tim rarely gave his top managers useful feedback, by saying they needed to focus more on this or less on that, why he didn't agree with a particular decision, or that the person was spend-ing too much money. "They just decided," says one former executive who felt he was sandbagged. "Black smoke would come out, and you'd be gone."

In Berrien's case, Tim walked into his office just before a *High-lander* ride to celebrate Moira's engagement (a cruise that featured an expensive fireworks display near the Statue of Liberty), and said, "We're making a change. . . ." Forbes wanted Berrien to move to a nonoperational role and focus on key large-client relationships as chairman. Berrien wanted no part of that and quit. Spanfeller, who to the end resisted integration, also left, but insists it was on his timetable. "He had to go," says a source close to an Elevation principal. "He wasn't willing to make that leap."

With their departures, in a classic "all fingers in the light socket" move, *Forbes* reorganized the sales and marketing groups, giving the title of president to *four* different people, with similar-sounding responsibilities and a reporting structure that looked like a kid had drawn a series of overlapping Xs, dotted lines, and equal signs on an iPad.

The resulting internal announcement was a mix of corporate speak and impenetrable job descriptions. One senior executive only half-jokingly offered a reward to any employee who could figure out what was really going on. Sales and marketing staffers quickly declared the acronym for the "office of the presidents" to be "OOPS." Not long after the OOPS implementation, the business masthead disappeared from the magazine. "No way to put it in writing without looking absolutely ridiculous," recalls one executive.

The restructure was intended to be the long-awaited and yearned-for "unsiloing" of digital and print sales. But instead of two silos, there were now *four.* "It was a disaster," says a former department head. "Endless time was spent in meetings trying to sort out the stepping on toes, duplicating effort, stuff that was falling through the cracks, and the problems of inevitable territory grabs as the presidents competed with each other."

But nowhere was the silo mentality more deeply entrenched than in editorial. Each magazine piece, from six-page covers down to a two-paragraph investment brief, was meticulously fact-checked, a procedure that involved a reporter verifying every word, number, and name in a staff writer's copy. "If you miss an error the writer will be okay," Jim Michaels would tell fact-checkers, "but *you'll* be gone."

No such scrutiny challenged a Forbes.com writer. Everything on the Web was about speed, volume, and "hits"—how many people clicked on a particular story. Higher traffic meant more revenues. To generate hits, writers were encouraged to put lots of "tickers" of prominent in-the-news companies in their stories. For instance, even if Microsoft weren't a major (or even a minor) player in a particular story, inserting its name, albeit in a contrived way, was supposed to help give the piece more traction.

Pressed to file four or five stories a day, to give context and added value to the breaking "commodity" news the wire services reported, Forbes.com writers were in constant hook-and-hurl mode. Finish one story, go onto the next, do it all over tomorrow. If there were errors of fact, they could be corrected online, and virtually nobody would notice. Spanfeller would proudly say that "his" edit staff churned out about one hundred stories a day, more than twice the number of stories the magazine staff did every two weeks.

Two different worlds, joined by a common name but about as far apart theologically as you could be. Which is one reason Tim Forbes had wanted the Web operation to be separate, given a chance to grow up on its own without being stepped on or restricted by its older sibling.

But the dot-com bust, along with the vaporization of the Forbes .com public offering, enabled the split mentality to be perpetuated, as edit staffers started using their share-appreciation-rights award letters as wallpaper and holed up in their separate camps. The Web staff, then at Twenty-third Street, remained ten blocks away from the magazine.

The two staffs built up walls and stereotypes between each other: print writers were seen as overpaid and lazy, writing maybe two stories a month, taking long lunches at the nearby Gotham Bar and Grill, and living it up on expense accounts that dwarfed those of dot-comers who rarely got a chance to travel anywhere. Web writers were dismissed as giggly twenty-three-year-olds in high heels and skirts who churned out silly lists and other fluff not worthy of the *Forbes* brand: The infamous "Top Ten Topless Beaches" list was the most frequently cited example.

Magazine writers resisted requests to do Web stories, which they considered insignificant. More importantly, no magazine writer believed Baldwin when he said Web stories counted in the complicated system he used to calculate annual productivity for each writer. Baldwin himself frequently made fun of Web stories in staff meetings and once told the Silicon Valley bureau he didn't want anyone spending "more than a day a month" on Forbes.com work. When magazine writers did pitch ideas to the Web, their phone calls or e-mails were often ignored.

Though giving lip service to the magazine as the "core" of the company, Forbes.com executives privately dismissed the print part of the company as irrelevant, since magazine stories generated no revenue for the site. It was a message embraced and repeated within Forbes.com, one that traveled quickly and frequently to 60 Fifth Avenue.

Web editors resisted attempts by magazine editors to recruit their best writers to do print stories. Why? Because those writers produced stories that generated lots of traffic, and Web editors got an incentive payment if they exceeded their monthly traffic goals. In other words, *no, you can't have him (or her) because that'll hurt my bottom line.*

There were different policies, standards, and procedures on just about everything. The magazine paid its summer interns up to twenty dollars an hour. Forbes.com proudly paid nothing, despite the fact it's against federal labor laws to not pay someone who brings "value" to a company. Forbes.com even tried to hire an out-of-work *lawyer* one summer as an unpaid attorney intern. Anyone who resigned from the Web site was escorted out the door immediately. At 60 Fifth, there was no set policy, and in the post-Michaels days, even someone who left for a competitor might be allowed to stay on for a brief time.

The magazine staff got a hot meal catered every other Friday night from the *Forbes* town house for people working late on the close. At Forbes.com they were lucky to get pizza, though the editors made a point of holding cupcake parties for staffers' birthdays. Vouchers for travel home by Elite Limousine's black town cars weren't available to Web edit staffers. Reinforcing the upstairs-downstairs divide was the rumor circulating on Inauguration Day '09 that the magazine staff was being treated to a catered hot lunch, with wine, in the boardroom to watch Obama's swearing in. The fact was a small group of writers gathered spontaneously in the conference room next to Baldwin's office that morning to watch the festivities. Someone brought bagels. Somebody else went out to get two bottles of cheap champagne to make mimosas. But what actually happened didn't matter. The silo stereotypes persisted.

Meanwhile, the money continued to drain away. For years, operating income had funded Bob and Kip's expensive habits, and the family, in general, had borrowed heavily to sustain its lifestyle. "They were very heavily leveraged," says a source close to Elevation. All that spending plus the duplicative, profligate funding of Forbes.com—separate building, staffs, technology, and support departments—helped force the asset sales and the search for more capital.

McNamee left the board in 2009, after butting heads with Tim Forbes as to how aggressive the company should be. In the view of those in a position to know, McNamee felt Tim wasn't moving fast enough integrating the company and bringing it fully into the digital age. Elevation in fact found it totally frustrating not to have more control over strategy. The brothers regularly dismissed their ideas, with the attitude that Elevation didn't have the voting authority to impose them. *We don't have to do that.*

Elevation filled the opening on the *Forbes* board with Bret Pearlman, a numbers guy who has pushed to reduce costs. But some of the moves have seemed counterproductive, sort of like a school trying to save money by teaching kids only the letters *A* through *K*.

In the summer of 2009, the bean counters decreed it was too expensive to run air-conditioning on the news floors after 6:00 P.M.

The shutdown had the effect of slowly microwaving the staff that had to work late, often past midnight, to put the magazine to bed. Employees now wait for the next inevitable next round of cuts (there have been five since October 2001). D'Vorkin may also turn the jobs of some full-time support employees—designers, photo editors, copy editors, and production staffers—into part-time positions, since writers are now going to be expected, among other things, to start doing their own photo research. And a search for a new editor (from the outside) has begun.

Meanwhile, to fend off gloom and dismay, CEO Mike Perlis has circulated a peppy memo listing eleven "core values," which all employees should presumably memorize and embrace. To the editorial staff, the hands-down favorite was #11: "Forbes is fun." Now that's breaking news.

31

"KNOW YOUR AUDIENCE!"

"FOR GOD'S SAKE, BILL, know your audience!" Roger McNamee bellowed. "*Bloomberg* is a news service for traders!" McNamee's outburst, directed at *Forbes* editor Bill Baldwin, would have been routine in the rough-and-tumble boardrooms of Silicon Valley. But it stunned the polite, genteel group of senior editors Tim Forbes had invited to a fancy dinner in the Forbes Galleries on April 28, 2008, to meet with some of Elevation's partners. Open confrontation is not part of the *Forbes* culture.

McNamee was lashing out at Baldwin's admission that he'd killed a story on an esoteric investment vehicle because a similar piece had appeared on *Bloomberg*. Taken alone, the incident would have been unremarkable, but along with other probing questions McNamee asked during the dinner—and a later incident where McNamee was overheard yelling at Baldwin in his office—it was clear that the 40 percent owner was getting increasingly impatient not only with Baldwin's narrow view of the *Forbes* mission but also with the company's lack of progress toward integrating the print and Web operations, a step McNamee felt essential to leveraging the brand effectively. McNamee went on to tell the diners that the current "deleveraging" economic environment the country faced was a "unique moment in time" that called for *Forbes* to "get in front of that for our readers to meet their almost desperate need for the right insights."

As the meeting broke up, Tim Forbes approached me and asked if I could blueprint an argument for merging the two "silos," along with some competitive context on how other media companies were dealing with the same challenge. The report, he added, should go directly to him. Not through Baldwin.

I delivered the twenty-eight-page document entitled "Steps Going Forward" to Forbes on June 4, 2008. Quoting *Bloomberg* editor-in-chief Matt Winkler, "If you stop growing, you die," the report urged that *Forbes* take "bold steps and not fret about possible failure."

The report cited the integration progress, or lack thereof, at several media companies, including the *Times*, the *Journal*, *The Daily Telegraph* in London, *BusinessWeek*, *Newsweek*, and International Data Group, which publishes *PCWorld* and *Macworld*, among many other magazines. IDG had successfully moved several of its publications to online only and has virtually eliminated the barriers between Web and print.

How important is it to integrate? When former *Journal* reporter and editor Robert Merry arrived at *Congressional Quarterly* in 1997 as chief executive, he found an incredible waste of resources. CQ had 150 reporters, editors, and researchers covering the Hill, more than any other news organizations. It had a weekly news magazine, a daily forty-page newsletter, and a password-protected paid Web site, cq.com, each with its own "silo." Reporters from each platform would often show up at the same Senate hearing, stumbling all over each other, not always getting along, creating resentment and rivalries.

Merry moved quickly to tear down the silos and create a single pool of reporters feeding all platforms, with a single editor in charge of everything. "It's the only way you're going to get real coordination," Merry said. "If you report up to separate silos, you're not going to get it."

Like *Forbes*, the *Times* used to have its Web and print staffs in different buildings. But with its move to its new building on Eighth Avenue, reporters from the "continuous news desk" work right in the main newsroom alongside metro, national, business, and sports reporters. And at least one CND reporter is "embedded" in each department, doing spot coverage, updating it during the day, and often doing the story for that night's paper as well.

It's what *Times* executive editor Bill Keller calls a "platform agnostic" newsroom. It's not so much about mechanics, Keller says, it's about philosophy and attitude. "If you're the foreign editor, it's about thinking of the foreign report on the Web as your domain along with the paper . . . It's about taking responsibility and having it in your brain."

"Steps Going Forward" correctly assumed *Forbes* wasn't about to order up big changes immediately. But it proposed several interim steps, including acceleration of a "prisoner exchange" program whereby at least one reporter from each platform was always working at the other, pairing print and Web beat reporters on specific coverage areas (finance, energy, etc.) together to work on breaking stories, and putting both staffs in the same building.

The report didn't address in any detail the rising importance of social media as a marketing and communications tool for publishers. That to me seemed very much a "Phase Two" issue. But I did underscore the urgency for the mindset change that print veterans would have to quickly embrace. What *Forbes* and others were facing was the rapid unbundling of a highly vertical business. The old-model distribution networks had suddenly become irrelevant since the Internet had made distribution available to anyone. Just as the telecom industry was unbundled as a result of the AT&T breakup decades ago, so was media now facing new challenges—and opportunities.

I believed our new competition was going to be just as much Google, Yahoo!, and even Twitter and Facebook, rather than the *Journal* or *Fortune*. "You have to kind of let go of what journalism was, at least intellectually, and almost zero-base it," says Jay Rosen, an associate professor of journalism at New York University. "Managers have to create a culture of experimentation in organizations that haven't had that, and have to become entrepreneurial when this is something they haven't needed before."

Rosen cites an example of how sclerotic old-school print thinking at *The Washington Post* led to an embarrassing error in the paper. Seems that a bunch of kids organized a snowball fight on a street corner via Twitter. An off-duty cop happened to be driving by, and his car got hit by a snowball. The cop got out and brandished his pistol—an event captured by any number of the snow throwers' cell phone cameras.

When the *Post* did a brief story for the next day's paper, a reporter called the police department's public information office for comment and clarification. The flack solemnly said there was no gun, the cop didn't wave it. That the reporter would believe such an "authoritative" figure rather than people on the scene who'd captured the incident on camera shows just how much of a gap remains to be closed. "This can only happen in a culture that hasn't adapted to the Web," says Rosen, "and it's like this mistake means *The Washington Post* has no credibility at all."

Fair enough, but there's an important distinction between one hundred people using their cell phones to record an event and real journalism, calcified as some of its traditions and procedures may be. What's missing from raw footage streamed to the Web is an authoritative voice, the result of years of source cultivation, the building up of levels of trust that allow a reporter to put something in context. It's something that only established news outlets such as the *Times, Washington Post,* CNN, NBC, or CBS News, and, increasingly, the *Journal,* can do: flood the zone with reporters on a major story and report not just there was a massacre of Congolese Tutsi in Burundi or a student riot in Paris, but also knowledgeably examine the economic and political reasons behind it. Most people need an expert to filter, prioritize, and context information. A fire hose of information without that is useless.

Yet now anyone can call himself a journalist.

"Hey, I can do that."

No, you can't.

32

SELMA WITHOUT HOSES

W E'RE FACING A SHITSTORM in our market." With such un-*Forbes*ian language, Tim Forbes scared his top editors on Halloween 2008. "We're not even staring down a black hole," he added. *"Everything is black."* Forbes had summoned the group to the second-floor boardroom to put in motion the most drastic changes to date at *Forbes*, though the editors didn't know it when they walked in.

At the head of the table, beneath a giant LG flat-screen TV in a space where a glum-faced portrait of Steve used to hang, sat Tim Forbes, in suit and tie. To his left, wearing ties but no jackets, was the magazine's leadership, including me, Baldwin, and Tom Post (code name: Compost), the other managing editor, a former English professor who learned the rigors of working for idiosyncratic bosses by being a writer for Peter Jennings at ABC. He wore a mustache and eye glasses that made him look vaguely like a shorter version of Groucho Marx, which suited his reputation as an incurable punster. Postman distinguished himself sartorially by often wearing vests and a fancy, large-linked pocket-watch chain, which dangled out of his right trouser pocket and connected to a belt loop.

To Forbes's right was the suit-and-tied FDC crew: editor Paul

Maidment, a witty, affable Brit with bushy eyebrows and a some-times unfathomable accent. Originally interviewed by Baldwin for a job as a financial editor at the magazine, Maidment's impressive mix of Web and print work at the *Financial Times* made him a per-fect candidate to run Forbes.com edit operations following David Churbuck's departure.

Sitting to Maidment's left was his deputy, Carl Lavin (code name: Honk), a man with curly black hair who liked to speak in jargon, using words like "data points" and "metrics" when "numbers" would do. From *The Philadelphia Inquirer*, and before that, the *Times*, Lavin had the amusing habit (widely imitated by others) of raising his voice at the end of a sentence for emphasis: "I'll get back to you ON THAT!" The boss began with a brief history of Forbes.com, a summary that made Maidment and Lavin increasingly fidgety, as if they were about to hear something really bad (like the closing of Forbes.com). Forbes then got to the point: He wanted a complete integration of Web and print, first sales, then edit. Fast.

All the reasons he'd been citing for keeping the two operations separate—as recently as only six months ago—were out the door. It was an astonishing about-face, and given the 180-degree pirouette, Elevation's fingerprints seemed to be all over the thumbscrews. But it didn't matter who finally pushed the button. In crisis mode, Forbes now wanted a game plan in place before Thanksgiving, less than a month away.

"There will be issues, some you will anticipate, others that you won't," he said. "Identify them, wrestle with them, work them out, and tell me how you're going to do it." He wanted another meeting quickly. Baldwin suggested two weeks. Forbes snapped back: "One week!" "No sacred cows," he added. "Start from scratch. How would you build something from the ground up?"

Then, if possible, Forbes turned even more serious. "Priority num-ber one," he said, peering over the top of his glasses. "*Do it without harming the magazine or the Web. Don't screw this up, okay?*"

Doing the job properly I knew would take lots of thought, con-sultation, and sign-off from various constituencies to make it work.

Even with a general blueprint in hand, having only a few weeks to come up with a complete tactical plan seemed ridiculous to me. But as a senior executive told me, "Remember, this isn't a company, it's *Forbes*." Right.

The sea change that had been rumored for months was finally coming. But upstairs in his office after the meeting, Baldwin didn't seem to get it. "Well, this sounds evolutionary to me," he told me and Post. Whoa! Had Unabomber been to a different meeting? "Bill, I think Tim has something more drastic in mind, like having one staff, everyone doing everything, cross-platform content, all that stuff," I said. "We're going to have to cut people. This is huge."

"We'll see," said Baldwin, in body language suggesting he didn't believe that his life and everyone else's were about to change in ways that nobody even then imagined.

As an editorial "transition team" worked to meet the Thanksgiving deadline, Baldwin, at least for a time, remained in arms-folded mode, allowing Maidment to fill the leadership vacuum and start setting the agenda.

That Maidment was the one who called the first transition meeting, in an offsite conference room at the nearby W Hotel, was a sign that the integration was beginning to look like a hostile takeover by the digital troops, reinforced by years of mutual resentment and political nonsense.

Patrick Lencioni's *The Five Dysfunctions of a Team* reads like a working script for the *Forbes* transition group—"lack of trust; fear of conflict (resulting in veiled discussions and guarded comments); lack of commitment (even though agreement may be feigned during meetings); avoidance of accountability (failing to call peers on actions and behaviors); and inattention to results (where egos and career development get in the way of the team's collective goals)."

While there was general agreement that the merged staff would be responsible for providing content to both print and digital, planning broke down when faced with the structure already in place on the Web where coverage teams were already focused on certain key areas—technology, lifestyle, entrepreneurs, etc. Each of those teams had a "channel editor" responsible not only for the coverage topic but also for meeting monthly traffic goals. So it soon became clear that in most cases, magazine writers would simply be absorbed into existing Web teams with demanding new requirements for daily production.

So who would supply copy for magazine covers and other important departments? Worried the flow of print stories would suffer, print editors schemed to create a separate team made up of the magazine's most talented writers to focus on magazine stories. The team would carry the unwieldy title of "Corporate Intelligence," and report directly to Baldwin. The group would be headed by Larry Reibstein, the well-liked and extremely competent editor of Outfront, a leadoff department filled with newsy material written in a snappy and sometimes irreverent style. With Baldwin's approval, we then made the changes to the org chart without consulting the digital side.

But Maidment and Lavin immediately saw through the ruse. "What's Corporate Intelligence?" they both asked, nearly in unison, when seeing the new plan. Logically arguing that a group set aside to focus on the magazine would run counter to the whole integration theology, they insisted some of those writers report instead to Dan Bigman, a widely admired editor recruited from the *Times* who had great breaking news instincts and supervised the Web site's corporate, Wall Street, and Washington coverage. We caved, but a line had been drawn.

Further underscoring the "hostile takeover" scenario: The decision by Tim Forbes to put the combined editorial staff in the much cheesier Forbes.com quarters at 90 Fifth Avenue, a block and a half up the street, instead of the iconic headquarters building where the magazine staff had been for decades. The combined sales staffs would be at 60 Fifth, along with the support departments. There was room at 60 for a downsized print/Web editorial staff—if the combined sales staff was at 90—but the main argument presented was that it would be too costly to move the television studio to 60 Fifth, since Forbes wanted the video crew to be easily accessible to the whole staff. (Never mind that less than a year later, Tim Forbes decided to move everyone back to 60 Fifth, including the TV studio.)

Putting his thumb on a scale clearly now tipping in favor of digital, Lavin convinced Baldwin that he, Lavin, should be the one to approve the expense accounts of the combined staff and be the one to decide where everyone would sit—two key functions that fed Lavin's growing ambitions of "managing across the newsroom." Baldwin, clearly taken to the woodshed by Tim Forbes for dragging his feet on the integration, suddenly became a convert, at least on the surface.

Individually, these minor issues didn't amount to much. But taken together, they reinforced magazine writers' fears that *they* were the ones now being treated as second-class citizens, and that, in the new world order, print wouldn't be all that important. An impression that turned out to be correct.

What Tim Forbes was really looking for, of course, were big cost savings. He got it. The plan called for initially cutting seventeen people in early January 2009, followed by another round of eleven, for a total savings of $2.4 million, or 8 percent of the $30 million in the combined print and Web budgets. The cuts were heavily skewed toward magazine writers, not Forbes.com staffers.

Under the "no sacred cows" rubric, two departments previously thought to be untouchable were to be eliminated or drastically cut back: the two-thousand-square foot analogue library packed with books and periodicals few people even looked at anymore was to be closed, the books given away to other libraries or booksellers. The fact-checking pool would be dropped to four from seventeen and merged into a new News Operations unit that would report stories, handle research queries, and do limited fact-checking on random pieces. On one level, the idea of eliminating fact-checking for all but the most important of stories made sense: Make writers accountable for their own work and ask those who consistently turned in sloppy copy to leave—basic Journalism 101 in place for years at the *Times* and the *Journal*. But it would also eliminate a *Forbes* trademark—an intensive, integrated training program for new hires and a cheap libel insurance policy.

The new organization chart was edit's own version of OOPS. There was a Politburo at the top made up of Baldwin, Maidment, and *five* managing editors, the latter instantly creating a new acronym, OMES, sort of a meditation-sounding mantra for the "Office of Managing Editors." The concept of having two coeditors at the top with equal rank—Baldwin for print, Maidment for digital—simply reinforced the old structure, particularly to the outside world.

"So who's really in charge?" would be the most frequently asked question by puzzled media reporters who called the *Forbes* communications office. It was another sign of management hesitation: lots of hand-wringing, no decision. Tim Forbes simply wasn't ready to suck it up and appoint someone to run the whole show. Said one senior executive at the time: "His name is on the building, he should just do it." Which meant that the "new" *Forbes* would at first seem much like the old *Forbes.* Two "equal" voices at the top really meant no voice. United in theory, the staff would still be emotionally divided—a reality that'd be played out in the months ahead, until the numbers started to look really bad again.

With the plan in place, complete but for a few minor tweaks, we all agreed we wanted to proceed immediately. But Tim Forbes put it off until after New Year's, arguing that layoffs just before Christmas wouldn't go down too well. Moreover, Steve had gone on record earlier in the year with a staff note saying there'd be no more layoffs in 2008.

But everyone knew the hurricane was coming. Gallows humor prevailed at the decidedly unfestive editorial holiday party in the Galleries that year. Sample: "How many Forbes brothers does it take to ruin a company? Four."

Most revelers were decked out in palpable tension and fear. Louisa Kroll, a valued senior editor in charge of the billionaires issue, seemed particularly on edge. Approaching me while I was in the middle of a conversation with other writers, Kroll stepped into the group and said,

"So why don't you just announce it? We know you're done with the planning."

"Actually we're not," I lied, trying to deflect the issue.

"Yes you are!"

"Excuse me, I think I need a refill."

Nobody really had a stress-free Christmas break, fretting their new 2009 desk calendars might not have any months beyond January. Sure enough, staffers arrived back after the holidays to find a category-five storm hitting shore in full fury, upending desks and blowing their occupants several zip codes away. Three big rounds of layoffs, in January, March, and October 2009, followed. I "retired" in May.

33

THE PRINCE OF DARKNESS
(PART II)

Those most sure they have it, most usually haven't.

—Malcolm Forbes

W ITH GREAT APPREHENSION, EDIT staffers filed into the fifth-floor newsroom at 90 Fifth Avenue On January 20, 2010, to hear Tim Forbes talk about "editorial direction" going forward. Bureaus outside New York—or anyone who had access to the special 800 number—could dial in to listen.

What they heard was not reassuring.

Citing the chaotic media environment, Forbes described the "enormous implications" of how plummeting CPM Web costs and "automated" media buying were driving revenues out of television and print onto Web sites, and how the *Forbes* sales staff had to "get a place at the table" by selling large cross-platform packages.

Then on to how editorial was going to change. The answer: Audience fragmentation required incorporating the tools of social media (Twitter, Facebook, etc.) to help drive traffic, plus a substantial increase in outside contributors, most of whom would be paid very little or nothing.

"People are eager to be affiliated with and be published on *Forbes*," Forbes said. "There are legitimate questions on how we maintain voice and quality, but if we select [the outsiders] wisely, we address much of that. The risks are manageable," he added.

"The right contributors," he said, "bring not only their content but [also] their own audience." Aha. More traffic. More revenue. "Audience fragmentation is not necessarily our enemy," Forbes said. "We can use it to our advantage. This does not mean we'll abandon our unique coverage: entrepreneurs, the rich list, mutual funds. We will continue to produce the very essence of *Forbes*. But it's also desirable and possible to publish popular content with mass appeal."

The slippery slope: a tilt toward the sensationalist might goose traffic, but also potentially might fuzz the brand's focus with a cacophony of amateur bloggers keystroking in their pajamas.

Forbes then addressed an issue that bothered many writers: The heavy new emphasis on "slide shows," the Web-based minigalleries of ten captioned photographs, attached to a very short story. The "slides" are used to illustrate traditional business topics like "10 Job Hunting Tips from People Who Actually Found Jobs" and "TV's 10 Biggest Flops," but increasingly, broader, very un-*Forbes*ian things like "What Stars Are Wearing Lucky Jeans?" and "10 Healthy Snacks."

Page views still matter, Forbes explained. Slide shows, particularly in a newly installed more viewer-friendly format, hold value from an advertising perspective. "We want to become a larger more intelligent destination for the worlds of business and upscale lifestyle content," he added. "Size does matter in a world of fragmentation." Forbes might have added that slide shows leverage hits in another way: embedded software makes them "automated," so once a viewer clicks on the first slide, the rest will automatically appear, each new slide counting as an additional click. And if the viewer leaves his computer to get a sandwich, when he returns, the system will be merrily clicking through every other Forbes.com slide show, running up the hits.

Lewis D'Vorkin had been whispering for months in Tim Forbes's ear about the low-cost-content business model he devised at True/ Slant, an aggregator of freelance bloggers he founded in 2009. Forbes was intrigued enough to make an investment in the company, whose financial results could be characterized as those of a "start-down." True/Slant billed itself as "News Is More Than What Happens," with posts such as "Can Sex with Channing Tatum Make Winona Ryder Hot Again?" and "Undercover Taxidermist Busts Illegal Hunters in Missouri." One article began: "Once on a flight I ate a cheeseburger-in-a-bag. It was a wonderfully microwaved beefy dough ball of cheesy-type goo. It tasted amazing!" Do we really want to read on? Will this be the new "feel" of *Forbes?*

Could be. D'Vorkin's initial role at *Forbes* was described as that of a "consultant," but anyone who could breathe and count backward from ten could see where this was heading. Not long afterward, in late May, *Forbes* announced it was buying the rest of True/Slant and bringing D'Vorkin on board as "chief product officer," to be in charge of all editorial. Baldwin and Maidment would now report to him.

Wearing an untucked shirt, jeans, designer sneakers, and an expensive watch, D'Vorkin told a group of senior editors in the boardroom on May 25, 2010, "within eighteen months this will be a rearchitected entity. Everyone has to collaborate." To another group he said, "If this goes down, we all go down together."

The "rearchitecting" process began almost immediately. At the end of one meeting, D'Vorkin said he wanted some editors to stay, pointing around the room saying, "You, you, you, you, and you." Baldwin, whose comments were dismissed as "That's not where we're going," wasn't one of those pointed to. Maidment, who clearly wasn't buying into the new plan, resigned in June; in July, Baldwin was removed as editor and given an office on the eighth floor, far removed from the newsroom. At his farewell party, Baldwin said when he became editor in 1999, he told his wife, Cathy, "I'll be back to writing soon." It took a while, but now he's back to doing just that.

34

DEATH BY A THOUSAND HACKS

When the joy of the job's gone, when it's no fun trying anymore,
quit before you're bounced.

—Malcolm Forbes

D'VORKIN'S GOAL IS A blend of full-time staffers and "hundreds and hundreds, if not thousands," of freelance contributors, many of whom won't be paid. Which prompted what surely was Carl Lavin's defining legacy at *Forbes*. Presumably trying to wow D'Vorkin with his knowledge of history, Lavin proclaimed in a meeting: "Well, Thomas Jefferson didn't get paid for writing the Declaration of Independence!" To the relief of many, Lavin soon departed, but not before sending out one last odd e-mail with links to Web stories he really liked. Consensus reaction: "Oh, just shut up and leave."

Forbes editors were now to be "curators of talent and marketers of stories," D'Vorkin announced, saying nothing about the traditional editor's role of drawing out the best ideas from writers, then working collaboratively to craft high-quality pieces of journalism. "Speed," he's said, "is the new accuracy." With our new kind of journalism, he said, "there's no beginning, middle or end. It's a conversation. It's all organic. The audience is your editor and should guide your reporting. Find out what they want to know." As if to underscore that he's in charge of products not people, when executive editor Melanie

Wells, the longtime head of marketing coverage, walked in to tell D'Vorkin she was leaving for another job, his response was, "What exactly do you do?" Under the new system, Wells didn't report to anyone in particular, and thus didn't know whom she was supposed to tell she was quitting.

The message conveyed over and over again: Journalism as *Forbes* used to practice it—hierarchical, elitist, and top-down—is no longer important. Moreover, *Forbes* in print has a "negative feel" to it. "We need to be less contrarian," D'Vorkin says. In other words, be more like everyone else.

Early in 2010, Bruce Upbin, a managing editor and one of the sharper knives still left in the drawer at 60 Fifth, derided True/Slant as "crap" in an edit meeting. More recently, however, Upbin has recanted, and has made it clear he's now giving three-star reviews to the Kool Aid D'Vorkin has been serving up: an arrogant bouquet, perhaps, but a nice finish. Upbin has encouraged writers to peg *Forbes* stories to the top ten most searched topics on Twitter and Google. "Go to google.com/trends and find out what people are searching for, then write off that. Find associations to break stories, even if they don't exist."

That seems like the strategy of "content farms," which the *Times* recently characterized as outfits that turn out "sometimes mindless articles based on what people are searching for." Demand Media, for example, uses software to track Google searches, generates headlines based on those searches, "and pays small amounts to freelancers to write the articles," the *Times* wrote. Sound familiar?

In a similar vein, in the summer of 2010, Lavin sent out an e-mail listing the hot Google searches of the day and asking staffers to exploit that. Reflecting the skeptical, fatigued view of most writers, Mike Ozanian stepped up to the plate and hit a "reply all" line drive right back to Lavin, saying, "What does this mean? Am I supposed to stop everything else I'm doing and chase Lindsay Lohan?" Giving Ozanian the digital equivalent of a standing ovation, staffers sent e-mails high-fiving him for the skewering. Lavin then sent an unsatisfactory response, prompting Ozanian to ask again, "But what does this mean?" No reply this time.

Some respected writers (not at *Forbes*) have seen content explosion as further evidence of the dumbing-down of culture. One example: This "enormous multiplication . . . is one of the greatest evils of this age; since it presents one of the most serious obstacles to the acquisition of correct information by throwing in the readers' way piles of lumber in which he must painfully grope for the scraps of useful lumber."

Just another sclerotic print editor lamenting that his role is being "amateurized" out of existence, under the pandering mandate of ever-increasing traffic goals? No, it was Edgar Allan Poe, bemoaning in 1845 of the new proliferation of books, thanks to Mr. Gutenberg's invention. This resulted, writes NYU journalism professor Clay Shirky in *Cognitive Surplus,* in a "massive downshift in average quality," but also prompted experimentation in new forms such as novels, newspapers, and scientific journals.

Coming soon is a "less-layered" structure at the magazine, so more writers can move toward effectively self-publishing their stories. Such disintermediation would be a big change from the Michaels days of at least two editors line-editing or totally rewriting each piece, which was then fact-checked and subjected to queries by the copy desk, and at one time, by a separate proofreading staff. Which D'Vorkin once dubbed the "Star Wars Bar" because of its odd-looking characters, including a dead ringer for Jabba the Hutt and a man who wore a fur hat with ear flaps all year long.

D'Vorkin has brought several people over from True/Slant (now shut down) as well as some AOL staffers. He's hired a Brooklyn-based Web-focused design firm, Athletics, to spiff up the Web site and the magazine, sending shudders through the print art department, which is newly vulnerable: The outside designers show up often to "consult" on the "look" of the magazine and now have a big say in cover presentation, previously the sole domain of veteran art director Robert Mansfield, whose prior unquestioned authority is now being challenged, if not undercut. "It's like being told to make a cake without a recipe," says one art director. "You put something together, and then an outsider says 'no, that's not what we want.'" The classic foreshadowing of more changes on the way.

Noting that nearly 25 percent of the editorial budget goes toward copyediting, art direction, photography, and production—almost certainly a sign those are the next groups to be thinned out—D'Vorkin has imposed a cookie-cutter template design for the magazine. Which means there's less layout work for the art directors. It's now all just paint-by-numbers, rather than an issue-by-issue creative effort. And at least for a time, until staff howls reached high decibel levels, and Steve Forbes himself complained, the consultants embraced photo manipulation in extremis to give the pages what they believed to be a "hot" look. In the fall of 2010, the art department hired Paris-based photographer Benoit Decout to set up a shoot with Bernard Arnault, Europe's richest man and the head of the $24 billion (in sales) conglomerate LVMH, whose storied brands include Dior, Louis Vuitton, Givenchy, Thomas Pink, Dom Perignon, Veuve Clicquot, Guerlain, Château d'Yquem, and TAG Heuer watches.

After the formal cover shoot, Decout convinced the very busy Arnault to stroll several times by a store window filled with Dior fashions. Dressed in a black suit, black tie, white shirt, and black shoes, Arnault looked to be the very model of fashion that he is. The resulting photo was stunning and elegant. But D'Vorkin's consultants believed it was too cluttered, and Photoshopped out the background, making it look as if Arnault were passing in front of a boarded-up storefront. Even worse, his tie and shoes came out in a lurid taupe, a color the stylish Arnault wouldn't be caught dead wearing. The whole effect was cheesy and inappropriate. Needed only was a quote balloon above Arnault's head with the Men's Wearhouse slogan *"You're going to like the way you look, I guarantee it."* E-mailed one appalled *Forbes* subscriber: "The LVMH article photos look cartoonish and make the article look as though it's an infomercial."

Forbes subscribers over the years have read many stories of "disruptive" business transformations. The Internet has already vastly changed the music and movie industries, with consumers now being able to instantly download tunes and films to their laptops. Traditional publishing is now having its turn in the bucket, with Kindles, e-readers, and iPads flooding the market. Bestselling author Seth Godin's new series *Idea Manifestos* is being driven primarily through the Kindle store. "I can reach 10 or 50 times as many people electronically," he told Mediabistro. "No, it's not 'better,' but it's different."

With editors being asked to assemble stables of outside bloggers and contributors, as many as 150 each in some cases, D'Vorkin's projection of "hundreds if not thousands" doesn't seem implausible. One "not better but different" plan is for most bloggers to post their material directly onto the Web site. No editing. When asked by a staffer what this would do to the quality of the *Forbes* Web site, D'Vorkin replied, "I don't understand the question." In an entertainment society that's all about heat and buzz, *Forbes* seems to be embracing what news futurist Ken Doctor has called the "race to mediocrity" and the "good enough" standard many believe is dragging quality down across all media.

Who might some of these "thousands" of new *Forbes* bloggers be? Certainly some credible, established authorities will appear. But there are also a lot of amateurs out there who think they're journalists simply because they have a smartphone and an iPad. Writing recently in the *Columbia Journalism Review,* Nicholas Spangler, a former feature writer for *The Miami Herald,* described some of the "freelancers" he worked with briefly at Demand Media, which, among other things, produces "commercial content" for 350 Web sites, including those of *USA Today* and the *San Francisco Chronicle.* Spangler's colleagues included "mechanics who'd always wanted to do creative writing, laid-off sports editors and one ex-Special Forces soldier/ex-cowboy who likes his new job because he doesn't 'have to get up before daylight to go out in sub-zero weather to break ice to water cows that want to kick my head off. Best of all, I don't have to see people.' "

Already, there's been some trouble. One freelancer who did a couple of tech stories for the Web site threatened a company with a bad story unless it gave her some of its products. And several outside bloggers have taken photos off the Internet for their blogs without getting proper permission from the photographers who own the images—creating a potential copyright nightmare for the *Forbes* legal department.

Forget the issue of editing what outsiders might say—what is their unspoken agenda? Are they pushing a thinly veiled PR pitch? Are they stock touts? What about accuracy? A few months into the new strategy a talented young *Forbes* writer wrote a jargon-filled commentary on a recently filed lawsuit. "Oracle suing Google over its Java-based mobile operating system is like an only child finally adopting his first dog," part of it read. Thanks for the simile. But apart from such muddled prose, some of the story was also quite wrong, judging by the quickly posted comments: "Your comments are misleading," "If you had spent even a little bit of time researching . . . ," and "You may want to check your facts." At the end of the comments, the author wrote: "I don't claim to know everything; thankfully I have smart readers like you guys to keep me honest and factual."

Flawed as the piece appeared to be, D'Vorkin praised it for generating "engagement" with the *Forbes* audience, thereby generating traffic—and for being an example of what he wanted more of. The message to the staff was clear: You don't have to necessarily get your facts right, just generate lots of traffic fast. "It's the sausage factory in real time," D'Vorkin helpfully explains.

When "coeditors" Baldwin and Maidment were running things, they rewarded two writers each month who had exceptional scoops with $1,000, one for print, one for Web. There's no more financial incentive, but Upbin started handing out something called the "engagement ring" to writers who corralled lots of interactive chat, an award met with a resounding thumbs-down by the staff.

In the fall of 2010 some editors were asked to *quadruple* their monthly traffic numbers, mostly through increased quotas for slide shows, prompting dismay and gloom from those editors who have tiny staffs and see no way they can possibly meet these new demands. "This is no longer journalism," says one departed editor. "It's just data pushing."

Revealing were the submitted "battle plans" of the various channel editors explaining how they hoped to meet their ambitious new page view goals for the last quarter of 2010. Typical was the pessimistic outlook of Frederick Allen, who runs the Leadership channel that focuses on career advice and job issues. Allen, an erudite and thoughtful Harvard graduate, was previously managing editor of *American Heritage,* where he used to focus on big ideas and historical insights. These days he's focusing on math: Based on an average of 75,000 page views per slide show, Leadership needed nineteen slide shows in October, twenty-seven in November, and twenty-one in December "to meet our page view goals of 1.41 million, 2.03 million and 1.59 million respectively," he wrote.

Allen conceded meeting those goals would be a "real challenge" with his staff of only one writer, a two-day-a-week intern, and "half" of Helen Coster, who splits her time between Leadership and another group. Allen's full-timer, Susan Adams, is one of the most talented writers on staff, and is pulled in many directions, as the magazine depends on her to contribute smart stories for nearly every issue. Calling for ramming speed, Allen lashed his rowers to produce two more slide shows a week and committed himself to updating six old articles each month that previously got lots of hits, "so that they can be presented as new." Slide shows like "America's Highest-Paying White Collar Jobs." He also pleaded, without success, to get the help of another intern and permission to assign an "experienced outside contributor to write one slide show article a week." But that would cost money.

All staffers have also been encouraged to sign up with something called Foursquare, a location service that would mesh with their Twitter posts. *"Your readers should know where you are!"* said D'Vorkin, in all seriousness.

Seeing where all this was headed, over a dozen magazine staffers have left, replaced by young Web types who have no institutional knowledge of *Forbes*. The exodus is just fine with D'Vorkin, who says the departees "didn't have the right DNA."

To long-time *Forbes* journalists who spent years doing substantive multisource stories, being told to blog in a chatty "cocktail party voice" is inherently offensive. "It's like being the Polish immigrant who used to advise the king," says one veteran writer, "and is now running a candy store in Brooklyn." These staffers feel they're in a sort of purgatory, a transitional period of purifying punishment where the pain comes not from fire but from a dumbed-down world of sound bites, workers being flayed to turn out more hits, demands for tweets, a loud Babel of finger-waving ideologues, and the moans of those ordered to write about Paris Hilton.

With an infusion of eager, young, Web-savvy staffers who, if asked where they were on the day Kennedy was shot, would probably answer, "Ted Kennedy was shot?," there's now more enthusiasm than complaining in the newsroom, helped in part by D'Vorkin's frequent cheerleading staff memos. "The problem with the old Forbes.com," says one staffer, "is that it was an old media company run by old media guys not grounded in new media. The assumption was that just because they were running a Web site, it was going to work."

Elsewhere, some souls are already emerging from purgatory. Having put *The Wall Street Journal* through the journalistic equivalent of a sex change, News Corp.'s Rupert Murdoch has done away with the lengthy Page One leaders that used to be the hallmark of that paper, stories that former managing editor Paul Steiger described as the vital "scoops of ideas" that simply no longer exist.

Some die-hard *Journal* traditionalists may be dismayed at what Rupert has wrought. But while *Journal* stories may be shorter, there are more of them, and it's now a *real daily newspaper*—covering everything from sports to politics, culture, art, music, and natural disasters, along with the *Journal*'s traditional mix of company, market, and investment news. Since taking over, Murdoch has increased the *Journal*'s circulation back over 2 million, relegating *USA Today* to second place at 1.9 million for the first time in many years. The weekday circulation of the *Times*, Murdoch's main target, has fallen to 928,000, the first time since the 1980s that the paper has been under one million.

More significantly, in a move that likely would have been counterintuitive to the Forbes brothers, Murdoch in early 2011 rolled out his new iPad-only newspaper, The Daily, an attempt to return the digital world to a business model where readers pay for news—ninety-nine cents a week. It will eventually have a staff of nearly one hundred. There were mixed reviews after the launch, but if the U.S. media market has learned one thing, it's that Rupert is not a man to bet against.

To the editorial staff, D'Vorkin, who considers himself sort of a transformational "futurist" figure with a revolutionary lexicon to match, has shown a slick deck of slides the advertising crew prepared that outlines the business model and how it will work. The key buzzwords are "engagement" and "conversation." "A good journalist breaks the story," D'Vorkin says. "A *great* journalist turns it into a conversation and continues it."

This appears to be the model of Dan Gillmor, who wrote *We the Media: Grassroots Journalism by the People, for the People.* In that, Gillmor argues that news should be a *conversation among* ordinary citizens rather than some kind of elitist lecture delivered with a wagging finger. "If you want to converse with a journalist," counters Andrew Keen, author of *The Cult of the Amateur,* "invite them to your local bar for a few drinks."

No, the argument is to put journalist, reader, and marketer into a ménage à trois conversation pit, which D'Vorkin describes as a "much more scalable content creation model" where they can duke it out in a digital version of an ultimate fighting cage. Reality TV! Cheaper to produce than a scripted series!

But how much interaction do Web readers really want—and how much of what they read do they actually retain? These days, everyone is interlinked to more people than it's possible to hold in the mind at one time, says William Powers, author of *Hamlet's Black-Berry.* Resulting, he adds, in the panicky feeling of "being plugged into an infinite crowd from which there's no unplugging."

The gold standard for "engagement" so far seems to be The Huffington Post, now a part of AOL, which claims almost 4 million, or 18 percent of its 26 million unique monthly visitors, weigh in with reactions to news stories each month. It's a model that D'Vorkin covets. Said the *Times* of the AOL deal: "One of *The Huffington Post*'s strengths has been creating an online community of readers with tens of millions of people. Their ability to leave comments on Huffington Post news articles and blog posts and to share them on Twitter and Facebook has been a major reason the site attracts so many readers. It is routine for articles to draw thousands of comments each and be cross-linked across multiple social networks."

Anne Nelson, who teaches new media at Columbia University, is skeptical about bullish promises of high levels of conversation from readers of any Web site or blog. "Only about .02-.03 percent of English-language Wikipedia users, for instance, actually wind up actively contributing to the Web site," she says. For viewers of You-Tube, she adds, "Only about 1 percent comment."

As for what and how people read online, Nelson cites the work of Danish Web consultant Jakob Nielsen, who's done studies of eye tracking of Web pages. Unlike print readers, whose eyes tend to zig-zag across the page and scan most of the words, the eyes of people reading on backlit screens move in an *F* pattern: They first look at the top of the content, reading horizontally, usually not all the way across, then scan again lower down the page, but this time not reading as far, followed by a vertical scan to the bottom of the page. The result is what's on the middle and/or the right side of the page typically isn't read at all.

Each year in class, Nelson gives her students two long articles to read, often from *The New Yorker*—one online and one in print. Few students can really sum up what they've read online, if they can finish the piece at all. Those who read the print story did so to the end and had far higher retention of and appreciation for what they'd experienced. It's the difference, Nelson says, "between surfing fifty web sites and retaining very little the next day, and reading *War and Peace* and remembering characters and scenes ten years later."

Which raises the question of Web addiction, what's productive and what isn't. Increasingly, studies at Columbia and elsewhere show that what UCLA psychiatrist Gary Small calls "brain fog," a condition stemming from so much continuous partial attention that nothing is really ever absorbed—it never moves from the in box to the file cabinet—is becoming more prevalent.

Nicholas Carr, author of *The Shallows: What the Internet Is Doing to Our Brains,* writes that constant Web usage seemed to be changing "the very way my brain worked." How? He was having trouble paying attention to one thing for more than a couple of minutes. My brain, he realized, "wasn't just drifting. It was hungry. It was demanding to be fed the way the Net fed it—and the more it was fed, the hungrier it became." The Internet, he sensed, "was turning me into something like a high-speed data-processing machine, a human HAL. I missed my old brain."

Columbia University graduate students asked to keep track of and "evaluate" their Internet usage came up with a startling conclusion: much of what they do on the Web is not productive and the mind-set of having access to a profound amount of information is more important than learning. "Interactions that started as productive ceased being so as I followed trails of information that while interesting, were not what I was actually looking for," wrote one student. Internet addiction, which is now being treated as a clinical disorder in China and Korea, has even spawned a recovery program called reSTART, which includes forty-five days of psychotherapy and group counseling in a warm-and-fuzzy rural Washington State venue.

So far there's no anecdotal evidence of *Forbes* readers having to enroll, but the "conversation and engagement" rollout is still in its early phase. Already, *Forbes* is selling "content space" to advertisers via something called AdVoice. "If an auto manufacturer is in the midst of a new-car launch and has a great story behind the creation of a high-performing engine," says Kevin Gentzel, *Forbes*'s chief revenue officer, "they should be able to tell it and to stream into our tech topic flow, or automotive topic flow."

At first glance these AdVoice pieces seem harmless enough in print, with the paid content in a different typeface from main edit. But unlike a separate advertorial insert, this copy appears directly up against and on the same page as regular *Forbes* editorial, set apart not by a solid column rule but by a dotted line, subtly suggesting the barrier between them is porous and subject to osmosis. Certainly some readers are confused. "The Nov. 22, 2010 issue seems to have content that may in fact be advertising," wrote one subscriber to Steve Forbes. "I can't say I hate your new format, but I can't say I love it either."

The fuzzed line between editorial and marketing showed up in D'Vorkin's A Brief Word column in front of that issue. With a nod to social media, so "many more knowledgeable content creators can provide information and perspective and connect with one another," D'Vorkin did something that no top editor at *Forbes* had ever done before: *welcome* a major advertiser—Cadillac—"as our first AdVoice print partner in our special report on Champions of Free Enterprise." Don't look for a tough piece on GM any time soon.

On the Web site, the ad/edit blurring is more problematic. Though "flagged" with an AdVoice slug, the sponsored blogs have raised howls of concern and derision from not only the public relations community but also the American Society of Magazine Editors. "Advertising supplied content should not look like editorial content," says Sid Holt, ASME chairman. "This is a bedrock principle." On one level, what D'Vorkin is attempting is similar to what the cookie brand Oreo is doing on Facebook—using content produced by ad agency copywriters schooled in the tricks of engagement to communicate with its 15 million friends. There's even a carefully planned editorial calendar, but it's about as far removed from journalism as it could be.

Certainly, a Web site comprised of "thousands" of bloggers will have the effect of democratizing the dissemination of information. Life will appear more egalitarian, with so many voices invited to participate, like 2010's New York gubernatorial debate. It featured a cast of seven, including a hooker and a candidate from The Rent Is Too Damn High party along with the two principals, Republican Carl Paladino and the ultimate November winner, Democrat Andrew Cuomo.

Just as the presence of seven candidates battling for recognition prevented any substantive discussion in a limited amount of time, the sheer volume of unedited amateur content that D'Vorkin is soliciting is bound to trivialize what should be informed debate, framed by experts, into what Andrew Keen calls a degeneration "into the rule of the mob and the rumor mill." Says Jürgen Habermas, a noted European social thinker, "The price we pay for the growth in egalitarianism offered by the Internet is the decentralized access to unedited stories. In this medium, contributions by intellectuals lose their power to create a focus."

D'Vorkin's AdVoice model, however, may address a legitimate concern many companies now have—that with fewer reporters to pitch ideas to and shrinking space in magazines, they're frustrated in not being able to get their messages out. Cisco and Salesforce .com, for instance, have already approached laid-off business journalists to ghostwrite stories for executives for about one to two dollars a word to appear on their own Web sites—or as advertorial content for elsewhere. So a story ghostwritten by an ex-*Forbes* writer could conceivably show up running in *Forbes* or the Web site right next to a piece by a *Forbes* staffer.

The logical extension would be to cut the number of writers and trim the salaries of those who remain, so that compensation would be partially based on how much traffic stories generate. When asked in a meeting whether salaries would be cut, D'Vorkin snapped, "I'm not going to go there." (D'Vorkin has been told to tone down his rhetoric and not be as harsh.)

A high-ranking insider explains the new *Forbes* strategy this way: divide a pyramid into thirds. On the bottom are the masses, the broad "drive-by" audience whose heads are turned by a clever headline on a newsstand or a captivating Web story. In the middle are the "fans," loyalists who are regular readers of the magazine, attend conferences, and would wear a *Forbes* baseball cap. At the top are the "fanatics," who in addition to the baseball caps would probably tattoo the *Forbes* logo on their arms and no doubt give up their new BMW 335is convertibles to have a lengthy one-on-one with Steve for an eyeglass-fogging talk about the gold standard.

Now turn the pyramid upside down. Hook the masses with thousands of bloggers (at least one of them should be writing about *something* you're interested in); they fall into the funnel, get converted to fans, and, eventually, fanatics. One option being discussed to increase the number of fanatics is bringing the *Highlander* out of mothballs and use it for frequent "investor cruises," charging top dollar to generate additional revenue.

But can *Forbes* monetize all that blog content at CPMs of pennies on a large enough scale to make a difference? "We don't know," concedes a high-level *Forbes* insider. "It might. It might not." New CEO Perlis has told staffers he's counting on mobile to be an important new digital platform to exploit.

"Lewis's model assumes that people will go to *Forbes* to discover things," says a former Forbes.com senior editor. "The problem with that logic is that everything begins with a search. A reader doesn't differentiate whether a story is hosted by *Forbes*, Cisco, or Yahoo!"

There are some similar models out there that seem to work, albeit on a different scale. For years, *Scientific American,* unable to afford many staffers, made do with a small edit staff and paid $500 an article to prominent scientists. The Huffington Post operates with a small edit staff but a stable of over three thousand bloggers in addition to original reporting on politics, media, and business. But to date, it has yet to make any money. And, of course, *The New Yorker,* the perennial National Magazine Award winner, relies heavily on outside contributors.

The closest in-house model to what D'Vorkin is looking for no longer exists. Under the direction of Tunku Varadarajan, an editor who arrived at and departed from *Forbes* with the speed of a slide show, the Web site's Opinions section for a time reflected Varadarajan's extensive connections to the Conservative intellectual and academic community. He lured such notables as Susan Lee, of the *Journal*'s editorial page, to contribute commentary for virtually no cost. The section was focused and powerful. But when he left in a huff after only a few months in the job, his contributors vanished overnight. And whereas Varadarajan's focus was narrow—commentary focused on a Conservative track—the new "voice" of digital *Forbes* is now many voices, fuzzing the traditional focus, or at the least, drowning it out in a sea of online upchuck.

35

HAIL MARY

WITH FOURTH AND LONG and the home team's winning streak on the line, the first cover officially on D'Vorkin's watch, written by an outsider (Dinesh D'Souza), had a sensationalist subject (Obama is being influenced by a ghost), created lots of buzz (though not the right kind), and paid scant attention to accuracy (no fact-checking). Baldwin reportedly refused to run it when he was still in charge.

"How He Thinks" (September 27, 2010) argued that Obama's alleged antibusiness stance was inspired by the views of his father, who grew up during Africa's struggle to free itself from European rule and who embraced anticolonialism as his life's passion, thoroughly believing that the rich countries of the West "got rich by invading, occupying and looting poor countries of Asia, Africa and South America." Never mind that the elder Obama, whom D'Souza described as a polygamist, wife beater, and serial drunk driver, left his family when Barack was a young child and that the two of them met only twice.

Obama came to believe, D'Souza wrote, that capitalism and free markets are code words for "economic plunder," and he grew to "perceive the rich as an oppressive class, a kind of neocolonial power within America."

In Obama's worldview, "profits are a measure of how effectively you have ripped off the rest of society, and America's power in the world is a measure of how selfishly it consumes the globe's resources and how ruthlessly it bullies and dominates the rest of the planet." Obama wants to tax the rich even more, supports the Ground Zero mosque, views some of the Muslims fighting Americans overseas as anticolonial resisters, and gave tacit approval to the Lockerbie bomber, "this murderer of hundreds of Americans, to be released from captivity."

Steve Forbes echoed D'Souza in Fact & Comment in that same issue, arguing that Obama wants to "increase government power over the economy and the 'rich,' while making Americans more impotent abroad." Included was a doctored photograph showing a smiling Obama chatting happily with Lenin. It may have been amusing, but using blatant fakery to make a political point was offensive to the editorial staff, so much so that the art department initially refused to alter the photograph.

Reaction came quickly. The White House lashed out, calling the publication of the story "stunning." The *Columbia Journalism Review* called the cover "a fact-twisting, error-laden piece of paranoia" and "the worst kind of smear journalism—a singularly disgusting work."

Forbes was put in the awkward position of admitting that no fact-checking was done on the story until after it appeared. Wrote the *Times*: D'Souza's essay "seemingly stitched some intellectual heft to what has long been a fringe idea of the far right—that Mr. Obama's Kenyan roots and Hawaiian boyhood make him a lesser American."

The cover didn't go unnoticed in the ad world either. One Mad Man says the article and the doctored photo together created a "mini shitstorm" within some agencies concerned that in a newly desperate effort to stand out and reverse its slumping sales, *Forbes* would be doing even more "facts don't matter anymore" stories.

"Any normal company—Bank of America, Procter & Gamble, Chevrolet—wants to stay far clear of a sensationalist crowd-sourcing mentality," says a former *Forbes* sales official. "Advertisers will watch what happens very closely. If more covers like [Obama] come in the future, they'd rather sponsor *Family Guy*."

Partial redemption of sorts came with a December 2010 cover, a regular old-fashioned (i.e., reported with more than one source) profile of Julian Assange, the shadowy WikiLeaks operative. Beautifully timed, the cover hit the stands the same week as WikiLeak's latest dump of diplomatic cables captured headlines and serial coverage by the *Times* and other major papers. Written by New York staffer Andy Greenberg, the story got good media pickup, prompting a staff shout-out from Perlis, who said "We're all flying high on the amazing exclusive cover story this week . . . and its impact on all our products and the media world." Unfortunately, Perlis didn't stop there and promptly did a cannonball into the swamp of management-speak, channeling Carl Lavin by praising the "ongoing maximization of our product re-architecture."

To his credit, D'Vorkin has succeeded in tweaking the magazine's design so that it's much cleaner and more consistent looking, with a singular style, a "vessel for content," as he calls it. "It worked for *The New Yorker*, and it will work for us," he's said. In several staff meetings earlier this year, he called his main challenge to "fill the vessel" with "tight" stories that don't appear to have been extended just to fill space.

"We want to put money and resources into big opening spreads and the covers and not into the ancillary stuff that nobody cares about," he said. Nobody, however, has asked him what parts of the magazine he thinks "nobody cares about."

A new feature to be rolled out in a big year-end issue and cover: What *impact* rich people have, not just on society, but on all aspects of life. D'Vorkin explains the focus this way: "It's nice to be rich, but what are you doing with it?" Statistics guru Mike Ozanian is working on the algorithms to sift the relevant data.

A broader question is whether the blog explosion is diluting the

Forbes brand, or, as Tim Forbes argues, merely extending it. Simon Sinek, the marketing expert who studies brands and how dangerously astray they can go, believes *Forbes* has already passed the point of no return into fatal dilution. One of his standard presentations at conferences is to discuss the qualities of two companies he ranks as two of the best brands in American business—Apple and Southwest Airlines.

Both, he says, remain true to the passion of their founding purpose. In Apple's case, it was Steve Jobs's passion that everything the company does reinforces its commitment to challenging the status quo. That Apple makes terrific products is almost beside the point; it's why they do it that makes them seem authentic and stand out in the marketplace. Similarly, Herb Kelliher at Southwest Airlines deeply believed that the company's driving vision was being the "champion of the common man." "You are now free to move about the country," Sinek explains, is more than a tagline, it's a cause.

Listening to Sinek's spiel at a *Forbes* conference for chief marketing officers a couple of years ago was Moira Forbes. Impressed, she approached Sinek afterward, introduced herself, and asked if he'd consider including *Forbes* as another example of good branding in his future presentations. Sinek was polite but blunt. "I don't think so," he said, "it's a very different company now." Tellingly, Forbes didn't ask for a follow-up meeting to have Sinek explain in detail why he felt the *Forbes* brand was in trouble. She just thanked him and walked away.

Sinek's diagnosis is simple: *Forbes* no longer embodies the "why" of B. C. Forbes's original vision, that capitalism is not on this earth to makes millions, it's here to create happiness. Everything B.C. wrote reinforced this cause, and he passed the torch seamlessly to Malcolm, who personally embodied the vision with his happy spending, and toys like the *Highlander*. The torch, what Sinek calls "that clear sense of purpose, cause and belief," still burned brightly. But when Malcolm passed it to the next generation, his eldest son buried it in the sand, feeling personally uncomfortable trying to fit into his father's shoes. The deconstruction has wiped out most of the symbols, and *Forbes* is now just pushing its piece workers to turn out more data for distribution.

A tale from another industry is perhaps an instructive parallel. Pan American World Airways was once America's most iconic carrier, the first to cross the Atlantic, the first to order a Boeing 747, and many other firsts. But when financial trouble hit in the 1970s, it began unloading its most valuable assets—the Pan Am building, the Intercontinental hotel chain, its Pacific routes, and finally its lucrative Kennedy–Heathrow routes.

What's left today? The building, the hotels, the name, and the famous "blue meatball" logo. But they're all under new ownership, and thriving, whereas the storied airline is just a memory, showing up in the occasional retro movie. Would the Forbes family have been better off today if they'd sold off the media part of the business and kept everything else? "What could go wrong did," writes a former Pan Am executive Barnaby Conrad. "No one who followed Juan Trippe [the founder] had the foresight to do something strongly positive. It was the most astonishing example of Murphy's Law in extremis. The sale of profitable parts was inevitable to the company's destruction. There were not enough pieces to build on."

It is possible to keep an editorial focus and still develop an effective digital strategy. The *Financial Times,* for example, without diluting its core competence—global business and finance—has been rolling out new digital-only products, a twice monthly newsletter on emerging markets called *Tilt*, and separate reports on China and Brazil. The ft.com Web site subscriber base reached nearly two hundred thousand by the end of 2010, up 60 percent from a year before.

In his drive to remix journalism at *Forbes,* what D'Vorkin has put in motion cannot be reversed. There is no midcourse course correction option. It's too late for that. In any case, Scottish pride and "stick-to-itiveness" would not allow it. The brothers are in this to the end, whatever the final script reads, whether or not it involves a sale. (If *Forbes* is sold for parts, Rupert Murdoch might be tempted by the profitable Asian operations and the database of world billionaires.) Elevation's investors ultimately won't care about the underwater

Forbes deal, because the firm's 1.5 percent investment in Facebook would more than cover its $250 million *Forbes* investment if, as hoped, a lucrative "social network" public offering mirrors Google's remarkable market success.

Some *Forbes* officials welcome the darts of competitors who deride what they're doing. "*Forbes* is now in a realm of its own choosing, where we can ignore people who say it's wrong strategy since those competitors won't do it," says one insider, who adds, "Just stop reading David Carr," the *Times* media critic who's been skeptical of D'Vorkin's strategy. For his part, D'Vorkin insists his is a winning plan: "We're out there first. First movers win big. We're opening up our platforms and letting everyone play."

One reader who doesn't want to play anymore wrote: "My husband and I have been *Forbes* subscribers since 1980, and we are letting our subscription lapse. The magazine deteriorates visibly from issue to issue, and the D'Vorkin regime is already too nausea-inducing. Way to ruin a brand, guys!"

Perhaps publications, like people, simply have lifespans, and the *Forbes* of B.C., Malcolm, and Michaels is merely entering its hospice phase. Whatever happens, years from now, the legacy of this remarkable family likely won't just be a dusty set of bound volumes sitting on some ignored library shelf, digitized lists of rich people, or coffee-table books with pretty pictures of balloons, private jets, yachts, and castles.

It will be in the collected work of the journalists who came out of *Forbes* and went on to do great things elsewhere—people like Gretchen Morgenson, Allan Sloan, Nina Munk, Lisa Gubernick, Dana Wechsler Linden, Joshua Levine, Laura Saunders, David Churbuck, Peter Newcomb, Norm Pearlstine, Elizabeth Corcoran, Ed Finn, Peter Kafka, and many others. Like the many scattered seeds of executives from Sun or GE, they all moved on to other achievements, while continuing to take their cues from the *Forbes* DNA they all so deeply absorbed.

It's hard to know today how much the brothers are hurting financially from the new economic realities. There's certainly evidence that life isn't what it used to be. Bob has given up his $127,500-a-year rental apartment in London. In a building adjoining the Grosvenor Hotel, Apt. 71 had a view of Hyde Park, three bedrooms, a dining room, full kitchen, a lounge, two bathrooms, and full access to all the hotel's services, including room service and twice-daily housekeeping. Now bereft of the *Tool* and use of business or first-class travel, both Steve and Kip have resorted to flying economy, occasionally calling upon the sales staff for help getting upgrades. "Who are our friends at British Air?" Kip inquired last year of one sales executive. Mr. and Mrs. Forbes were headed to London and had nothing but coach tickets. It seemed a bit presumptuous to the executive, who recalls, "It was like 'drop everything you're doing and get me some Lord and Taylor gift bags!' " Another salesman got a call from Steve seeking an upgrade on Air France. After learning the deep discount fare Steve obtained couldn't be upgraded, the salesman simply put the difference on his corporate American Express card.

With the town house now up for sale and the entire staff having to vacate 60 Fifth in four years when the sale/leaseback deal expires, only the magnificent Château de Balleroy in Normandy, untouched by the Germans in World War II because they used it as a hospital, remains in the real estate portfolio as a place for the family to frolic. That, too, is surely soon to go.

Media turmoil and recession aside, the collapse of the family's hold on their company has come in part because the brothers wanted to live like their father while at the same time trying to shroud his memory, removing all the strings from Malcolm's exuberant capitalist guitar. And they frittered away funds that could have been more smartly deployed. As a friend still there told me, "It's 3:00 A.M. The waiter has finally brought the check."

I have no quarrel with the digitization of media. It's the new reality. Wrist-to-forehead whining is counterproductive. Just deal with it. Journalists who can't *should* do something else. Lewis is a very smart guy, and nothing was going to change under the old regime. Something drastic had to be done. And fast.

But from my old-media perch, it's been poignant to watch what I believe to be the erosion of a unique voice in American journalism. Over the past two years, I've wondered what Jim Michaels would think of an editorial mission that goes against much of what he worked so hard to build and protect over the years. Of sound bites like "speed is the new accuracy" and "the sausage factory in real time." Or how an editorial voice that once set the standard for logically reasoned insight is discouraged because it is now seen as too confrontational.

Here's one way of looking at it. Travel one hundred miles north from Manhattan to the historic village of Rhinebeck, which dates back to 1686 when a group of Dutch settlers crossed the Hudson River from Kingston and bought some land from the local Iroquois tribes. It was there in the Grasmere section of the Rhinebeck Cemetery that Jim Michaels was laid to rest in the fall of October 2007.

These days, if the ground beneath Lot D-22 seems unsteady, it's probably not seismic activity.

It's more likely the irate occupant trying to break out.

Spoiling for a fistfight.

NOTES

Since this book is largely a memoir, with heavy reliance on personal recollections, observations, and notes on events, I made a conscious decision, along with my editor, to take a minimalist approach to these notes—and to flag only those references that reflect the original thinking of others or where the source material might otherwise not be immediately apparent.

BOOK I

5   *To enter Malcolm Forbes's . . . bedroom* Christopher Buckley, "Malcolm Forbes at Timberfield," *Architectural Digest,* March 1988, author visits to Timberfield.

6   *Painted in Forbes's favorite colors Capitalist Tool* description, author's travels on the plane: Malcolm Forbes, *More Than I Dreamed* (New York: Simon & Schuster, 1989).

6   *Dr. Kruesi's foreboding proved to be correct* Kruesi quote about how Forbes died in his sleep: George James, "Malcolm Forbes, Publisher, Dies at 70," *The New York Times,* February 28, 1990; medical protocol for pronouncing someone's dead: Eric Gender, M.D., Mount Sinai Medical Center, New York, NY.

7   *The family sought proceeds from Mass Mutual* Former *Forbes* senior editor on delay of insurance payments: James R. Norman, "What (Money) Makes Steve Run? Amid the Aura of His Vast Wealth, Some Serious Questions Linger over the Funding of Steve Forbes's Quest for the Presidency," *Media Bypass,* March 1996.

8   *Forbes wanted to be buried* Laucala description, native revolt, George Harrison reference, sale, author interviews: Forbes, *More Than I Dreamed.*

9   *"Any sons who inherit"* Private letter to his sons, February 8, 1949: B. C. Forbes, on file in the Special Collections Library, Syracuse University, Syracuse, New York.

11 *"He was so many things"* Bob Forbes eulogy, as quoted in *The Chicago Tribune,* March 2, 1990.

12 *Which of course raised the question* Story references: Michael Signorile, "The Secret Gay Life of Malcolm Forbes," *Outweek*, March 1990; "Malcolm Forbes Had AIDS and Killed Himself," *Globe,* March 27, 1990.

12 *The mainstream press generally steered clear* Elizabeth Taylor quotes: Landon Y. Jones, "Elizabeth Triumphant: After a Harrowing Spring, a Revitalized Taylor Talks About Her Health, Her Passions, and Her War Against AIDS," *People*, December 10, 1990.

13 *Now what do I do? . . . Once escorting a group of Japanese businessmen* Author interviews with former employees approached by Malcolm.

14 *"Guess what? I'm having dinner with your dad tonight!"* Author interview with former employee.

19 *Malcolm thought it was amusing* Cross-country balloon anecdotes: author interviews, Malcolm Forbes, *Around the World on Hot Air and Two Wheels* (New York: Simon & Schuster, 1985).

25 *Not far from Washington Square* 60 Fifth history: James W. Michaels, "Sidelines," *Forbes,* September 1967.

27 *The boss's surroundings reflected* Malcolm quotes: Forbes, *More Than I Dreamed.*

27 *Malcolm's eldest son* Details of bequests: *Last Will and Testament of Malcolm Stevenson Forbes,* signed July 8, 1988, on file at the Surrogate's Court of Somerset County, NJ.

31 *"So what do you guys think of this house idea?"* Author interview with source close to those who had direct knowledge of the meeting and the Panorama House project.

34 *Beyond objects Victoriana* Walker auction details: David Hewitt, "The William Aikens Walker Affair," *Maine Antique Digest,* June 2000.

34–36 *Kip got into a bidding war* Details of Jefferson auction, aftermath, quotes: Benjamin Wallace, *The Billionaire's Vinegar* (New York: Three Rivers Press, 2009); Patrick Radden Keefe, "The Jefferson Bottles," *The New Yorker*, September 3, 2007. Lincoln's opera glasses quote: Time.com, August 2, 2010. Malcolm reaction, quotes: Forbes, *More Than I Dreamed.*

37 *"Forbes is to art, bric-a-brac, toys"* Buckley, "Malcolm Forbes at Timberfield." Obsessive behavior: Elizabeth C. Hirschman, "Consumption Styles of the Rich and Famous: The Semiology of Saul Steinberg and Malcolm Forbes," *Advances in Consumer Research* vol. 17 (1990).

37 *Malcolm's trove of Fabergé* Fabergé egg background: Forbes, *More Than I Dreamed.*

38 *Except for Kip's passion* Information on Forbes's toy soldiers: Richard Scholl, *Toy Soldiers: A Century of International Miniatures* (Philadelphia: Courage Books, 2004).

38 *Malcolm had a particular passion* Forbes, *More Than I Dreamed*; author interviews with sources close to the family.

39 *Also auctioned off* Toy boats: Jacques Milet, Robert Forbes, and John Ehrenclou, *Toy Boats* (New York: Scribner, 1979). "The Forbes Toy Collection Sells for $2.4 million at Sotheby's," Katy Mantyk, *The Epoch Times*, December 22, 2010.

39 *Built at the De Vries Lynch shipyard Highlander* Details: multiple author visits, www.forbeshighlander.com; Forbes, *More Than I Dreamed.*

40 *On one particularly epic 1987 . . . voyage* Amazon trip anecdotes, quotes: Christopher Buckley, "Adrift Up the Amazon," *Condé Nast Traveler*, November 1987; Forbes, *More Than I Dreamed.* "I'll see your kings and raise you" reference: Christopher Buckley, quoted by Tony Allen-Mills, in "Puff Daddy: Should Christopher Buckley Carry a Government Health Warning? His Satire Defending Smokers' Rights Has Inflamed Washington's Policy-Making

Machine. And Now His Savage Cynicism Is About to Light Up the Big Screen," *The Sunday Times* (London), June 11, 2006.

41 *If Forbes's guests weren't wined and dined on the boat* Balleroy description: Forbes, *More Than I Dreamed*.

41–43 *In Tangier* Malcolm's seventieth birthday detail, quotes, color, Elizabeth Taylor anecdotes: author interviews with participants; Judy Baumgold, "That Party," *New York* magazine, October 2, 1989.

50 *Flirtatious but ultimately bowing to celibacy* Si Newhouse references: author interviews, Steve Fishman, "Si Newhouse's Dream Factory," *New York*, March 31, 2009.

52 *It wasn't so much that Veteran's Day wasn't held* Barney Kilgore quote: Richard J. Tofel, *Restless Genius* (New York: St. Martin's Press, 2009).

BOOK II

58 *The land was filled* Historical account of New Deer: Francis H. Groome, Ordnance Gazetteer of Scotland, www.scottish-places.info/towns/townhistory4054.

58 *Further back in time* Characterization of the toughness of clan chiefs: Edward Burt, *Letters from a Gentleman in the North of Scotland to His Friend in London* (Memphis: General Books, 2010).

59 *Young B.C.* Early days of B. C. Forbes, quotes and newspaper clippings: *B. C. Forbes Collection*, Special Collections Library, Syracuse University, Syracuse, NY; Forbes, *More Than I Dreamed*; Arthur Jones, *Malcolm Forbes: Peripatetic Millionaire* (New York: Harper & Row, 1977); Christopher Winans, *Malcolm Forbes: The Man Who Had Everything* (New York: St. Martin's Press, 1990); all quotes from former *Forbes* staffers from author interviews.

69 *Appearing on September 15, 1917 Forbes*, September 17, 1917, first and subsequent early issues.

71 *Was B.C. anti-Semitic?* Anti-Defamation League, Sidney Hillman correspondence: *B. C. Forbes Collection*.

72   *B.C. professed to be concerned* Letters from New York Central and Erie Railroad executives: *B. C. Forbes Collection.*

73   *Was his relationship with sources too cozy?* Letters from Stutz Motor Cars, Ogden Armour, and Thomas Wilson: *B. C. Forbes Collection.*

73   *After a visit to Detroit* Letter from B. C. Forbes to son Gordon about new Dodge car: *B. C. Forbes Collection.*

73–74   *B.C. brought his Conservative ideology* Rugg, teacher controversies, news clips: *B. C. Forbes Collection*; Fact & Comment excerpt from *Forbes.*

74   *B.C.'s syndicated column* McCann Erickson survey: *B. C. Forbes Collection.*

75   *One reader, and an apparent old friend* Seavey letter and B.C.'s reply, Venezuela Syndicate tip nutrition letters: *B. C. Forbes Collection.*

77   *To resolve what was becoming a formidable clash* Baptism formula, B.C. as daunting father: Jones, *Malcolm Forbes.*

78   *B.C. was smart enough* Tex McCrary transcript: *B. C. Forbes Collection.*

78   *"We blame all our financial troubles on you."* Nasty reader letters: *B. C. Forbes Collection.*

80–81   *One weekend in 1933* Duncan's death, aftermath; *City of Dunc Weekly News,* basement flood, Malcolm off to Hackley School, Malcolm letter to Gertrude Weiner: Jones, *Malcolm Forbes*; Winans, *Malcolm Forbes*; Forbes, *More Than I Dreamed.*

82   *Which prompted Malcolm* Early Keynesian quote: Forbes, *Sayings of Chairman Malcolm.*

82   *B.C. worried* Lobster letter to Wally, letter from Wendell Willkie: *B. C. Forbes Collection.*

84   *Nation's Heritage* "Snooty" letter from B.C. to Gordon: *B. C. Forbes Collection*; Robert Heimann background: *Princeton Alumni Weekly,* May 16, 1990.

87   *Back in Englewood* Chancery Court filing: "Wife of B.C. Forbes Files Support Suit, Charges Financial Writer and Publisher with Cruelty," *The New York Times,* September 21, 1943.

87   *B.C. had a different view of things* Adelaide "going berserk" letter: *B. C. Forbes Collection.*

88 *Did the relationship with Gertrude go beyond the platonic? Last Will and Testament of Bertie Charles Forbes,* signed April 2, 1952, on file at Surrogates' Court, Bergen County, NJ.

89 *It's clear the sons relied* B.C.'s two letters to Gordon: *B. C. Forbes Collection.*

91 *Though trying to focus on the magazine* Malcolm's state senate race: Forbes, *More Than I Dreamed.*

91 *Meanwhile, B.C. had formulated a succession plan* Letters from B.C. to his sons, correspondence between B.C. and Gordon: *B. C. Forbes Collection.*

92 *In addition to the distribution of* Forbes *stock Last Will and Testament of Bertie Charles Forbes.*

93 *Ironic in light of another campaign forty years later* Interview with a former employee whose friend was the mother of Steve's classmate.

93 *During the gubernatorial race* Campaign photo with no voters in sight: Forbes, *More Than I Dreamed.*

95 *Hard by the shores of Lake Erie* All Dewey Michaels, Jim Michaels, Al Boasberg historical tidbits, Albert Michaels, Jean Briggs, and Michael Ellis.

99 *On January 30, 1948, Michaels filed* Michaels's private e-mail, as quoted by Subrata Chakravarty in "The man who broke the story about the Mahatma's assassination," indiaabroad.com, November 19, 2007.

99 *Michaels's reporting showed up the next day* Stories of Gandhi's assassination and funeral: *A Treasury of Great Reporting* (New York: Simon & Schuster, 1962).

102 *When he heard a rumor that someone on the staff* Mack anecdote reported to author by meeting participant.

BOOK III

116 *The best response to a wealth ranking* Fidel Castro's rant about his ranking: Kate Palmer, "Castro Lashes Out at 'Absurd' Claims," ForeignPolicy.com, May, 2006.

120 *In Michaels's view* Reference to how Barney Kilgore transformed *The Wall Street Journal*: Tofel, *Restless Genius.*

120 *Not realizing that rewriting Michaels was the equivalent of a death sentence* Chakravarty, "The man who broke the story."

121 *Later, Michaels would cite* Stanley Brown, *Editor of the Year*, Adweek, March 1983.

124 *At* Forbes, *Queenan feasted* References to Queenan's stories: "Ben and Jerry's, Purveying Yuppie Porn," *Forbes,* November, 1989; Vancouver Stock Exchange, "Scam Capital of the World," *Forbes,* May 1989; "Heterosexual AIDS, Straight Talk About AIDS," *Forbes,* June 1989.

127 *Reading all the coverage* Details on discovery of Vince Foster's body: James B. Stewart, *Blood Sport* (New York: Simon & Schuster 1996).

127 *So Norman started digging* Author's personal involvement with story and with Norman's resignation; *Media Bypass*, August 1995; beyondweird.com; www.mail-archive.com; www.book-of-thoth.com/archives—printpage-7903.

149 *I admired Baldwin tremendously* Red Holzman reference: Howard Beck, "In Every $10 Fine, a Tribute to Holzman," *The New York Times,* February 23, 2010.

153 *Summing it up* Morgenson and Baldwin quotes: Dean Stockton, "The Most Important Financial Journalist of Her Generation," *The Nation,* July 6, 2009.

159 *Churbuck's techies embedded* Nude Lindsay Lohan photos, *New York*, February 2008; Forbes.com, February 27, 2008.

163 *A perfectly pleasant and charming young man* Three Stooges reference adapted from *David Letterman's Book of Top Ten Lists and Zesty Lo-Cal Chicken Recipes* (New York: Bantam Books, 1995).

176 *But in a decision that left many staffers at 60 Fifth scratching their heads* www.telegraph.co.uk; interviews with former *Forbes* sales executives.

180 *Under the radar Social Register* material: "Oh, Dear Bunny, What Will Become of the Social Register?" *Rittenhouse Review,* June 12, 2002.

181 *Tight-lipped but grinning* "It Was a Hoax: Lenin's Not for Sale," *The New York Times,* November 7, 1991.

185 *But behind any controlling, competitive personality* Generalized personality "type" descriptions from Bert Shaw, a Woodstock, NY, therapist with extensive experience in family dynamics.

186 *Spurred on by the left-wing* Princeton environment during the time Steve Forbes attended: *Bric-a-Brac* yearbooks, 1966–1970; the 1970 *Nassau Herald*; Don Oberdorfer, *Princeton University: The First 250 Years* (Princeton, NJ: Princeton University Press, 1995).

186 *Not for young Steve* References to Cannon Club: Ross Leiner, "The Rise and Fall of Cannon Club," *The Daily Princetonian,* November 22, 2008.

187 *Also oddly removed* Steve Forbes's senior thesis on file at the Seeley G. Mudd Manuscript Library, at Princeton University.

188 *More detached than his brothers* Shaw.

190 *The most approachable and at-ease brother* Lydia Raurell on the Viennese waltz and the cha-cha: Robert Janjigian, "Lydia Raurell of Palm Beach Realizes Ballroom Dancing Dream, Authors Book," *Palm Beach Daily News,* January, 2009.

190 *On the other hand* Firing of longtime assistant: *Barton v. Forbes Inc.* 1995 WL 3011 (S.D.N.Y.) Decided Jan. 4, 1995.

194 *So every time D'Vorkin walked through the photo department* Interview with a former *Newsweek* employee who personally witnessed the incidents.

194 *"He was very forward-thinking"* Meredith White, quoted in "Darth D'Vorkin Arrives at Forbes," by Zeke Turner, *New York Observer,* July 13, 1010.

197 *But he couldn't say why* D'Vorkin's bankruptcy filing, as reported in the *New York Post,* August 5, 1988.

197 Forbes *had already been on D'Vorkin's radar* D'Vorkin's early meetings at Forbes: D'Vorkin's own recollections in "A Brief Word," *Forbes,* October 11, 2010, author's conversations with Michaels and Minard.

199 *Comedian Vaughn Meader's* . . . The First Family, Cadence Records, 1962.

201 *Still, the Helms connection was not particularly helpful* Role of for-

mer aides to Senator Jesse Helms: The Center for Public Integrity, *The Buying of the President, 1996* (New York: Avon Books, 1996).

202 *But the Crystal Owl Award* James Aley, "That Highly Prestigious Crystal Owl Award," *Fortune*, March 4, 1996.

202 *Forbes's campaign's centerpiece* Steve Forbes, *Flat Tax Revolution* (Washington DC: Regnery Publishing, 2005); Steve Forbes, *A New Birth of Freedom* (Washington DC: Regnery Publishing, 1999); Charles Lewis and the Center for Public Integrity *The Buying of the President 2000* (New York: Avon Books, 2000).

203 *For a time* "What Makes Steve Run?" Jeanie Kasindor F, *Fortune*, February 5, 1996.

204 Time *described him* Richard Stengel, "A Brass-Knuckled Gentleman: Steve Forbes," *Time* December 4, 1995.

206 *"Owning a seascape is not an endorsement of pornography"* Characterization of Forbes's reaction to attacks of his supporting homoerotic art: Elizabeth Bumiller, "Politics: On the Trail: In Political Quest, Forbes Runs in Shadow of Father," *The New York Times,* February 11, 1996.

206 *Forbes also helped drive the final nails* Richard L. Burke, "Fight for Religious Right's Vote Turns Bitter," *The New York Times*, February 10, 1996.

BOOK IV

213 *"I don't know how many of you"* Bryan and Urstadt Ari Levy, "Elevation Partners: The Ups and Downs of Private Equity," *Bloomberg Businessweek*, May 6, 2010.

214 *Big investors like these* General private equity description distilled partially from *Private Equity*, by Harry Cendrowski, James P. Martin, Louis W. Petro, and Adam A. Wadecki (Hoboken NJ: John Wiley & Sons, 2008).

216 *Today that per-page rate* CPM numbers and page rate numbers from interviews with former senior sales executives.

222 *Not only did the separate silos send the wrong signal* Characterization of being pulled in different directions: Patrick Lencioni, *Silos, Politics, and Turf Wars* (San Francisco: Jossey-Bass, 2006).

223 *They all could have included instruction manuals with only two words* Adapted from *David Letterman's Book of Top Ten Lists and Zesty Lo-Cal Chicken Recipes* (New York: Bantam Books, 1995).

225 *The resulting internal announcement* OOPS characterization from interview with former senior executive.

228 *Elevation filled the opening* Teaching only letters A through K reference adapted from *David Letterman's Book of Top Ten Lists and Zesty Lo-Cal Chicken Recipes* (New York: Bantam Books, 1995).

233 *The report didn't address* Unbundling parallel between media and telecom: Om Malik, "Old Media Is Being Unbundled, Just Like Telecom Was," Giogaom.com, February 23, 2011.

235 *"We're facing a shitstorm"* Tim Forbes remarks reconstructed after the meeting in author's personal diary.

241 *Nobody really had a stress-free Christmas break* Desk calendars without any months beyond January reference adapted from *David Letterman's Book of Top Ten Lists and Zesty Lo-Cal Chicken Recipes* (New York: Bantam Books, 1995).

243–244 *Citing the chaotic media environment* Tim Forbes remarks transcribed via 800 call-in number.

245 *Wearing an untucked shirt* D'Vorkin remarks reported by various meeting attendees.

248 *That seems like the strategy* Discussion of content farms: Claire Cain Miller, "Seeking to Weed Out Drivel, Google Adjusts Search Engine," *The New York Times*, February 25, 2011.

251 *Who might some of these "thousands" of new* Forbes *bloggers be?* Concerns voiced by a journalist: Nicholas Spangler, "In Demand," *Columbia Journalism Review*, November 4, 2010.

253 *Revealing were the submitted "battle plans"* Copy of Frederick Allen report obtained from a *Forbes* source.

253–54 *Seeing where all this was headed* "Ted Kennedy was shot?" Billy Crystal line from *When Harry Met Sally,* Columbia Pictures, 1989.

256 *The gold standard for "engagement" so far* AOL purchase of The Huffington Post: Jeremy W. Peters and Verne G. Kopytoff, "*Betting on News.* AOL is Buying The Huffington Post," *The New York Times,* February 7, 2011.

257 *Columbia University graduate students* Author interview with Anne Nelson, whose students reported on the effectiveness of their Internet use.

258 *On the Web site, the ad/edit blurring is even more problematic* How *Forbes's* sponsored blogs are raising concerns from the American Society of Magazine Editors: Nate Ives, "Does Forbes's First Sponsored Blog Look Too Much Like Editorial?," *Advertising Age,* November 4, 2010.

265 *Partial redemption of sorts* Perlis remarks obtained from copy of staff memo.

265 *To his credit* D'Vorkin comments to staffers transcribed via 800 call-in number.

267 *What's left today?* Barnaby Conrad comments in his *Pan Am: An Aviation Legend* (Emeryville, CA: Woodford Press, 1999).

268 *One reader who doesn't want to play anymore* Disaffected Subscriber: www.bnet.com/blog/technology-business/forbescom-don-8217t-steal-our-content-we-took-it-fair-and-square-update/7533.

BIBLIOGRAPHY

Aldrich, Nelson W., Jr. *Old Money: The Mythology of America's Upper-Class*. New York: Alfred A. Knopf, 1988.

Balen, Malcolm. *The Secret History of the South Sea Bubble*. New York: Fourth Estate, 2002.

Bruce, Duncan A. *The Mark of the Scots*. New York: Citadel Press, 1998.

Buchanan, Josephine, ed. *Scotland Insight Guide*. Singapore: Apa Publications GmbH & Co., 2007.

Burt, Edward. *Letters from a Gentleman in the North of Scotland to His Friend in London*. Memphis: General Books, 2010.

Byron, Christopher. *The Fanciest Dive: What happened when the media empire of Time/Life Leaped Without Looking into the age of High-Tech*. New York: W.W. Norton & Co., 1986.

Carr, Nicholas. *The Shallows: What the Internet Is Doing to Our Brains*. New York: W.W. Norton & Co., 2010.

Cassidy, John. *Dot. con: How America Lost Its Mind and Money in the Internet Era*. New York: Perennial, 2002.

Cendrowski, Harry, James P. Martin, Louis W. Petro, and Adam A. Wadecki. *Private Equity*. Hoboken, NJ: John Wiley & Sons, Inc., 2008.

Clurman, Richard M. *To the End of Time: The Seduction and Conquest of a Media Empire.* New York: Simon and Schuster, 1992.

Conrad, Barnaby. *Pan Am: An Aviation Legend.* Emeryville, CA: Woodford Press, 1999.

Cremin, Aedeen. *The Celts.* New York: Rizzoli International, 2000.

Denton, Robert E., Jr., ed. *The 2000 Presidential Campaign: A Communication Perspective.* Westport, CT: Praeger, 2002.

Devine, T. M. *The Scottish Nation: A History, 1700–2000.* New York: Penguin Books, 1999.

Doctor, Ken. *Newsonomics: Twelve New Trends That Will Shape the News You Get.* New York: St. Martin's Press, 2010.

Forbes, Malcolm. *Around the World on Hot Air and Two Wheels.* New York: Simon & Schuster, 1985.

———. *The Further Sayings of Chairman Malcolm.* New York: Harper & Row, 1986.

———. *More Than I Dreamed.* New York: Simon & Schuster, 1989.

———. *The Sayings of Chairman Malcolm.* New York: Harper & Row, 1978.

Forbes, Robert L. *Beastly Feasts!* New York: Overlook Duckworth, 2007.

Forbes, Steve. *Flat Tax Revolution: Using a Postcard to Abolish the IRS.* Washington, DC: Regnery Publishing, 2005.

———. *A New Birth of Freedom.* Washington, DC: Regnery Publishing, 1999.

Forbes, Steve and Elizabeth Ames. *How Capitalism Will Save Us: Why Free People and Free Markets Are the Best Answer in Today's Economy.* New York: Crown Business, 2009.

Forbes, Steve and John Prevas. *Power, Ambition, Glory.* New York: Crown Business, 2009.

Gillmor, Dan. *We the Media: Grassroots Journalism by the People, for the People.* Sebastopol, CA: O'Reilly, 2004.

Herman, Arthur. *How the Scots Invented the Modern World.* New York: Three Rivers Press, 2001.

Howe, Jeff. *Crowdsourcing. Why the Power of the Crowd Is Driving the Future of Business.* New York: Three Rivers Press, 2008.

Jones, Arthur. *Malcolm Forbes: Peripatetic Millionaire.* New York: Harper & Row, 1977.

Kaye, Jeff and Stephen Quinn. *Funding Journalism in the Digital Age.* New York: Peter Lang, 2010.

Keen, Andrew. *The Cult of the Amateur: How Today's Internet Is Killing Our Culture.* New York: Doubleday, 2007.

Lane, Randall. *The Zeroes: My Misadventures in the Decade Wall Street Went Insane.* New York: Portfolio, 2010.

Lasch, Christopher. *The Revolt of the Elites and the Betrayal of Democracy.* New York: W. W. Norton & Co., 1996.

Le Herman, David. *David Letterman's Book of Top Ten Lists and Zesty Lo-Cal Chicken Recipes.* New York: Bantam Books, 1995.

Lencioni, Patrick. *The Five Dysfunctions of a Team.* San Francisco: Jossey-Bass, 2002.

———. *Silos, Politics, and Turf Wars.* San Francisco: Jossey-Bass, 2006.

Lewis, Charles and the Center for Public Integrity. *The Buying of the President.* New York: Avon Books, 1996.

Lewis, Charles and the Center for Public Integrity. *The Buying of the President 2000.* New York: Avon Books, 2000.

Lowenstein, Roger. *Origins of the Crash: The Great Bubble and Its Undoing.* New York: Penguin Books, 2004.

Maclean, Fitzroy. *Highlanders: A History of the Scottish Clans.* Woodstock: Overlook Press, 2007.

Mahon, Gigi. *The Last Days of The New Yorker.* New York: McGraw-Hill Publishing Co., 1988.

Mann, Thomas. *Buddenbrooks.* New York: Vintage Books, 1994.

McNamee, Roger and David Diamond. *The New Normal: Great Opportunities in a Time of Great Risk.* New York: Portfolio, 2004.

Milet, Jacques and Robert Forbes. *Toy Boats.* New York: Scribner, 1979.

Negroponte, Nicholas. *Being Digital.* New York: Alfred A. Knopf, Inc., 1995.

Oberdorfer, Don. *Princeton University: The First 250 Years.* Princeton, NJ: Princeton University Press, 1995.

Parkin, Godfrey. *Digital Marketing: Strategies for Online Success.* London: New Holland Publishers, 2009.

Partnoy, Frank. *Infectious Greed: How Deceit and Risk Corrupted the Financial Markets*. New York: Henry Holt and Company, 2003.

Peterson, Theodore. *Magazines in the Twentieth Century*. Urbana, IL: University of Illinois Press, 1964.

Phalon, Richard. *Forbes Greatest Investing Stories*. New York: John Wiley & Sons, 2001.

Pool, Ithiel de Sola. *Technologies of Freedom*. Cambridge, MA: The Belknap Press of Harvard University Press, 1983.

Powers, William. *Hamlet's Blackberry: A Practical Philosophy for Building a Good Life in the Digital Age*. New York: HarperCollins, 2010.

Queenan, Joe. *Closing Time*. New York: Viking, 2009.

———. *If You're Talking to Me, Your Career Must Be in Trouble*. New York: Hyperion, 1999.

Quinn, Stephen. *Conversations on Convergence: Insiders' Views on News in the 21st Century*. New York: Peter Lang Publishing, 2006.

Quinn, Stephen and Vincent F. Filak. *Convergent Journalism*. New York: Peter Lang Publishing, 2005.

Raurell, Lydia. *A Year of Dancing Dangerously: One Woman's Journey from Beginner to Winner*. New York: Overlook Duckworth, 2008.

Scholl, Richard. *Toy Soldiers: A Century of International Miniatures*. Philadelphia: Courage Books, 2004.

Shirky, Clay. *Cognitive Surplus: Creativity and Generosity in a Connected Age*. New York: Penguin, 2010.

———. *Here Comes Everybody: The Power of Organizing without Organizations*. New York: Penguin Books, 2008.

Sinek, Simon. *Start with Why: How Great Leaders Inspire Everyone to Take Action*. New York: Portfolio, 2009.

Singh, Shiv. *Social Media Marketing for Dummies*. Hoboken, NJ: John Wiley & Sons, 2010.

Smith, Randall. *The Prince of Silicon Valley: Frank Quattrone and the Dot-com Bubble*. New York: St. Martin's Press, 2009.

Srodes, James L. and Arthur Jones. *Campaign 1996: Who's Who in the Race for the White House*. New York: Harper Paperbacks, 1996.

Thiro, Rosalyn, ed. *Scotland*. New York: DK Publishing, 2008.

Tifft, Susan E. and Alex S Jones. *The Patriarch: The Rise and Fall of the Bingham Dynasty*. New York: Summit Books, 1991.

———. *The Trust: The Private and Powerful Family Behind The New York Times*. New York: Back Bay Books, 1999.

Wallace, Benjamin. *The Billionaire's Vinegar: The Mystery of the World's Most Expensive Bottle of Wine*. New York: Three Rivers Press, 2009.

Winans, Christopher. *Malcolm Forbes: The Man Who Had Everything*. New York: St. Martin's Press, 1990.

Wolff, Michael. *The Man Who Owns the News: Inside the Secret World of Rupert Murdoch*. New York: Broadway Books, 2008.

Zarrella, Dan. *The Social Media Marketing Book*. Sebastopol, CA: O'Reilly Media, 2010.

INDEX